Female Entrepreneurs

Leading Australian Businesswomen

Leiza Clark

This book is dedicated to my daughters Brittani and Imogen.

First published in Australia in 2006 by
New Holland Publishers (Australia) Pty Ltd
Sydney • Auckland • London • Cape Town

14 Aquatic Drive Frenchs Forest NSW 2086 Australia
218 Lake Road Northcote Auckland New Zealand
86 Edgware Road London W2 2EA United Kingdom
80 McKenzie Street Cape Town 8001 South Africa

10 9 8 7 6 5 4 3 2 1

National Library of Australia Cataloguing-in-Publication Data:

Clark, Leiza.
Young female entrepreneurs.

ISBN 1 921024 04 6.

1. Businesswomen - Australia. 2. Women-owned business
enterprises - Australia. 3. Entrepreneurship - Australia.
4. Success in business - Australia. I. Title.

338.04082

Publisher: Fiona Schultz
Managing Editor: Martin Ford
Designer: Karl Roper
Production Manager: Linda Bottari
Printer: Toppan Printing Co. China

Acknowledgements

My sincere thanks and gratitude goes to the amazing women who have participated in taking part in this book and who shared their valuable and inspirational experiences in business.

All the ladies interviewed for the book have generously given their time without any financial rewards, and by doing this they have helped in contributing, so that *100 per cent* of proceeds that I receive from this book will be donated to the National Breast Cancer Foundation to help with ongoing research to find a cure for breast cancer, and for that I cannot thank them enough.

For my husband Robert and my two beautiful daughters Brittani and Imogen, who have shown incredible patience during the process of compiling this book, I thank you for your unwavering belief, support and inspiration, I couldn't have completed the book without it.

To my parents and friends thank you for your input and continual encouragement during this process.

I am grateful to Anne-Maree Webster, Linda May and Gillian Peterson. I thank them for their incredible support during this project.

Thanks also goes to Stephen Ungar for his invaluable advice.

To Selwa Anthony, my author agent, and to Martin Ford from New Holland Publishers, thank you for your assistance and expertise.

I'd also like to thank Sue Cameron and Renee Hampson from the National Breast Cancer Foundation for making it possible for me to donate the proceeds to breast cancer research.

About the Author

Leiza Clark's background has been predominately based in retail management and human resources before she moved to freelance writing. She completed her journalism training at the Australian School of Journalism in 1999.

Leiza has written a range of training manuals and videos for companies such as Crazy Clark's Discount Variety Stores, Red Onion Restaurant, Sweeny Studios and The Com Stores. She's also supported her husband's business in HR. (Her husband Robert founded Crazy Clark's Discount Variety stores, a retail company consisting of 115 retail outlets throughout Australia. In 2000 the business was sold to Miller Retail Limited.)After her two daughers were born she became involved in community radio with 4RPH, reading news and finance while studying interior decorating and art. These days, besides writing, Leiza is involved in residential property development with her husband while they raise their two young daughters.

Although this is her first book, she has had over 15 years experience in interviewing, training and writing. Leiza holds memberships with the Queensland Writers Centre, the Australian Media, Entertainment and Arts Alliance, the Australian Journalists Association, the Australian Businesswomen's Network and the Queensland Interior Decorators Association.

Leiza's passion is to provide a book to the market than can help and inspire women to have confidence in themselves, recognise opportunities, and learn what steps to take to achieve their dreams.

The inspirational women in this book have shown incredible courage, guts and tenacity. They've recognised opportunities, taken risks and have strived for excellence with their businesses. These ladies have proved to be true entrepreneurs of today.

The purpose of this book is to give people an insight into how these successful business women started out and prospered in today's competitive world of business.

The extraordinary women in this book will pass on valuable knowledge, experiences and suggestions, with the hope of encouraging and motivating more Australian women to go out and take the first step in starting their own businesses.

CONTENTS

INTRODUCTION

In 2004, while on an interstate flight I came across an article in the *Business Review Weekly* that caught my interest. It was an inspiring article entitled 'Why Women Entrepreneurs are Rare'. I thought to myself, 'This is great; there should be more resources out there like this article to support and motivate women who want to start a business or who are already in business and need a bit of direction'. And I thought 'Where can women go to find such information?'

Over the next few weeks, I started to take an active interest in this topic, looking for books about Australian women who have built and pioneered their own successful businesses.

However, there's not much print information out there for women, except magazines with short articles or the Internet. What I was searching for was a good reference book, something based on genuine business experiences, and preferably interview-based, on young aussie females and their personal business successes and failures, yet I had no luck finding one and so I decided to create one.

I began by pursuing young successful women that were accomplished in varied backgrounds and businesses, to hear their stories, in the hope that they could be role models and mentors to anyone wanting to start a business.

When I started interviewing I came across a common link between all the women I'd spoken to: They were not in business for money but because they loved what they were doing, they were all incredibly driven yet down to earth and modest about their success.

Writing, researching and interviewing for this book has been an incredible experience; being able to meet and talk with Australia's top young business women and hear about their lives, how they established their businesses and their journeys to success.

I believe no-one can offer better advice about how to succeed in business than the women in this book. They give personal accounts of their highlights, challenges and sacrifices. These talented young women have overcome adversity by never giving up on their dreams. Their undeniable tenacity and determination has proven them to be true entrepreneurs of today.

The book is based on relaxed candid interviews, including all their imprecisions and anecdotes, in order to provide readers with an insight into the true women they are, how their minds tick and the way they express themselves. This book

- Discusses how these 20 dynamic women pioneered their own businesses.
- Describes how they started out and got their first break, their approach and attitude towards business.
- Reveals their trials and errors and how they balance their personal lives with business.
- Offers resources for women wanting to start a business within Australia.
- Gives practical guidance and tips from each lady interviewed.
- Provides a list of valuable business contacts and networks.

My aim is that this book will serve as a blueprint to anyone starting a business, and I hope it encourages more women to consider going into business and fulfilling their dreams.

This book could not have been written without the input of these extraordinary women interviewed.

I would sincerely like to thank them for making a difference and for being role models to the women of Australia.

One hundered per cent of the proceeds that I receive from this book will be donated to the National Breast Cancer Foundation to help with ongoing research to find a cure for breast cancer.

Leiza Clark

SONIA AMOROSO
CAT MEDIA

At the tender age of 22, Sonia had a vision, and with passion and determination she has successfully built an empire in just seven years. Sonia and business partner Peter Nicholas established Cat Media in1998, which is one of the fastest growing health and beauty organisations in Australia today, exporting to over 30 international markets and distributing to more than 4500 retailers within Australia, and continuing to grow at a rapid rate.

Researching, producing and cleverly marketing over 50 winning product lines such as Fat Blaster, Reducticarb, Horny Goat Weed, Mood Lift, Monoease, Naturopathica, Skin Doctors, Vein Away and Jungle Bronze, Sonia's goal is to launch two or three new products each month.

Sonia has been recognised as a market leader by her peers, heading a team of over 100 staff with a turnover of $43.2 million; there is nothing stopping this extraordinarily talented woman. Her enterprising talent has not gone unrecognised either, receiving national recognition with numerous awards such as Ernst & Young's 2003 Young Entrepreneur of the Year Award, and Sydney's Business Review Awards in 2004—and the list goes on.

◆

Can you give me a brief overview of Cat Media?

I guess the name's a little misleading because we don't have anything to do with cats or media really other than my nickname being Cat. What we do is develop, distribute and market a variety of health and beauty products under the two brand names Skin Doctors Cosmeceuticals and Naturopathica.

We also have a third range called Kamouflage, which has some quirky little cosmetics like Jungle Bronze, which is quite popular. There are two products in Jungle Bronze; one's a bronzing body gloss and the other a spray on self-tanner. We've just released a product called Liquid Jewels. It's for a younger market, fun and quirky, whereas the Skin Doctors range is a serious cosmeceutical line, very much focused on solving all the different problems that women have in beauty; everything from anti-ageing products, products for wrinkles and pigmentation, as well as cellulite and stretch marks. Basically any problem with acne or any type of blemish on the body that a women will have throughout her life, we have the solution; that's what Skin Doctors is all about.

Naturopathica is a range of ailment specific neutraceuticals, so basically we provide total solutions to ailments by combining a number of proven herbs and nutrients in one formula and all at proven doses. This range covers ailments such as arthritis and menopause, and includes products for sexual enhancement and weight loss—obviously Fat Blaster being our number one product. Fat Blaster is actually Australia's number one weight loss product. Again the philosophy is basically the same as Skin Doctors except with Naturopathica we help people with different types of health problems.

Really, is Fat Blaster Australia's Number 1 weight control product?

Yes, Fat Blaster holds about 76 per cent of the weight loss supplement market. There are 132 players in this market and we hold the bulk of it. Actually we hold more than that now, 76 per cent was just for Fat Blaster, now we have another product called Reducticarb. It's one of our new products so that would definitely increase our hold on the weight loss market.

That's a brilliant result, to hold that much of the market.

Fat Blaster in its first year single-handedly grew the whole category by over 100 per cent.

How would you compare the sales and growth of the cosmeceutical skincare ranges against the Naturpathica products, for example, the weight control pills?

Until probably a year ago, Naturopathica's success with Fat Blaster was the dominant part of the business, but with the recent release of Relaxaderm and some of our other cosmeceutical products they are probably about even. The incredible thing about the cosmeceuticals is the international growth. The category of cosmeceuticals has just started growing on a global scale and opportunities for the products are huge. It's growing at about double the rate of the normal skin care industry so it's a pretty exciting time for this category of products and we're launching it all over the world right now. So I expect the skin care and the anti-ageing side of things to really take off. That will certainly change the dynamic between the two companies.

Let's go back in time. Can you tell me about your childhood, where did you grow up?

I grew up in Five Dock, in the western suburbs of Sydney.

Do you come from a large family?

I have two brothers, so there were five of us in the famil; Italian background.

Where did you do your schooling?

I went to Domremy Ladies College, it was a Catholic convent school. Two blocks away from my house, which was handy. Then I went to the University of Technology in Sydney.

Did you have any great schooling achievements?

When I was younger I was reasonably sporty, I did gymnastics and athletics. As I grew older at high school that kind of changed a little as my priorities changed. Other than that, I always loved music and singing, which I was very passionate about at school.

Is it true that you sing in your spare time?

Yes. I do like to sing and I write music as well.

You are a woman of many talents. Sonia, what is your current age?

I'm 32 years old.

Do you think your parents have influenced your decision over the years, to go into business for yourself?

Definitely not. It's quite funny, even recently when the company had Fat Blaster hit No. 1 and the company was going extremely well, my mother asked me when I was going to get a real job.

What was your ambition when you left school?

When I left school I wasn't sure what I wanted to do. It wasn't until I went out into the workforce and experienced reality, experienced a little bit of sexism in the workplace and became acutely aware that my career path would be directly influenced by whoever my superior was. I didn't like the idea of that, so that's when I decided to go to university to eventually work for myself. I completed a Bachelor of Arts in Communication.

Originally I enrolled to pursue a career in journalism but then I took a subject in advertising, and I knew from that very first lesson, that this is where I wanted to be. This is what I was going to do, something in marketing and advertising.

That was fantastic that you had that realisation of where you wanted to be in business so early. What was your first job?

It was at AMP, General Insurance. I had a variety of roles, but mainly a systems support role training people how to use basic programs.

Where did you go from there?

I applied to university and was accepted, to my great joy! I enrolled in the course and loved it and because I was majoring in advertising, the course gave me the tools I needed to create fully produced ads autonomously. While I was there I met my business partner, Peter. He was an avid marketing student and I was very excited about advertising and production and things like that, and we just gelled and knew that there was such opportunity out there for us and so we took that opportunity and we embarked on a number of projects together. My course gave us the opportunity to produce quality ads, as we would use the facilities at the university and it was great. The university was fantastic, because a lot of my personal projects became university projects and vice versa, so I was able to do both at the same time by studying at university and working on the business.

We had no money in the beginning so we wouldn't have been able to afford to do it any other way. We were in a fortunate position to be able to use the university facilities to produce advertising material and then create an income that way, so it was fantastic.

I then went and spoke to a couple of credit controllers at publishing houses, knocked on their doors and said, 'Excuse me, Sir, can we have an account? And of course were met with, 'Well, 'no we don't give out accounts to just anyone; who are you?' Fortunately I was particularly persistent at that time. I'm not sure if I would be as persistent these days. One of them said 'NO', so I went back the next day and said, 'I think you should give us this account because we're going to be doing this, this and this, we'll build our advertising and we're going to be one of your biggest clients, one day.'

And here we are now, one of their biggest clients. They did say yes eventually and gave us an account, but only after about three or four times of asking.

We placed small ads and then with the income that we made from those ads, we re-invested it and placed half-page ads. After that, with the money that we made from the half-page ad we re-invested that capital and placed full-page ads. We just kept re-investing the money that we made and at the time we were only selling direct response, it wasn't like we are now and wasn't a retail product. It was just one product that we went out with and people would cut out a coupon or phone in and so the money was in our hands straight away. With that money we could pay our account and then buy more advertising. So that was basically how we built it up, we didn't have any initial funding.

Did you have the products manufactured yourselves?

Well, how we came up with the products is an interesting story. One of the first products that I did with Peter was researching a book. The book was to be on plastic surgery and its alternatives. We started looking at emerging trends in the cosmetic industry, for example, anti-ageing, and what (if anything) would work on the skin. There were a lot of new technologies coming into the market in terms of active ingredients, in particular alpha hydroxy acids, retinols, real 'resurfacing' agents. So what we did was contacted a lab and had some samples made up and gave these to volunteers to try.

We didn't really know what to expect at the time, but we thought that probably people would be pretty happy, but not ecstatic. We didn't know what to expect, but we were very surprised when people came back and said, 'Where can I get some more of this, I can't believe the dramatic change in my skin'. And it's from that first project that we realised there was a real market there that was not being addressed and we wanted to take the opportunity to address it.

Which was your first product and when was that released?

Vein-Away and it was released in August 1998.

Did you have a basic business plan in place when you started?

No, business plans are great tools when you need to have a group of people focused on the same thing to achieve goals, but at the time there were just two of us and we knew exactly what we wanted to achieve. We shared the same vision, and neither of us were business people and we didn't have a business background, but we both had marketing backgrounds and so I could go out and do the best marketing plan for you but probably wouldn't have done the best business plan. We just knew what we wanted.

You mentioned you started with direct marketing, can you elaborate?

We started to run direct response advertising in the televison guides in the Sunday newspapers, as well as *Woman's Day*, *New Idea* and *That's Life* publications at the time. It was very much women-focused publications. By direct response I mean the ads had a consumer response mechanism—either coupon response or phone order.

Did you do market research to find out what was the best source of advertising, for example, magazines and newspaper lift-outs as opposed to television?

No. We went straight into print because that's what we knew best at the time. And market research is something that I'm not a big believer in to be honest with you.

Why is that?

Well, because, people who do market research, for example, focus groups, I find don't get the right information. And that's because they go into these focus groups with a bunch of people sitting around a table, and in any bunch of people you're always going to have people who are a little stronger in character and their opinion is going to influence the other people in the group and you don't know whether the people in the room really care about what information they're giving or whether they only care that they just earn their $100 at the end of the session. So I don't put that much weight on them. I find the best research for our business is testing advertisements, and that's how we've always operated. It's far more cost effective, and it's always been our motto—'Test Test Test'. So we'll place a small ad in one of those publications and let the market dictate. Let the real consumers tell us whether they want this product or not. And that's the sort of market research that we do. We are then testing not only our products, but we are testing places to advertise. We'll test the various different publications to see what gets the best response. I can't see any better type of market research.

Has your consumer target market changed over the years?

No. We've actually got quite a broad market because we have so many different products. It's anything from 18-year-olds and in some cases younger now because we have acne products, to 70-year-olds. We've always had a very broad market because our products are far reaching, we appeal to a cross-age, cross-culture, cross socio-economic demographic.

What percentage of your products would be sold to men versus women?

Depending on the product, Fat Blaster is probably slightly more female than male. However, we find that we have a lot of male users who buy our hair removal products and our skin care products, and we also have male specific products like prostate formula, so it really depends on the product.

As far as advertising goes, what is your main form of advertising today?

I guess TV advertising is our biggest form of advertising and the most far reaching in terms of consumers. As far as TV goes, we do morning television with Kerri-Anne and *Good Morning Australia* and we also do print as print is still our forte, it is still where the strength lies and we do anything from women's magazines to newspapers and billboards; basically we advertise everywhere.

Did you network with anyone in the beginning, for example, was there anyone you could phone to ask advice?

Not so much that. We did join an American group at the time called NIMA, now called ERA. NIMA used to stand for the National Infomercial Marketing Association and ERA's now Electronic Retailers Association.

We would go to their overseas conferences and network with similar minded people in the direct marketing industry, and met some incredibly successful people within that industry and certainly picked their brains; yes, in that respect it was great. In fact, one of the ladies who we met back in those days is now our media buyer in America and she's certainly given very good advice along the way as well.

How and when did you break into the international market?

It has been a work in progess. We opened our first office three years ago in the United Kingdom and we have 20 or so staff there now. Basically we started the business in the UK the same way we started here.

We used the same model. Direct Response Advertising direct to consumers. And through advertising we've built up our brand image and reputation, and selling direct to consumers has created an income base for us. The reputation the brand developed gave us entry into the retail market in the UK and we are now in some prestigious retailers over there such as Fenwicks, Selfridges and House of Fraser.

Earlier this year we participated in a trade show called COSMOPROV in Bologna and from that we've secured some fantastic market penetration globally. At the same time, I sent a letter out to numerous department stores across America and we have had a great response from that. So at the moment we're filling shelves in stores around the world, with around 300 different department stores in the United States (as well as a few thousand GNC stores) and we also export to Sweden, Ireland, Spain, France, Netherlands, Hong Kong, Singapore, Norway, Cyprus, Greece, Denmark, Andorra, China, South Africa, Iran, New Zealand, Brunei and Indonesia. The upcoming markets are Taiwan, Thailand, Philippines, Turkey, Austria and Switzerland.

That is an incredible list.

Yes. And we're going into Boots, in England, which has been a long courting process, but we're finally going into their stores, which is exciting.

How many retail stores do Boots have?

They actually have around 1400 stores and the incredible part is that they hold over 40 per cent of the cosmetic market. We're just going into a new group in Hong Kong called SASA and they hold approximately 90 per cent of Hong Kong's market. It's just a fantastic time; it's so exciting to see people's responses to our products. There's like a coming of age in the cosmaceutical industry and a coming of age for our products. It seems that we were a little bit ahead of our time and now everyone wants these results-focused products.

It's really snowballing for you isn't it?

Yes. It's like a good virus. It's like, verbal, viral marketing. The name becomes known as a brand, particularly in America. I recently arrived back from a trip over there, visiting store groups, and in one of the stores in California my meeting was above the actual store, and they took me down to where our counter was and the staff were setting up the counter and it was right across from the Chanel counter, so we have some fabulous neighbours now. It's just going to take us, take the brand, up to a different level, and particularly being in America, and having that exposure in those sorts of department stores, it will trickle down globally.

How many outlets do you supply in Australia?

In Australia we physically supply 2700 pharmacies and health food stores, 250 beauty salons, 1300 supermarkets and 3 major wholesalers.

Amazing. What would you say was the most challenging thing you have had to overcome?

I guess the real challenge was in the early stages, and I suppose with any start-up company it's finance. Being able to fund growth potential was the major obstacle because we had no money. Realistically no-one was going to give us any money at that time, so we had to find a way to manage that in our own way. We funded the growth as we went with our marketing as I was explaining before. We'd place an advertisement, make money from that advertisement and then re-invest that money and grow it like an upside down triangle I guess. Just keep investing it, place more ads, make money from each of those new ads, re-invest that to make even more ads, make even more money and so on and so on to really grow it organically. And thankfully we had a fantastic market response to the products so we were able to do that reasonably quickly. We managed to grow the company from the 2 of us to 40 staff within a year.

It grew pretty fast, did you expect to grow so quickly?

I think in order to be successful, you need to start out with an optimistic viewpoint. It wasn't too far down the track that we were up to almost 100 staff. I guess it was between 1998 and 2002, and the sales went from $0-$32,000,000 turnover. That's quite a fast growth path and it was all with no funding.

What a great result for your first four years of business.

Yes, it was fantastic.

And more recently, what was the annual turnover for business in 2003?

$43.2 million.

What is the forecast for 2005?

$56.1 million.

As far as sacrifices, what do you believe was your biggest sacrifice in getting the business off the ground?

I don't really feel that I've sacrificed anything because I've enjoyed the process so much and I've learnt so much from it. I guess there has been some personal relationship sacrifices. Other than that, nothing really. It's been very rewarding.

Do you currently have a partner in life?

I do have a partner and we live together, but I'm not married.

Is he involved in your business?

No, he's not.

What sort of hours were you putting in weekly in the first year?

When someone asks me that it's really hard to quantify. Particularly when you start—and it's not as different as you go down the track—whether you're in the office or not, you're just always working. Your mind is always on the business and what your next project is going to be and how you can do something else differently. You become a chronic insomniac and God knows how many hours in the middle of the night you're up thinking about things or writing ads, so it's really hard to put a time limit on hours. I don't like to quantify hours worked as hours in an office because that's not how I work or how I live.

These days has that changed, do you take time out, for example, on the weekends?

I do take time off on the weekends now, I never used to but I do now. You have to. Now it gets a little too stressful if you don't. When you first start you don't mind it because it's all exciting, it's all new, it's like go go go. But eventually the stresses get a little bit too much and you need to have a break, but at the same time, it's not like you're not thinking about things on the weekend. You never really switch off. I'd still be doing some work. I'd still be checking something, still be thinking about an ad or a line, you know, a tag line, something like that. There's always that.

Have you ever found it difficult dealing with men in business, for example, in manufacturing, sales, finance, publishing houses?

No, and perhaps it's an attitude thing, because when it is your business, it doesn't matter. You're kind of the customer. You're in a position of power, no matter what.

There have been times that I've been in meetings and certain individuals you can tell aren't comfortable working with a woman or won't look a woman in the eye, but like I said, you're in a position of power so it's not really an issue.

Have you ever had to source external funding to help with the growth and changes?

Only since the Pan Pharmaceuticals debacle in 2003.

How did that affect the business?

Terribly. A number of products were affected for quite some time and thankfully our biggest product, which was Fat Blaster had alternative manufacturers, so that was a blessing, but yes it affected us pretty badly.

How many product lines do you currently produce?

Between 45-50. We have new products coming out all the time with probably 3 or 4 in the pipeline at any given time.

Where are your products produced?

In Australia.

Obviously with the overseas expansion the business calls for you to travel. How often are you travelling?

It changes all the time depending on what's going on here or what trade shows we have and what's going on overseas. I guess over the last four or five months

I've spent two or three of them overseas, but it's not always that much, and sometimes it could be more. It all depends on what is called for.

You mentioned earlier that you have a business partner. What would you say are the advantages and disadvantages of having a business partner?

It's always advantageous to have someone to bounce ideas off. Peter Nicholas, my partner has a very similar vision to me, similar ideas, and that's a good thing. Disadvantages? I think the advantages far outweigh the disadvantages. I mean there are certainly some disagreements and arguments that you have along the course but I think that's a good thing because if you agreed on everything then what would you need each other for? I think it's great—and very important— to have more than one perspective. It's important to have disagreements, important to have strong opinions from both sides so you can come to the right path together.

How many employees do you have currently?

Globally it's a little over 120, the bulk of whom are in Australia.

What would you say have been the greatest moments with your business?

I guess Fat Blaster would have to be one of them; creating an entirely new concept within the weight loss category. It was really the first multi-ingredient weight loss supplement in Australia. It was marketed in a very different way, as I mentioned earlier, growing the entire weight loss category by over 100 per cent in its first year.

We were awarded the Australian Journal of Pharmacy Health Product of the Year Award and that's significant because it's the first time a natural product has ever won, and it's also significant in that the competition that we were up against included Panadol, Nurofen, Nicorette and Zyban, and yet we won.

One of the other great things that I think was a highlight of the business was the launch of our Relaxaderm cream. I'm very passionate about our Skin Doctors range and to launch a cream that in sales volume was matching Fat Blaster was fantastic. This is an incredible achievement in Australia, as this product was selling more units of Relaxaderm in a week than the biggest selling cream in Australia's department stores was selling in a year.

That's sensational, you must have been ecstatic with that response.

Yes, and we made that much of an impression on the market with this product and that was a huge achievement. One of the other highlights of course was winning the Ernst & Young Young Entrepreneur of the Year award.

You've also had a lot of exposure through winning that award haven't you?

Yes, we certainly have. That's been very rewarding and exciting and a huge achievement.

Have you or the business received any other awards?

We have been very blessed to have won a number of awards. The most recent was of course Ernst & Young Entrepreneur of the Year in the Young category. We also recently won some awards from the prestigious Australian Journal of Pharmacy, namely, AJP 2004, Best Public Relations, Highly Commended Health Campaign for Relaxaderm and AJP 2004 Best Pharmacy Health Promotion Carotenoids for Naturopathica and DSM. The Sydney Business Review's Business Woman of the Year Finalist 2004 and The Sydney Business Review's Sydney Graduate School of Management MBA Scholarship. Other awards we have won are Business Review Weekly BRW Fast 100, National Pharmaceutical Services Association, DIANA Awards for finalist in most outstanding new products—Fatblaster Complementary Healthcare Council Awards for exporter of the year, Champions Small Business Awards—Westpac won the export business category, finalist Cleo Best 'o' Beauty and New Woman finalist Anti-aging for Relaxaderm and our tanning product Jungle Bronze.

What's predominately your role within the business these days?

My role, other than the responsibilities of being managing director in a corporate sense, is more a marketing role. I guess you could call it 'Creative Director', but it's a little more intricate than that because I still write a lot of copy, I still get very much involved in production of everything from print advertisements, design concepts and actual content in the ads and I write and produce all of our TV work as well. My role is incredibly varied—I present on TV and act like the 'face of the company' in a way, so there's a PR element to my role as well. I also do a lot of work for the groups that we deal with overseas. I can't even begin to list all the different things that I do.

How would you describe your management style, or your staff culture?

We have a great culture, It's very young, it's very dynamic and I guess the most important thing to me as a leader or manager is to really be able to communicate our vision of the company—not just share that with all the people that work with us but really have them believe in the vision—become part of the vision and make our dream their dream. Our staff believe in what we do and that we really do change people's lives, and I think it is really important that it's felt, experienced and owned by every staff member from the Senior Management Team through to people in the warehouse and the receptionist.

Everyone needs to know that they make a difference in this company and they are part of the success of this company. I think that's vitally important.

How do you personally motivate yourself on a daily basis?

Well, it's not really difficult because I love this company so much and I love what I do so much. I enjoy the process so it's not hard for me to get motivated because all I have to do is think of a new project or a new product launch that's coming up or think about the department store launch in the United States and I'm buzzing already.

Product success is very motivating. As soon as you start to feel that something's going to work, you want to go out there and work it even more and then make another product just as good or better; it just leads to more motivation.

Is that what motivates you the most—product success?

Yes, it's very rewarding in a number of ways. This business is very rewarding. Because it's an incredible thrill to release a product onto the market and release a marketing campaign that you know you've had a lot to do with, and then have the public respond to that. I sometimes think of it as like an entertainer who performs before a crowd and gets instant feedback and that is what gives them the biggest thrill. I find it kind of the same—consumers respond to our products and then I feel that warmth, that connection. It feels great that we're doing something to touch people's lives because our products really are life-changing.

Menoeze is a fantastic example of that. When we launched that product onto the market the response from people was unbelievable. One lady who was on HRT had been airlifted to hospital a number of times and was so violently ill she was literally on death's door! It was incredible to hear her story about how she started taking Menoeze and her life went back to normal.

We have great communication with our consumers and people do ring in or write to us and tell us their experiences with our products and that in itself is incredibly rewarding—and incredibly motivating as well—knowing that you're changing people's lives.

How do you prioritise your time on a daily basis, are you a big list writer?

I've got to say I've never been a great organiser. One of my little secrets—I'm not so great at time management, but I know what's a priority and it gets done one way or another, even if it's at 12 o'clock at night.

Do you have a technique you use to achieve your goals?

I guess the only thing that's worked for me is having a passion for my business and my industry and really believing in myself, my team and what I do and what we all do. I mean that true belief, which is sometimes hard to find in oneself, but I'm sure if you search hard enough you'll find out what the thing is that really makes you want to do something, want to make a difference.

Have you ever felt vulnerable in the business?

Pan Pharmaceuticals. I was very vulnerable at that time.

Can you elaborate? for example, did you have all your products produced through Pan?

No, thankfully they didn't produce all of our products and we had alternate suppliers—but we did have supply problems. The whole industry had supply problems because Pan manufactured most of the industry products. That was a very difficult time and I guess I felt a little vulnerable.

If you had to start over would you do anything differently?

Probably not. I know a lot more now,. Certainly if I would do anything differently it would be to take the knowledge that I have now and start again. But I think the formula that we have works very well and the same formula that we had when we first started is the exact same formula that we use in our business today but on a grander scale. So I would have to say we'd do it the same way all over again.

Have there been any mentors along the way, anybody that specifically stands out, as role models that you admire?

I always get asked this question and I always have difficulty with it because I find (which is why I like the idea of this book so much) there is a huge lack of female role models for young women to look up to. I have to say my business partner is very inspirational in that way and I guess in a way you can say we've both been mentors to each other, which is another great advantage of having a business partner that is so like-minded.

I've always liked the story of starting on the kitchen table and ending up with a multi-million dollar corporation, because that's where we started, we didn't have anything else. Actually I don't think we even had a table to work on; it was a couch. Having come from there, the rags to riches stories were the sort that appealed to me. People like Lillian Vernon who started literally on her kitchen table in direct marketing, selling belts and bags and turning that into one of the biggest catalogues in American history. It's an amazing story. So she was very inspirational to me.

Is there a book that you would recommend for someone wanting to go into business?

The books that I tended to read and take inspiration from were advertising books. They weren't so much business books so it might not really be relevant for everyone because this is a kind of a strange business really. I mean we are a very unusual business model.

We are very marketing driven, of course our innovation—our research and development are a core strength as well. But it is very unusual for a company to be both.

What would you say would be the best advice you were given?

Probably find your USP. Know what's unique about your product or service. Your USP is your unique selling proposition. That would probably be the best advice, that and Test Test Test. Before you spend loads of money on something—test the market. Learning how to minimise your risk and exposure is one of the most important business lessons you will ever learn.

Where do you go from here; what's your plan over the next 5 years?

Global expansion definitely. We've already started, so the path is set to grow an international brand, building up the business the way we have done here.

◆

Three key strategies for Cat Media's success

1. USP—unique selling product. I was speaking earlier about the multi-ingredient formulations, that weren't being done when we launched products. There were a lot of one shot vitamins out there so unique products and unique categories would be one.

2. Unique and aggressive marketing would be the second thing that has made us successful. We created our own style of marketing, a hybrid between direct response techniques and branding techniques, the advantage is that we market our products ourselves. I think the passion and the belief in the products comes through, which can often fall to the side when creativity is given to an agency.

3. The third is an incredible team, a team of people that allows us to be creative, to come up with fantastic products. We also have a very fast speed to market, which is important in our industry. The speed at which we can get products onto the market is very unusual and it's a real strength for us.

Sonia's words of advice

1. Know what is unique about your product and what is unique about your company. Understand why someone would come and choose you rather than go to anyone else. It's the first thing you need to think of. You need to know what it is about your product or service that people will want. And why they will want it.

2. Understand and know your own strengths—and make sure that you focus on those strengths. You can't be everything and you shouldn't try to be.

3. Surround yourself with the best people, the best advisors you can find in the areas that you're not too sure about,;make sure you have the best people around you.

4. Find your passion. It's probably the most important one because passion I think is everything in success. You need to love what you do for so many reasons. One of which is, if you don't have passion you're not going to be able to find the drive that you need to get you through. Not just the day-to-day running of the business, but the hard times—because there are always hard times—particularly in the beginning. There are always hurdles along the way and if you don't love what you're doing it's harder to stick to those things. If you don't believe in what you're doing it's difficult. You need to have that passion as a backup. And also when you have that passion it inspires the people that you need to help you. It inspires your team and it inspires you as well so passion is the No. 1 tool to have. I believe it is essential to business success—or any success for that matter!

5. Be an egomaniac! Jokes aside, it's important to have a steadfast belief in yourself. I think that's really important. To believe. To dare to dream. To know that anything's possible. That you will succeed. I know it sounds a bit like pop psychology but it's so true. You need to have an innate belief that you will be successful in whatever you do. You will find that most successful entrepreneurs always knew they were going to be successful. It's not arrogance, it's just that if you don't believe that you're going to be successful, then you won't keep trying. You're not always successful first up and you need that belief (just like you need passion) to keep trying. After all, if you don't believe in yourself, how are you going to make anyone else believe in you?

BARB DE CORTI
ENJO

In 1985 Barb De Corti immigrated to Australia with her husband. Unable to speak a word of English, she spent the first two years learning the language and establishing herself as an aerobics instructor, after learning that her qualifications as a practising accountant in Austria were not recognised here in Australia.

In 1993 she was introduced to Enjo cleaning products by her mother-in-law, while on a visit back to Austria. Barb's son was 10 at the time and asthmatic, and the Enjo products were recognised in Austria for being environmentally friendly and less toxic. Barb started using them and after a short time she noticed her son's attacks became less and less, and the products she was using were cleaning better than anything that she had ever used. Barb became a huge advocate of them, promoting them to her friends and family and within a short time all of them were using Enjo products as well.

It was then that her husband suggested she bring products into Australia and try selling them. They invested $40,000 of their personal savings into the products to get the business off the ground. It wasn't easy sailing, it took tough years to build the business to where it is today.

The Enjo cleaning products are exclusively imported by Barb to Australia, she also established a 40 per cent partnership with the company that distributes the products in the USA. She has an annual turnover of $80 million and has over 1500 distributors that will increase to 4000 by the end of 2006. Barb's goal is to have Enjo cleaning products in 30 per cent of Australian homes by 2010.

Could you give me an overview of your business?

We are a direct selling company and our reasoning behind this is that our product needs to be demonstrated. The basic infrastructure for how we promote our products is through independent sales consultants throughout Australia, who run their own businesses promoting the Enjo products through in-home demonstrations.

Can you tell me what's so special about the Enjo products?

They are fibre-based cleaning products—in the form of cloths and gloves. They clean 90 per cent without chemicals. Enjo doesn't replace the chemicals. It's a very simple process. In the olden days they used a brush and water, and nowadays we're more sophisticated and have come a long way with technology, so we use fibre technology to do the cleaning with water only.

I would imagine it would be fantastic for all those people who are chemically sensitive.

Yes. It's an amazing product. I'm always astounded that people don't jump faster at the chance to change over because we're talking health—their own health—and people have still so little understanding about what's really going on with chemicals, but it's an educational process.

Let's go back in time. Where did you grow up?

Austria. I came to Australia 18 years ago in January, so that would have been 1987.

Did you come from a large family?

I come from a family of eight—the oldest of eight. My youngest brother is only 23. I grew up in a little village—not very wealthy at all, but brought up really healthy and close to nature. We had a small farm at home; we were nurtured and loved, and always brought up with a 'can-do' attitude, so a very fortunate upbringing.

Did you complete all your schooling and go onto university or college?

Yes. I completed my high school degree and did accounting in college, so I'm a qualified accountant and also have a background in textiles. I was always quite interested in fabrics, so through my apprenticeship I worked for a knitting yarn company learning about the different wools and cottons.

Do you believe that your childhood and your upbringing influenced your decision to go into business for yourself?

No. Apparently as a child I never did anything without a purpose, so everything I do is very outcome-focused. I suppose I was always just a very tenacious person.

What was your ambition when you decided to leave college? What did you want to do?

To marry, have two children and stay at home. All I wanted was a little cottage and my own family. But once I actually started to work, that all changed. I really enjoyed working and always strived for more, so it was in me already—inherent.

What was your first job?

My first job was as an accountant in Austria. I married at a very young age. I was 18 and still going to college. I then finished college and had my first child, Mark— I was only 19 when he was born. So after Mark was born I had my first job as an accountant.

Where did you go from there?

Then we moved to Australia—the first time around, because my then-husband had a job here and so we came to Australia for two years. I spent most of my time learning English while we were here. Unfortunately his father died and we had to go back to Austria for a couple of years to sort the business out. Then we decided to immigrate to Australia, and based ourselves in Perth. I continued to learn English, and was an aerobics instructor part-time because you didn't need to have a full knowledge of English to be able to instruct. I did that for six years and I loved it too because I'm quite fit and health-oriented, so that was a great job for me.

How old were you when you first moved to Perth?

Twenty-four years old.

What led you to start your own business and why?

Basically we came across this new product while we were visiting family in Austria. My son was a really bad asthmatic at the time, and I'd spend quite a few sleepless nights making sure he didn't suffocate. It was quite stressful for us all at that time.

So, I was always on the lookout for different cleaning solutions—being such a clean freak—I was known as the bleach queen. Then my mother-in-law said there's this cloth that you clean with using only water. I looked at her and thought impossible—especially coming from my mother-in-law, and I thought this is insane—they can't clean as good as my chemicals. Anyway, I tried out the product when I came home and to my surprise they really worked.

Even within the first week of using it I could see an improvement in my son's breathing. We eventually found out what brought on his asthma attacks—years later after having researched our product—it was basically the chemicals I used to clean with prior to using Enjo. At the time I didn't give it much scientific thought—all I wanted was just to have a healthy child.

I wasn't even thinking of starting a business. But the products worked so well, and I kept telling my friends and people through aerobics, and they started saying, 'Barb, I want those products. Where can we buy them?' So I decided to bring a couple of gloves in and sell them to my friends. My husband at the time said we should just start a business with it. He encouraged me to pick up as importer for the product—that's how it all started.

So was your husband working at the time or did he start the business with you?

Yes, he was running his own computer company at the time; we had very little money—having just migrated to Australia. We didn't start the business for financial reasons—we didn't think we were going to be millionaires—it was the fact that it was such a great product, and we thought everybody should have it because of the obvious health benefits and for the environment. It started out quite altruistically, but then it developed into a business. I originally brought $40,000 worth of gloves into the country, and it took us three years to sell. Now on a good day we'll sell anywhere between $500,000 and a $1 million worth.

In the early days you would go out there and demonstrate the product yourself?

Yes, and I loved it. In the beginning I was the only consultant and I would have to demonstrate the products. It was great because you would always get that wow effect from people, when they'd see that the products really worked.

What year did you establish the business?

Last year we celebrated 10 years in Australia, so it must have been 1994.

How old were you then?

I'm now 41, so I would have been 31.

Did you do any market research when you brought the products out?

No, I didn't even look into it.

How did you get your name and the products out there in the early days?

I talked to the school about it, I talked to people at counters—my butcher, my hairdresser,. Those people started using the product—they then told other people—and that's basically how it grew in the early days. Within two months I had another consultant—Joan Wragg. Joan is still an Enjo consultant, and she is one of our top people. I learnt a lot from her—such as the fact that you have to get out of your comfort zone, talk to people. That was basically her advice and that's what I did. I had no sales experience whatsoever. The only thing I had was that I believed in the product, and I get on with most people.

Have you ever had to do any advertising or any marketing?

In the early days it was just word of mouth, but now I have a huge advertising budget—especially in the last four or five years. We advertise on television and in magazines. To de-stigmatise the whole industry. To get the brand name known and to support our consultants!

Did you network with people in business when you first started?

No, I'm not a network person in that regard. It's just not me. I had friends to talk to and things like that, but I didn't seek out women's groups or women in business and that sort of thing, I found I'd rather stay away and just chisel away myself.

Did you have a business plan?

I had one after three years, and only because I heard on one of the motivational tapes I was listening to that you had to have a business plan. I knew how to do a budget, but I didn't know how to put a business plan together. So I went to the library, got myself a book and started to put a business plan together, which was terribly complicated at the time.

It made my job a lot easier and we became more successful very quickly because we had direction. I would say it is imperative to have a business plan.

Once you devised your business plan, did you meet the projection that you'd set in your business plan?

Actually I was way off—we overshot it by quite a lot. I found that the things I would focus on would grow. I worked a lot myself, which meant I did all the demos, so I couldn't really focus and work on the business because I was too busy working in it. I actually made a plan to recruit people into the business.

While putting the business plan together I came to realise that to really make a big difference to people's lives through Enjo, I needed more people to help me to promote it. That's basically when I started to focus on offering a business opportunity—starting to recruit people into the business and basically letting people know what a great business it is.

Once we had consultants on board the turnover was tremendous—it exceeded all our projections because we grew so much quicker. We approached our past customers and they became consultants, and we still do the same now. Our best customers became our best consultants because you need to love the product to understand it and to want to make a difference.

How many distributors do you have now?

About 1500, and we're aiming for 4000 by the end of 2006.

How do you manage the consultants regarding training, etc?

We have training managers in each state who look after my team managers. There are certain levels—we have senior managers and we have team managers. The senior manager will train all new consultants so it's uniform throughout Australia; the team manager nurtures the consultants, they're there like a coach. They have weekly contacts with the consultants regarding advertising, monthly specials and so on. We do a lot of training, not so much on how to sell but more on self-esteem and building team motivation. Every month I get out there with all my team managers—for a week I'm on the road. All our managers have refreshment trainings once a year; they come to Perth, which is our head office; we do refresher training with them for three days. Also all our new management comes to Perth where we do induction training for four days, so we do a lot of hands-on training. I know all of my 130 managers by name and have a relationship with them, I know about their families, their children, their ambitions. They in turn have the same with their consultants. We keep it, despite the size, quite intimate. It's not like a big operation.

It sounds like you keep it very personal?

That's just how I am. It works well for me, so I don't have to become a hard-nosed business person. You can create a fantastic business by showing compassion and empathy, and having a business brain as well. And you can run a successful business without having to constantly look at the bottom dollar and give the people you work with as little as possible so you become rich. That's not what Enjo's about at all—we look after our consultants very well and they look after us in turn by being very loyal and helping us to build our dream. We're very fortunate.

Do you actually sell outside of your direct sales team, such as via a website?

No, not at all. We only support our consultants through our website. But no ordering is done via the website or through retail outlets.

How did you break into the international market?

My ex-husband is running the American market, and he's based over there. Enjo is sold in about 10 countries in Europe, so it is quite a substantial company now around the world. The USA belongs to Enjo Australia, but the rest of the world is run by the Enjo manufacturer, but using the same business model—we all work on the same business model.

How many international distributors do you have in the USA?

Because we've only just started over there, we have about 40, but it's early days. We've only been there for a year and it takes a while to establish. We're very happy with what we've achieved there so far.

It sounds like you've done well considering you've only been there one year.

Yes—we did very well because we already had the knowledge which we gained here in Australia, so certain mistakes and detours we made in Australia, we didn't have over there so we went into the US with a concept, a business plan, and knowledge as well as the support from Enjo Australia, with all the print material and creative marketing—we basically just passed it on to Enjo in the USA.

How did you come up with a training model?

From my own personal experience. I've always believed there are different types of ways that people learn, and it was important to me that we created a program that would be suitable to many people. We made sure it was simple and hands-on training. There still is a lot of theory but it's put into practice so people learn much easier and quicker. We developed that training here in Australia and now Enjo has taken it worldwide.

What would you say were the major challenges or obstacles you had to overcome in your first year of operating the business?

The challenge probably hasn't changed much to be honest—it's getting people to understand that just simply water with the cloth can really work. This is basically still our biggest challenge—after all these years of being in business in Australia and having sales in the millions, it's still a hard task to get people firstly to see the product, then to look after them to make sure they persevere with it because it's like everything else –changing habits can be hard—and none of us are very good at it. We find people try to resist change, so that's probably one of the hardest things for us.

Did you have to make any huge sacrifices to get the business off the ground?

No, I didn't have to. There were maybe a few lean years, but it's been such a rewarding business, I never feel like I'm working. It has its moments, but when I look at the big picture, I don't think I've made any sacrifices. I was fortunate enough to be able to run a business while bringing up my son. My marriage break-up had nothing to do with the business. It was just 24 years with the one person and it had run its course.

What sort of hours did you put into the business in the first couple of years?

Less than I do now. I just worked the hours required—I never counted the hours as such.

A 40-hour week doesn't exist when you run your own business. When you do run your own business, you have to like it so much that the hours don't worry you—you can't see it as work because you just do what's necessary, even now I couldn't give you the hours that I work. I wake up in the morning and the first thing I probably think is Enjo—what needs to be done.

Do you take weekends off to be with the family?

My son is currently in Queensland. He's 22 years old now and he's up in Brisbane and loves it there. So I take time off if it's needed, but I still give seminars on weekends—I give about 10 seminars a year, but I'm currently doing a diving course, so I make sure I take those weekends off. If I have a lot of weekends where I'm working, I take a Monday or Tuesday off. I seem to have a bit of a balance going there.

What was the annual turnover for business last year?

Last year we did $80 million.

When you say $80 million, is that only for Australia?

Yes, that's Australia-wide. Everything goes in a cycle, and we are just working on the next phase, and we know what our potential is.

What percentage of your own money did you initially invest in the business? You mentioned $40,000. Was that your own money or a loan?

That was our own money—our savings. Because it was so tough in the beginning, we had to sell our house that we owned, so there were a couple of things we had to overcome at the time. When we sold the house, we invested the money from it into the business, then eventually we bought another house and the rest is history. People now say Enjo's such a successful business, but we did struggle for the first three years. We lived on the bare minimum. I still remember telling our son that we just couldn't afford Christmas presents—there was a really big order at the time, and he said, 'That's cool, Mum, I can wait.' Within eight months when business started to go better, he got his late Christmas present. I also believe that's what's made him the person he is today—he's a wonderful human being.

What year did you first start making a profit?

In year four—1998.

Do you deal with debts and creditors internally within the business?

Yes, to a certain extent; however, I now have a team of people. A general manager and an accounts department of five people, so I don't deal with those things personally on a daily basis. I just have to make sure that we all run on budget, I'm more focused on marketing nowadays than anything else.

Do you currently have a partner within the business?

Yes I have two partners, my ex-husband is still a partner but he doesn't work in Australia. He joined me after three years because it was then big enough to financially support us, he was with Enjo Australia up until the end of last year, then he took over in the USA.

What would you say were the benefits of having a partner?

I think to bounce off ideas. That's why it's very important to work with somebody as a partner who is on the same wavelength but doesn't necessarily always agree with you. That's where my ex-husband was so great in the early days because he would question things I did so I'd have to explain it. I came across another person through sheer luck, and that partnership works well because we're not in a relationship so it doesn't interfere with our personal lives—it's purely business. It's good—I enjoy working with somebody.

How many employees do you have in the Perth head office?

Currently about 50.

Does the business call for you to travel regularly?

I travel approximately 10 days a month to the eastern states, with my business partner—we're regularly in touch with our managers over there. You can only see a certain amount from head office, you really need to visit regularly and being out there makes a tremendous impact on the growth of the company. Nobody else can talk about your vision and your goals as passionately as yourself, and I find being out there with our managers makes a huge difference because you immediately know if they're happy with a decision you made at head office.

What would you say have been some of the highlights of running your own business?

Receiving letters from your consultants who have succeeded; seeing them be rewarded for doing something they would never have seen themselves doing in a lifetime. The manufacturer of our products has a synergy meeting every year where all the top sales people in the world get together. Girls who join us as consultants and do well are suddenly in Hawaii celebrating their success. That is the most rewarding I would say. It's amazing to see them succeed and grow.

What awards or recognition have you received for the business?

We're one of the top-growing companies—have been in the *Business Review Weekly* (*BRW*) the last three years running for Australia's top 10 companies. We were a runner-up in the Entrepreneur of the Year Award by Ernst and Young ,which is a worldwide award. I was also runner-up for the Telstra Business Woman of the Year.

But I don't promote myself a lot to be quite honest because the focus should not be on me—it should be more on the company and on the people who make it a success. It's the same for any big business—you're only as good as the people around you, and I'm fortunate that I work with great people.

Have you remarried?

No, we're in the process of getting a divorce. Because we had no animosity, there was no rush but in the end we decided that we both wanted to move on. I'm happily single.

Was it difficult balancing the business and home life in the early days?

It was okay because during the day my son was going to school. When he was very little I could be home when he was at home, and most of the demos were held in the evenings. He would sit in the office with me when we ran the business from home for the first three years. In the evenings when my husband was home, I went out and did my demos. It all worked very well together in the early days. As things got busier and I had to travel a lot, my son was a lot older anyway, so it really worked well for us.

Could you describe your management style and what type of culture you build within your business?

I would say it is quite an unorthodox one because I'm very hands-on and feedback-oriented. I know my business and the people I work with, my management style is quite a strong one because when I believe in something I like to see it through, bearing in mind it's a two-way street.

How would you motivate yourself on a daily basis?

Knowing that every day it's just going to get better, that's basically it—you've put everything into it; you have a great product; you work with great people. I'm quite a disciplined person though—I get up at 4.15 in the morning; I do my reading for 45 minutes; I have my gym workout till 6.00, and then I have a shower and have my breakfast, and I'm gone by about 7.15. So I'm very routine-based. I haven't changed in years now.

If you're awake at 4.15, what sort of time do you finish work at night and go to bed?

Usually I finish at about 6.30, and I would be in bed by about 9.00 at night—asleep. Now you can see why I have no partner—no time.

What motivates you generally? Is it money, seeing people develop, growth of the business, helping others, recognition?

Basically all those things, except I don't work on recognition because I really believe that I'm the right person for what I'm doing—I was supposed to do what I'm doing. I'm convinced on that one. I love it when we help other people and fulfil their dreams. I'm motivated by seeing the product out there, making a difference in people's lives and health. It's the success of the company that motivates me, I also like the income because it gives me opportunities to have a lifestyle I never dreamed of—I can travel and I don't have to think twice if I want to purchase something. It makes my life easier and you can help others financially as well, it's a whole combination of those things.

What techniques do you use to achieve your goals?

On a daily basis I set goals, my main goal is to communicate with most of my people on a daily basis—with my consultants and managers. Our business is very people-driven, so it is always a goal to make sure that everybody feels they are part of the company, and then help them to achieve their goals. Also I set other goals to keep the business running at a very healthy level eg; how many demos do we need every month to achieve the next level, how many consultants need to be recruited, what incentives need to be put in place? These are basically looked at on a monthly basis, and worked at weekly with our marketing team.

We do yearly goals and business plans together for each year, then we break it down as to what needs to be done on a daily/weekly/monthly basis to achieve it.

If you had to start over, what would you do differently?

Perhaps learn quicker at how to run a business. We learned so much from what we did wrong which made us a better company I believe. One thing we've always strived for is to be different to everybody else, I must admit that when we went through huge growth where we grew 200/300 per cent a month, we lost it a little bit because we were so caught up in the success, every now and then you need a bit of stagnation to do a reality check. We do that because we want to make a difference and not become like everyone else.

How do you prioritise your time on a daily basis?

I just go very much with the flow and work by my business appointments. The only thing I'm diligent about is to make sure I answer all my emails on a daily basis, first thing in the morning and last thing in the evening so I don't make people wait.

Have you had any mentors or role models along the way?

I haven't had role models because I always thought I just wanted to be me, and if being me is not good enough to do what I'm doing, I shouldn't be doing it. Mentors—I definitely had people who constantly looked over my shoulders— now more than ever—I had one great mentor who is still a great friend of mine. He is an ice hockey coach for the Swiss national team in Switzerland. He's Canadian and has been to the Olympics, you can learn so much from sports coaches—if you take your eye off the puck, you get a goal which you don't want. He always told me you have got what it takes—just focus on the things which you're good at, and not the things which aren't important—and that is negative people and criticism.

That's basically the advice he always gave me when I was whinging about something. He said get over it if it happened, just don't make the same mistake again, learn why it happened and move on. That was a sporting analogy he always used.

Are there any motivational books that you've read that you would recommend?

I'm always reading something, I'm currently reading *A Beautiful Mind* by DeBono. I absolutely love it and again it brought me back to reality because you slip into the daily grind—you become like everybody else and suddenly you lose sight of yourself. The other thing I've read recently was *Attitude* by Justin Herald. I liked his book and it's easy to read. I've read *Solution Focus Coaching*, it's a brilliant book—I recommend it to everybody. Again it's about how what you focus on will grow, and if you focus on negativity, that's exactly what will grow. If your business struggles and you focus on the struggle, you can't go forward. Books like that I do enjoy, and I would read one a month.

Do you regularly undertake any business training yourself?

No. I like the way I do things and I don't expect to succeed in everything I touch, that is unrealistic and I like to know my own path—with all the potholes and trees and things in it.

Where will your business go from here and what's the plan for the next five years?

We're currently going through a new phase, and my goal is that 30 per cent of Australian households should be Enjo users in five years time. (Currently we have about 7 per cent of Australian households, so there's a long way to go.) I truly believe that the company we're working with has the latest in product development, that is why I'm very much Enjo—because I truly believe the customer is getting the best product that is available.

◆

Three key strategies for Enjo's success

1. I believe I have a great product.

2. I have a passion for the people I work with.

3. We surround ourselves with people who know more than you do in certain areas. Don't try to be an accountant or strategist if that's not what you're good at. If you're good with people, go out there and work with the people and give somebody the job of doing your accounts and dealing with banks. I think that often business owners try to be everything. Invest the money you can afford and surround yourself with people who know more in certain areas than you do.

Barb's words of advice

1. Believe in what you want to do. Make sure you have staying power. If you know yourself and you've quit everything you've started, you can be pretty certain you'll quit your business.

2. Don't work just for money. People always ask what do you think? What wisdom can you give me? What should I do when I want to start my own business? I say it's as simple as believing in the product you're promoting, having a vision and not doing it just for the money because you'll be very disappointed. You have to make sure you do it because you love it, and you have faith—and the rest just follows.

3. Attitude. I think what keeps people going and succeeding is all in the head—how you perceive things, how you see yourself. I have a philosophical outlook on business, and some people sometimes look at me and probably wonder how I ever made it.

4. Have a good business brain. I can read a spreadsheet; I can communicate with the bank, so business knowledge is necessary. If it isn't innate in you, I think it's important that you gain it. Don't just go and take risks without thinking it through, but don't be a pussycat either and think 'I don't want to get out of my box'.

5. Be self-motivated—that's also very important. You can't wait for other people to motivate you every day.

6. A healthy body/healthy mind. I personally couldn't do my job if I wasn't a fit, strong, healthy person. That balance has to be there. I look at some business people and I think how can you do what you do with the way you're out of shape. You can see them labouring. It's unbelievable. The quality of life just can't be there.

JANINE ALLIS
BOOST JUICE BARS

In the late 1990s Janine accompanied her husband to the United States, where she came across an idea that would change the course of her life and prove to be bigger than her wildest dreams. 'As a consumer I always struggled to find anything healthy to eat and drink when I was short of time, then I saw the juice and smoothie concept in the States and decided to introduce the concept to the Australian market.'

Janine built the innovative youth based retail business after she developed a business plan and pitched the idea to investors, raising $200,000 of which $20,000 was her own savings.

It was her own passion, determination and personal attitude towards healthy living that led her to develop the grab-and-go Boost Juice retail concept in Australia. Janine always takes a personal interest in every aspect of the business from developing the juice and smoothie recipes herself, to the strategic planning, staff training and store setups, besides day to day running of the business.

Her first store opened in Adelaide in May 2000, which she set up while still living in Melbourne, at the same time raising her three young children. Since then Boost Juice has had phenomenal success, becoming Australia's fastest growing juice franchise ever, with a network of 150 stores, and that is growing at a pace of one new store per day.

Janine admits that she never imagined that she would be leading a multi-million dollar empire, overseeing 1800 staff, and achieving staggering revenue of over $100 million per year, and with plans to expand into the world market over the next few years, there is nothing stopping this dynamic inspirational woman.

How would you describe Boost Juice Bars in your own words?

Boost Juice Bars are a juice and smoothie retail outlet and we're the largest juice and smoothie outlet in the southern hemisphere. It started in May 2000 in a store in Adelaide and expanded from there and now we have over 150 stores in every state of Australia except Tasmania and we have 2 stores in New Zealand.

Where did you grow up?

I grew up in the eastern suburbs of Melbourne in a place called Knoxville. I'm the youngest of four kids. Basically my parents were classic baby-boomers; Dad worked and Mum stayed home, and we lived in a 10-square green weatherboard house in a very underdeveloped suburb. I was born in 1965, so Knoxville was dirt roads and really out in the sticks. I remember at primary school it was really common to see black snakes and brown snakes.

Did you complete your schooling at Knoxville?

Yes, I went to a school called Knox Technical College, and I left there in Form 5 when I was nearly 17. It's equivalent to Year 11. After I left school, I took a junior media assistant/secretarial job at a company called McCann Erikson Advertising Agency, working in the media department for the General Motors Holden account. I was very keen to get into the work environment and earn money and be self-sufficient.

Do you believe that your parents influenced your decision to go out into business for yourself?

Not at all. My dad worked in middle management at a massive company in Bayswater called Fibremakers. My mum was a homebody, so their aspirations amounted to: if I got a secretarial job, how exciting, that was a fantastic achievement. Don't get me wrong—they were very encouraging, but there was no history of owning businesses. At school I just cruised along, was always after a good time, but really couldn't think beyond actually getting on an aeroplane and having an adventure overseas. When I was growing up, it was like, 'What do I want in life? I want to see the world', which is what I did. I told my mother at 21, much to her horror, that I was leaving for 3 months, and I came back 6 years later.

I imagine they're blown away with what you have achieved.

They are, and I couldn't do what I do without my mum's support. She is phenomenal, helping me with the kids, picking them up, dropping them at school, she's fantastic.

When I get home from work, the children are bathed—they're fed like I was fed as a child.

So there's a lot of consistency there and I honestly work guilt-free because I know that someone's with my kids who loves them as much as I do. They're all at school now so that's a little bit different. In the first two years of Boost, I worked from home. That's probably where the motivation came from to start my own business—I didn't want a part-time job because part-time jobs weren't that stimulating. I wanted everything: I wanted to have my family, I wanted to have an interesting job, I wanted to have stimulation, I wanted to pursue creative pursuits. But I had to create that myself because it didn't exist in the world.

So your first job was as a media assistant, where did you go from there?

I left McCann Erikson to take up a position at Australian Made, which was an agency funded by the government to promote Australian-made goods in Australia. I was hired to represent Victoria. I was still 17 at the time—it was a modelling assignment. That fell over because funding was pulled, so I thought I'd try modelling for a while—which I found quite boring.

I worked for Adidas—I had what was at the time a perfect sporting body, so I was a house model for Adidas for approximately 12 months, and while I was there I worked for a gymnasium called Vigour (which has now gone under) as assistant manager. From there I went into advertising for a small company as the accounts co-coordinator.

As I said, my aspirations were to travel, so I was working three jobs—I worked in a nightclub as the marketing person and I worked on the door at night, purely because the money was great. I worked day and night to earn enough money to go overseas.

I took a job in Camp America where you go to America and work in the summer camps for American kids, and I was fortunate enough to work with blind, deaf and mentally retarded kids over there. It was fabulous. Having grown up in Knoxville and not exposed to anything really outside the norm, it was a great eye opener for me.

After that I travelled around the States. I was a nanny in France for a while. I went to Germany, Spain and Portugal. Then I went back to France and got a job working on David Bowie's yacht. I did that for a couple of years, which was a great way of travelling because you basically went to sleep in Italy one night and woke up in France or Monaco. It was pretty amazing. I went to the Cannes Film Festival three times and did the Grand Prix two times, then did an Atlantic crossing away from the Caribbean so that was good fun—fun for a young person travelling.

From there I met a guy called David Putnam who was the producer of a movie called *Midnight Express*. He was also a bigwig in TV in England, and he suggested that if I went back to Australia he'd get me a job working for a company called Village. He was a director of the company.

So I eventually decided to leave Europe and come back to Australia, and got the job with Village Roadshow through his recommendation. I started managing one of the Village cinemas and after eight months I was transferred to Singapore to help set up their cinemas over there. When I came back to Australia again I worked for United International Pictures as a publicist for two years. That's when I met my husband and started having babies—and decided to start my own company.

What was your main reason for starting a business?

I wanted to create a business where people loved to go to work and were treated with respect. I wanted to do it my way.

What were the first steps in starting the business?

Find a hole in the market, look for evidence that your idea will work, sell the vision to investors, and get the money.

Were they silent investors?

Totally silent investors—they bought shares by putting money in—there were five of us at the beginning and the investors weren't actively involved in the business.

Where did you get the juice and smoothie recipes?

They were all made in my kitchen. We had a smoothie and juice fest where everyone who came over tried a new concoction. Fortunately, I have taste buds that match what most Aussies like. It was important to me that they were very healthy and that's why we use a live culture yogurt rather than sugar-filled sorbets

So, you started in 2000. What age were you then?

I'm 38 now, so I was 34 then.

When you did market research, was there anybody doing that sort of thing in Australia?

In the beginning there were a couple of people putting their toes in the water, but they don't exist any more, they were doing it for all the wrong reasons—they were doing it just for the cash. When we asked ourselves why are we doing this? None of us was actually in it for just the money. My husband had a fairly good job, so I didn't take a wage out for the first two years. He could just earn the money and I could just focus on building the business and working it.

Did you have a target market?

Yes—the target market was females aged 18-35, so we focused on that market. We did email marketing from the word go. We opened the door and started sending emails straight away and doing monthly newsletters. I personally inputted the first 6000 emails—I did everything.

I was running the stores, doing the accounts and marketing, and absolutely loved every single bit of it. That puts me in good stead now, because there's not one part of this business that I don't understand. It hasn't really changed, only got bigger, but I've had to change in the sense that I can't be involved in everything all the time.

Did you have anyone you networked with in the early stages?

In the early stages there was no-one. I was just so busy, and even now it's still so busy, yet I now try to surround myself with great mentors. But back then it was very much just learning, making mistakes, learning really quickly, making more mistakes, learning again really quickly, and also trying to get the right people around me.

Did you always plan to build up the stores and franchise them?

No, not when we first started. It was only once we were trading that we knew we were going to grow quickly. Whether that was going to be a franchise model or a company model, I wasn't sure. What I learned very quickly was that the success or failure of any business is the people, and I knew that I couldn't physically hire enough good people to be able to match my growth. And another point was that franchising is self-funded as well, so we considered it. Making sure we were always conscious of not just putting someone—anyone—into a franchise because we needed to fill one. Out of every hundred people who apply, only seven people get through because we are still so careful to get the right people. Quite often we don't get people involved who've had retail experience—it's all about their attitude and their understanding of the importance of customer service.

When did you actually decide to go out and franchise?

It was after the first year of opening. We came across a guy called Rod Young who definitely was a person who was an expert in the field and who was a fantastic person to get involved in the business. He worked for Deacon's, a law firm, as a consultant, setting up franchises. We were his very first clients, so it was perfect timing for him and perfect timing for us.

How did you go about setting up the franchise model? You mentioned you had Rod Young, who helped.

He'd been in franchising for years, so he knew what to do. Going to Deacon's was the best thing we could have done, as they're a reputable law firm which did it properly. At the time it cost us $60,000 and they said it was cheap. I think it cost a lot of money. But the good news was that we actually got a really good agreement and that has been an important part. It was the most important thing we'd done, in that whole process.

So what did you get for $60,000?

That was for our documentation, which to me, not having much experience in the law, nearly made me fall over.

For anyone wanting to set up a franchise, would you recommend taking the same path you took to other people?

I think it depends on the business. It depends on your motivation and what you want to achieve out of it, and I think it depends on who you're in business with.

I think if people franchise because they can make a quick buck that's when they'll fail. I think if you stop having fun, you should stop. If you're doing it just for the cash, then you'll get the wrong franchisee and guess what—your fun ends. So I think it depends really on what they're doing, what business it is, what they're looking for in their business and what they're looking for as a return.

What are the pros and cons with franchising?

You can't please all the people all the time, and you don't always get things right. In essence, every single one of our franchise partners is brilliant. Sometimes they forget that they're in their own business and they lack accountability. However, that is probably 2 per cent of the whole group. The other 98 per cent of them are absolutely brilliant. Even those 2 per cent, they've got their weakness, but they certainly have their strengths as well.

You mentioned you had five silent partners in the business in the beginning. Are all five still involved?

No, over the years we have exchanged silent partners for more active, hands-on partners. The originals were all very good friends—all of them did very well and were happy to take a good profit and move on. This allowed us to bring in Geoff Harris who joined us when we had about 20 stores—he's a co-founder of the Flight Centre. He's been great and we catch up once a month; we travel together to see the Boost stores. He's been an integral part of my personal growth as a business person. We have also brought on Mark Beason, a wonderful person who I have got to know over a period of time. Rod Young, who's an expert in franchising—he's got a small shareholding, and Simon McNamara, who had Viva and is now a critical executive and a share holder. The lesson is: never get into bed with someone that doesn't share the same ideology as you.

What do you think of the advantages and disadvantages of having partners?

Pick the right partners. Geoff Harris, for example, is absolute gold. Picking the wrong ones will hurt your business dramatically, with mixed direction, internal board room bickering and so on.

The key to having partners is to make sure you have the majority share holding. At the end of the day, that is the only way to make sure you can stick to your vision and keep total control. Unfortunately bad partners can kill a good business.

How did you break into the national market?

We expanded throughout Adelaide first—that was where we started our first store and because our first concept was already interstate, I'd already established systems and operations manuals and ran it remotely from where I lived in Melbourne. When we continued expanding throughout the other states it wasn't too difficult because everything was already in place.

Where did you set up stores after Adelaide?

We did a 25-site deal with a number of major shopping centres. This was really quite scary because we had put everything on the line including our house and every bit of cash we'd ever made. We signed a deal with Westfield and LendLease without any franchisees for it and without really having the infrastructure to grow that many sites so quickly, but we just did it. We went out with our chests puffed up saying how big we were and how much capital we had behind us and told them what we're going to do and what we're going to achieve. We basically talked big to try to be big and become big, and it worked.

In the early days, did you ever find it difficult dealing with men?

I always find being a female working in business an advantage, because quite often you're completely underestimated—that's why it's an advantage.

What were the major obstacles to start with?

The major obstacles were always people. The best thing I've done in business is get the right people, and the worst thing I've done in business is get the wrong people, and also not acting quickly enough when I know in my heart that they're not right for the business.

Was selling your house the biggest personal sacrifice you made?

Yes, a tear was shed at auction day—I sobbed—but it was a only material thing.

In the first year, were you working long hours?

Absolutely, but the thing is because you love it, it's not a chore. There was not one minute that I didn't think about the business. There wasn't one moment when I wasn't doing something to somehow move the business forward. I was fortunate that my husband, even though he had a full-time job, was involved or into it as much as could. Our Sundays consisted of us getting into the car and driving around the city streets looking at sites. So when you ask how many hours did I put in, I did hundreds; but it never felt like it because it was always this really exciting thing I was creating.

How did you husband feel about that?

He's had his moments of 'what about me' but because he drives me harder than anybody else he knew he had to compromise. I think he's really enjoyed seeing his wife and best friend grow and learn with all that we have done. Mostly our discussions are vibrant and full of new ideas and direction. It's never boring that's for sure, and being a high achiever himself he understands. We know Monday to Friday is a hurricane but we are very big on weekend family time, which is a good balance for me.

How many stores do you currently have?

We've got 150 stores in the group and we own 25 personally.

How many employees would you have now at head office?

At head office, at the support centre we call it, about 35 people, and Boost Juice employs about 700. The whole group, as in franchisees included, is about 1800 people.

How often do you travel to set up stores?

I don't set up stores any more. I have a phenomenal team that does that, but I see every single store that goes out for setup, and they definitely have my stamp on it. I travel nearly weekly. Every three months we do a Boost night, so I tend to get to every state every three months, and then there are other reasons to go to every state anyway. Probably once every two weeks I'll be on a plane somewhere. I hate being away from my kids, so I often drag one of them with me.

What would you say have been the highlights for you in running your own business?

I think the whole journey itself has been really good fun, so I think that's a highlight in itself. Just the people thing—seeing the people development is pretty amazing—seeing the difference you can make. A highlight was creating a business, overall, and hitting 150 stores. Another highlight was when we turned over a million dollars a week instead of a million dollars a year. There have been so many highlights. What we probably do wrong is not celebrate the successes enough.

What awards and recognition have you received for the business?

We won a retail award from LendLease—that was really exciting. I received the Telstra Business Woman of the Year Award, and even though it was a Janine award, it really was a Boost award because I wouldn't have got it without my team. There was also a People's Choice Award for Boost Juice and for *My Business* Magazine.

What was your group annual turnover for the business last year?

It's not a complicated business, but we actually have two businesses—we have the company stores that generate income and expenses, and we have the franchise network that does the same thing. So we turn over about, as in the company overall, $35 million. The stores turn over about $65 million annually.

Have you ever had to obtain external funding outside of the investors?

We have, but I'm one of these people who don't like debt. We recently worked with the Viva acquisition, and we took a loan out with the bank, but only used it for three weeks then basically we were on track again. Even with the recent acquisition of 20 per cent from the Beason family, which went into a separate fund and has never been touched, the company has been very positive in cash.

When did the company first start making a profit?

The first year we lost $34,000, which was pretty amazing considering we were opening all those stores, and then the second year we made about $500,000, and then really grew from there. So it was probably year two we hit profit—but always very cash positive, which is what I liked about Boost—there's your smoothie; there's the cash.

Does the company deal internally with debts and creditors with regard to franchisees?

No, because again, the great thing about being in the year 2005 is that the banks have a direct debit system. We didn't have it at the start, but when we discovered they had it, we transferred everyone onto it because it really helps the relationship too. It's only a line item that comes in with the bank statement instead of 'You haven't paid your royalties this month. Please write the cheque.' It's been really good. It takes the personal side out of it, so when we're ringing them, we're ringing them for good news, not 'you owe us money'.

Is your husband Jeff involved in the business these days?

He has a full-time job with a company called Aus Stereo, and he's on the Board of that company so he has a major position. But yes, he's absolutely involved in Boost Juice in a strategic way. Working weekends with me, he'll come in after work and meet with the marketing department—he's a phenomenal marketer. He has an amazingly creative mind and definitely thinks outside of the box and he helps me with that because I'm more logical and he's more 'out there'.

How would you describe your management style?

It's really evolved over the years. I probably started a bit soft but now I am told I am the model of the current trend of 'emotional intelligence'. I use a lot of intuition. I need total honesty. I give a lot and in return I get great commitment from my people.

How do you motivate yourself on a daily basis?

I think it's the same as every human being—sometimes even as a mother. Some days you think *I love my children but today I don't want to play. I'll play tomorrow—I'll be a mum tomorrow but today I just want to be myself and not have someone hang off me.* It's like business—some days 99.99 per cent of the days are great, but that 1 per cent of the time—when it could be that time of the month, it could be you just didn't get any sleep last night because the children were sick or just because, you don't want to play. But that is so rare because the other 99.9 per cent of the time I'm having an absolute ball and wouldn't give it up for anything.

What motivates you in general—is it money, recognition, challenge, helping others?

The physical money doesn't motivate me. Obviously money gives you freedom and that's really important in life, but I am very target driven, so if I said I'm going to deliver x profit or x target or x turnover, that drives me. It could be a large figure or a small figure, or it could even be a loss figure in some instances, but that drives me. If I promise someone I'll deliver on something, I will deliver on it—my word drives me. What motivates me is the love I have for it and the passion I have for it, so the motivation just comes because nothing infuriates me more than when I hear about bad customer service or people waiting too long, so it's really that care factor that also motivates me.

Do you use specific techniques to achieve your goals and are you a great list maker?

I'm very much into lists. I think I use Outlook to the tenth degree—I'm very much into tasks so there's a tracking form and everyone has clarity. Communication strategies are making sure that that is absolutely not negotiable, and those 9.30am meetings happen. Even if the Queen's here, she has to wait.

Have you ever felt vulnerable in business?

More so earlier on than now. But you always feel vulnerable in business—there's always that part of you that has that little bit of tiny fear somewhere down there. Even still to this day, I have everything I possibly own in the business, so if something happens, we lose everything. So yes I think you do feel vulnerable if you think of the enormity of what you've got on the line, but then I think life's too busy to be vulnerable. At the end of the day you think that whatever problem is thrown at you, you're sure there will be a solution for it. If not, I'll find one.

If you ever had to start over, would you do anything differently?

No, and the reason I say no is that I've had to learn some of these lessons to be where I am now. So I wouldn't do anything differently because for me, if I'd had a really good accounts person at the start, I probably wouldn't understand the accounts like I do now. I don't have accounting training, but I can sit with the best of them and know what I'm talking about now. But if I'd had good accountants, I might have just let them be. I would have to say that there's probably nothing that I've done in the past that I'd do differently now.

When you're away from work, how do you relax and unwind?

We're fortunate and very lucky to have a beach house, and that's where I'm a good mother, where I'm a good wife. That's where I try to get my 'me time' happening. We go away as often as we can.

Have you had any mentors along the way?

Geoff Harris is definitely a mentor—I just love him. He's great. Sometimes the mentors and the people around you that are the ones who surprise you the most. Jacinta Caithness who's in our company, she's only 24 years old and she has also been a form of mentor to me. Sometimes mentoring comes from areas where you don't have to be a 62-year-old business person to be a mentor. You can look around you and see people who do things that are very mentor-like all the time.

Do you read motivational books yourself?

I try to, I love reading books about people and their lives—what they've done and achieved.

Is there any book that you would recommend to someone wanting to start a business?

Yes, *Good to Great* I thought was an excellent book. Actually any books on people who have succeeded and how they did it. You're better off picking up a book on Gerry Harvey—on how he did it, and learn from his lessons—or someone like Richard Pratt, who had no formal education but just got on with it and did it.

Do you undertake any training yourself?

I'm really self-motivated, so I don't feel I need to go to someone to make me achieve what I need to achieve because I think I've already got that inbuilt. But I believe any sort of self-development course is great. Certainly a time-management course would be vital for anyone—it's certainly helped me.

What's the best advice you've ever been offered with regard to your business?

'If it's to be, it's up to me', and 'If nothing changes, Janine, nothing changes' is what Geoff Harris says to me. If you've got something wrong, and you don't change it, nothing changes and it will always be wrong.

What are the plans for the next five years?

The plans for the next five years are to establish Boost Juice as one of the most famous and loved brands in the world.

Three key strategies for Boost Juice's success

1. Not taking 'no' for an answer.

2. Having the power to blame yourself for everything—if everything is your fault, you can fix it. The second people say blame the weather or blame something, it means the power of change is out of your hands. So I think that if you make sure that everything is your fault, then that gives you the opportunity to fix it. It's really accountability and responsibility.

3. Tenacity—I think with business, it's not something that you can do part-time. You have to throw yourself it, you have to continue to go and go when everyone else says it's not going to work. It's that blind faith in yourself to keep going.

Janine's words of advice

1. You should have a business plan to get there—that's vital.

2. Try not to get into business with a partner if you can avoid it.

3. Try to find mentors who have actually achieved it in the past. Try to outsource or seek out the absolute right people to assist you to try to avoid making the same mistakes that they've made.

4. Don't do it just for the money because as soon as you do it just for the money, you make decisions based on that, which could tend to be very poor decisions.

5. Always maintain your integrity and honesty, and only do business with people who have the same integrity and honesty that you have.

6. Recognise that it's about people. Spend time rewarding and recognising the right people. Make sure you get the right people from the start. Staff are the success or failure of any business.

LORNA JANE CLARKSON
LORNA JANE ACTIVE WEAR and BODYWIZE

Lorna Jane Clarkson was an aerobics instructor and couldn't find the right clothing to match her active lifestyle, so she started making her own workout gear and the business grew from into a multi-million dollar leisure wear empire. Lorna Jane Pty Ltd was established in 1990, a Queensland-based company that manufactures, distributes and retails women's active, sports, swim, weekend and leisure wear.

Lorna started her business when she was 25. Now, at 39, with 21 stores around the country and overseas distributors in Japan, New Zealand, Vanuatu as well as international stores in Singapore and Hong Kong, she's is a long way from where she started 14 years ago, cutting out designs on the lounge-room floor of her home. With Lorna Jane's sales topping 10.5 million for the last financial year, there is no stopping her. Lorna Jane's passion to promote her healthy lifestyle has also led her to open the first Bodywize Women's Health & Wellbeing Club and Day Spa in Teneriffe, Brisbane, with a second club planned to open in Rosalie at the end of 2005.

Lorna Jane's story is quite exceptional in that she has been able to tap into a very unique niche market, not only in Australia but on a worldwide scale, competing with the likes of Nike, Adidas and New Balance. Lorna Jane is the face and person behind the business, and the epitome of health; she lives and breathes everything that her Australian brands represent.

Lorna believes her brand is more than just a fashion label for women, it represents a way of life—a culture. It is an opportunity for her to touch people's lives and influence the way that they live their lives, by asking them to put their health and wellbeing first. Whether it is through her Lorna Jane active stores, Bodywize Health and Well-being clubs, Bodywize Day Spas, H20 Water Company or her Bodywize magazine she is making a difference by educating her customers about the benefits of leading a healthier, more balanced life.

As the public face and creative force behind the business, Lorna Jane is still intimately involved in the design of the Lorna Jane label, producing swimwear, active wear and weekend clothing. Lorna Jane is also recognised as one of Australia's leading fashion labels and has been honoured with the most awards ever received by an active wear label within Australia.

Can you give a brief overview of the Lorna Jane brand?

Lorna Jane, the brand, is more than a brand—it is a way of life. We started an active wear company that was filling a gap in the market-place for fashionable functional active garments, but have emerged as a culture that represents health and wellbeing. When our customers wear our Lorna Jane or join our club they are making a statement that they are moving towards living a healthier more fun-filled life. As the brand has developed over the years, it's put me in a position where I can educate our customers on how they can improve their lives. By combining the Lorna Jane active wear label and Bodywize concepts, our message has become clearer. We feel passionate about helping people improve their lives.

Where did you grow up?

I was born in England, and came to Brisbane when I was 11 years old. I lived for a short while in Cairns but have been a Brisbane resident ever since.

Were you a high achiever at school?

I went to Springwood high School in Queensland and I wasn't overly studious—definitely not in the top five, but I was a hard worker and took school life quite seriously. I loved art and that's where you would find me at lunch time, working on my latest masterpiece. I think my mum still has some of them! God love her.

Do you believe your childhood influenced your decision to work in the health and fitness industry?

Not directly, but I have always been health conscious, it was part of my upbringing. I was brought up to respect myself and my body so I was never tempted to smoke or drink and always encouraged to exercise.

Were you always interested in fashion?

What girl doesn't love fashion? Some of my earliest memories are as a teenager coming out of my bedroom and my mother or sister saying, 'You are not wearing that, you have got to be kidding,' and then two months later they would be saying, 'Remember that top and skirt you were wearing, can I borrow that?'

What was your ambition when you left school?

I wasn't really sure what I wanted to do, so I studied dental therapy after graduating from Year 12, and I worked for five years as a dental therapist in Cairns before moving back to Brisbane. But I was always interested in health and fitness and taught aerobics while I was studying and part-time when I was a therapist.

What led you to start designing leisure wear?

As an aerobic instructor I couldn't find any active wear that I liked, so I started making my own. It was the '80s so they were pretty outrageous, and I was always getting asked about them, so I started making outfits for friends, other instructors and people who came to my classes. I spent my weekends cutting and sewing in my dining room. There was this one moment when I woke up and realised that this is what I wanted to do. I felt passionate about creating active wear; I quit my day job and turned my hobby into a full-time business.

Where did you go from there?

I opened a small studio in a fitness centre that I was working in; one room for manufacturing and the other as a small showroom. The business grew by word of mouth until we decided to open our first Lorna Jane retail store in 1991 in Broadway on the Queen Street Mall Brisbane. We have 22 stores throughout Australia and we intend to open another four or five stores in Victoria in 2005–2006. Our goal is to open 50 to 60 Lorna Jane stores across Australia. We've also set up a Lorna Jane store online where products can be viewed, and ordered and paid for securely over the Internet.

Where do you currently export to?

Currently we export to Japan, Taiwan, Singapore, Hong Kong, New Zealand and Vanuatu. The Lorna Jane range is sold to a limited market within Australia with approximately 20 distributors in selected gyms and boutiques.

Why did you decide to open the Bodywize Health and Wellness Clubs?

I really wanted to share the things that I have learnt in my life; about how to look after your health and how to get the most out of life. It has always been an ambition of mine to open a fitness centre. At Lorna Jane we make amazing products, but Bodywize was taking it to the next level. We can now speak to our customers on a daily basis and enrich their lives in so many ways, by encouraging them with their exercise, by showing them the benefits of going to the bath house or looking after their skin, having a massage or learning about nutrition.

Can you elaborate on Bodywize and why it's so different from other fitness clubs?

Bodywize is the first of its kind. It's a health and wellbeing club built to enrich people's lives through a more holistic approach to health and wellbeing. Members see our naturopath and beauty therapists before they use the club. They are taken by the hand and given a personal program to help them achieve their personal health and well being goals.

State of the art equipment, extensive yoga, pilates, group fitness and dance classes, personal training as well as a luxury day spa and Japanese bath house are just some of the many features.

The club also has a relaxation lounge and oxygen bar where members can relax, read a book or chat with friends while sipping complimentary herbal teas and breathing pure oxygen.

We have also opened a smaller Bodywize Express Studio, at Rosalie that offers yoga, pilates and circuit training. If this is a success, and we know it will be, we will start to open more in Queensland to start with and then Australia-wide.

It sounds exclusive and very unique.

Yes, it is definitely a 5-star facility, but with a relaxed and friendly atmosphere that encourages friendships and a sense of belonging. We will definitely be capping the memberships, the last thing we want is an overcrowded club.

How many staff do you employ?

Currently Lorna Jane Active Wear employs between 130-140 staff and Bodywize Health and Wellbeing Club has up to 40 employees. My mother looks after all the Australian payroll.

How many females versus males do you employ?

Lorna Jane predominately employs women, because the nature of the business is women's clothing. But I am proud to say we employ three males at Lorna Jane and four males Bodywize.

How would you describe the staff culture that you create within the business?

The Lorna Jane/Bodywize culture follows through to our staff; we have created a working environment that encourages all of our staff to exercise and find balance in their lives. We even allow them to arrange their working hours around having a swim at lunch time or going to an early morning yoga class, for example,.

What percentage of your own money did you initially invest into the business?

Initially I didn't have to outlay a lot of money. I began the Lorna Jane brand on 'a made to order' system, so there was no cost associated with inventory. I kept my overheads minimal and re-invested the profits.

Now that the business has expanded do you receive external funding?

We managed to self-fund Lorna Jane for quite some time. But rapid expansion requires the development of financial partnerships. We are currently working with the Commonwealth Bank, and they have been great; they understand our business and have supported us along the way.

Would you consider investors to expand the business?

Bringing investors onboard is definitely an option moving forward.

Has the business always been profitable?
We have only ever had one year when we didn't make a profit and that was during a big growth period. That year was a turning point for the business.

What was last year's sales revenue for both companies?

The revenue for both companies was excellent with Lorna Jane Active Wear topping $10.5 million for the last financial year and Bodywize Health Club achieving $3.5 million.

That is a great result. Does the business deal with debts and creditors itself or do you use an external company to assist you in this area of the business?

We control all our finances in-house. We have the benefits of remarkable cash-flow because of our privately owned retail stores.

And your husband Bill is your husband and partner in the business?

Yes, we have been together for 14 years and married for 10 years. We met in Cairns in the late 1980s, while I was working in Cairns as a dental therapist. When I left Cairns to go back to Brisbane, Bill followed. Bill is a former butcher and he also worked in the building industry before joining me in the business and his role is to oversee the retail operations of the business.

The business has enhanced Bill's and my relationship. We seemed to have always maintained the right balance for the business. We both understand the level of commitment and respect each other's opinions and don't take things personally; we keep the focus purely on the business.

Do you have other partners in the business and what do you think are the advantages or disadvantages of being in partnership?

We don't have any partners in the business at the moment, I think the most important things to consider in partnerships is that you share the same dream and each partner needs to understand their role and contribute passionately. Good communication is paramount and a total commitment to making each venture successful.

How do you decide on the locations where you propose to open retail stores?

We are always getting site offers, but you have to do your research; a good location for one retailer is not necessarily right for another. In saying that, once you make a commitment to a new shop, it is essential that you do everything in your power to make it work.

What have been the biggest highlights for you in running your own business?

I have to say winning the Fashion Awards would have to be one of the highlights and opening the first Lorna Jane store was a bit of a milestone. Opening the first Bodywize Fitness Centre was fantastic. But I must say the biggest thrill of all is when I see someone wearing a Lorna Jane garment or overhear a conversation about how much someone is enjoying it at Bodywize. I guess it's about being appreciated and making a difference in people's lives.

What is your main role within the business on a day-to-day basis?

Officially my role is the creative director. I'm head designer and I oversee all of the creative decisions within the company. I am the spokesperson for Lorna Jane and Bodywize and am responsible for maintaining the integrity of both brands.

Does the business call for you to travel regularly?

I travel at least three or four times a year to promote our products at overseas trade fairs, and to do product research.

How would you describe your management style?

My husband and I are very clear on the culture behind our brands and we encourage our staff to embrace this culture and the way of life it represents. Our management style encourages our staff to voice their opinions and bring forward new ideas. It is important that our staff believe in the company, its culture and all that it represents.

How do you motivate yourself daily?

Lorna Jane is the way that I live my life, it is the clothes that I like to wear, and it is the things that I enjoy doing. These brands are the result of the way that I choose to live my life, the concept motivates me, and the idea of making a difference in people's lives motivates me. I feel really fortunate to wake up every day and feel passionate about the way that I am living my life.

You seem to have it all worked out. Finding that perfect balance can be so hard for some people, how do you do it?

You have to have balance in your life. Yes there are times in business when you really have to put in the hours, but it is equally important that you allow yourself time to relax and recuperate. Life is a journey, you need to make sure that you enjoy yourself along the way. Bill and I have a house at the beach on the Sunshine Coast, It is a great place to relax and re-energise.

Do you set regular goals for yourself and the business?

We always have a one-year, five-year and ten-year plan. Bill and I have a running sheet that we look at monthly to reassess our dreams and where we are going, so we are constantly looking at the big picture and making sure we haven't diverted too far away from it; as the company gets bigger it's a little harder to do that. That is why a mission statement is a good idea, it is a consistent reminder of the core values of your business and what you are trying to achieve.

If you had to start over, would you do anything differently?

I think I would definitely do it differently. With the knowledge I have gained, I think I could now do what it has taken me 15 years to achieve in 5 years!

Have you had any mentors along the way?

Not really, but Bill and I read a lot and are consistently discussing strategies and business ideas with our friends and business associates.

Where does the business go from here? What's in store at Lorna Jane over the next five years?

We will continue to open more Lorna Jane stores in Australia in 2005-2006. Internationally we have plans to expand Lorna Jane into Canada and the USA. And with Bodywize we'd like to open Bodywize Health and Fitness Clubs throughout Australia.

We are in the process of putting together the Bodywize Wellness publication and have a water company, to promote the benefits of drinking pure water.

◆

Lorna Jane's words of advice

1. Wake up every day and be passionate about what you do.

2. Life is a journey, enjoy yourself along the way.

3. Surround yourself with positive like-minded people.

4. Follow your instincts; your first impressions are usually right.

5. Take time out to regenerate; it is amazing how much more productive you can be if you add balance to your life.

6. Never let the fear of losing stop you playing the game.

NATALIE BLOOM
BLOOM COSMETICS

Natalie Bloom, a graphic arts student, had her first taste of business when she developed her own greeting cards and candle-making kit from home. Using her initiative Natalie took a stand at a Melbourne trade fair in 1993, and secured a major lucrative order with Myers that was the turning point in her career.

Today, 11 years on, Natalie is an incredibly busy lady with three children under the age of three and a flourishing business to control. Recognised as one of Australia's leading entrepreneurs, she has single handedly pioneered a multi-million dollar cosmetic empire that exports globally to 14 different countries including the US, UK, New Zealand, Japan, Asia and Europe. Bloom's expertise is in manufacturing cosmetics, skin-care products, accessories and aromatherapy candles.

Her innovative, fun and quirky products have a big following with an impressive list of celebrity users including Kylie Minogue, Natalie Imbruglia, Princesses Eugenie and Beatrice, Liv Tyler, Christy Turlington, Victoria Beckham, Elle Macpherson, Britney Spears and numerous more.

Natalie has been hailed as an outstanding success for her clever, progressive products and marketing and she's helped put Australia on the world map for manufacturing excellence.

In 1994, Natalie was awarded the Business Opportunities/Optus Young Heroes Award and in 1998 was awarded Winner of the Minister for Youth Affairs' Young

Australian of the Year Award. Natalie was also announced Cleo's Young Australian of the Year in 1999 and has been awarded four times in the Gift of the Year Awards for innovation and excellence in Australian manufacturing.

Can you give an overview of your business?

We develop cosmetic products that have a playful yet sophisticated positioning. Although they're good quality products, they have a playful edge that is fun and accessible and user-friendly. Bloom is positioned as a niche brand so we're not a prestige brand or a mass brand.

What does your range consist of?

Colour cosmetic products is the key component of our product mix, which is 80 per cent of the range including a lip category, eye category and complexion. And then we also do skin care and some aromatherapy products. The key, our core competency, is in colour cosmetics.

Tell me about your origins, where did you grow up?

I've always lived in Melbourne. I'm the middle of three children.

Where did you complete your schooling?

At a school called St Catherine's in Melbourne. I completed Year 12 and went on to do a a Bachelor of Visual Communication at Royal Melbourne Institute of Technology (RMIT).

Did you have any great schooling achievements?

In the HSC I received the Art Award. It was the Art Award for the final year at school.

Do you believe your childhood, or your family, for example, influenced your decision to go into business?

I think I had a very grounded childhood and we had a really warm household, so I think that obviously has influenced my position in life and influenced my make-up.

Are your parents entrepreneurs themselves or were they in business?

My mum was a full-time mum, and my dad was in his own business, so that probably had an influence on me.

What was your ambition when you left school—did you know exactly what you wanted to do?

I always wanted to do graphic design. One of my art teachers early on, like in about Year 9 or 10 said that would be a great course to suit me, and I started to look into it and I think there was never any doubt that that wasn't the right decision. I was lucky because I was very focused and did whatever I had to do to make that happen. I did lots of work experience and worked at getting a folio together, and was focused, whereas I look at kids today who are leaving school and don't know what they're doing. When there's confusion it makes it really difficult to make decisions.

What was your first job when you finished your studies?

I worked in a very small design studio when I finished my degree—which was limiting from a creative point of view, so I was there for 12 months.

Where did you go from there?

I started the business—I started when I was 22.

How did you go about that?

Because I was a graphic designer, I was familiar with printing and the printing industry, and I printed a range of greeting cards that I just started selling, so I didn't have to do much. I just basically printed them and started to sell them in my spare time. It was never intended to be a business.

What's your age now?

I'm 33 years old.

Are you married?

I've been married for five years.

Is your husband involved in the business?

No. He had his own business for 13 years and he sold that business about four years ago and now he has interests in other businesses and various things.

How many children do you have?

Three—a two-year-old and 4-month-old twins.

How do you balance the domestic arrangements with home and work— do you have any outside help?

I've got a full-time nanny so that definitely makes it possible to be able to work, she predominantly looks after my two-year-old daughter. The day my daughter goes to crèche, the nanny looks after the twins in between feeding, so currently I don't know if I've got balance yet.

Do you go into the office daily?

I do a combination. Like today, for example, when Chloe's at crèche, it's really a day in the office. Depending on day-to-day meetings and what I have on my desk at the time, versus face-to-face and phone meetings; it varies all the time.

What led you from greeting cards to candles and cosmetics?

I was always passionate about anything natural and packaging in general, and I put together a candle-making kit that was really of the moment in the early 1990s when everything came as do-it-yourself kits. The kit had natural sheets of beeswax and wick, and you literally put the wick down and rolled up the candle. It was all very simple, there was no heating or melting of wax, and it was a really unique concept that started the business. I had no business plan, I had no real intention of what I was doing getting into a business. It was a hobby.

I then took it to a trade show in Melbourne and set up a stand. Myer came up to the stand and ordered 5000 pieces of this candle-making kit. That was really the beginning of the business. All of a sudden I had to learn how to invoice and how to manufacture in bulk, and it was a huge learning curve, and it was basically just to meet demand.

From candles, where did you go from then?

In my candle-making kit there was a bottle of essential oil to scent the candles, and when I went to research who to buy these essential oils from, I was exposed to the world of aromatherapy and it really struck a chord. Just from a personal point of view, I wanted to understand about aromatherapy, how to use essential oils, and it became quite a passion. It was not something that was around back then. It was only sold as a medicinal-type of product. I didn't understand how to use essential oils, and I think the general public thought it was a hippie sort of thing, but I saw there was a niche in the marketplace to produce a range of essential oils that was easy to use, so I put together an aromatherapy kit.

There were three different themes—relaxing, romance and an energy kit, and in each kit there were three tiny vials of essential oils that you could either use individually or combine two or three together. Or I'd suggest to mix the oils with olive oil from the kitchen to make massage oils. It was all very consumer-friendly, and we sold thousands and thousands of these kits.

It came to a point where I couldn't keep up with my ideas. We did massage oil and different essential oils pre-blended, I then did a lip balm that had essential oils in it (not fragrance oils). Everything on the market at the time was very synthetic and contained saccharin to make it taste sweet. When I went to a manufacturer and requested they create a lip balm that was natural and scented with essential oils they looked at me like I was crazy. In the end we produced a formula that we're still selling today; it was the catalyst to the range evolving into colour cosmetics, it was quite a turning point in terms of sales.

From there it became our objective to launch into colour cosmetic products. The next product was a lip gloss with a hint of colour, then lipsticks and lip liners; we had a very strong lip category.

Slowly we evolved into eye products and then complexion products. It was a very slow evolution process and probably not something I would recommend people do, but because I was young, naive, passionate and excited, I just literally let one product finance the next, rather than saying here's my business plan; I'm going to get capital behind me and I'm going to invest and I'm going to launch a brand. It was more one product going into the next, and I suppose there are benefits to that because we did everything with passion and excitement, but it took a lot of patience. I don't think I had the guts to just go and invest a million dollars into a full range. It turned out to be lip balms financing the lip glosses, and then lip glosses financing the lipsticks.

Where did you initially start manufacturing products?

Back then everything was manufactured in Melbourne. Not everything is now, but in those days it was.

Which products are manufactured outside of Australia now?

There are certain products where different countries have expertise, like all lip pencils are manufactured in Germany, so if you want the quality, you have to get your lip pencils from a certain factory, so they come from Germany.

There's a formula in one of our foundation ranges that Japan has the leading cutting edge technology to produce this formula, so we get that made in Japan. It varies product by product. But the majority of our product is still actually filled and manufactured in Australia.

For the products that are made overseas in Germany and Japan, do you have a warehouse in Melbourne where they are packaged?

Yes, we do it ourselves.

What sort of market research did you do when you commenced the business?

None. I didn't plan to start a business.

What was your target market originally?

I had no idea. I wasn't strategic in my thinking, but now when I think back it was people interested in innovative, fun products regardless of age, whereas now I think I target the market at 35-year-olds, and we're very focused on market research now. We really identify who the consumer is, and the business has become so much more sophisticated as it gets bigger.

How did you get the products out into the marketplace in the early days?

I was out there selling the product myself, and we employed a PR company fairly early on in the business. Initially I would send samples to the editors of magazines, but then probably in about 1994/95 we employed a PR agency to actually handle the public relations.

What do you find is the best form of advertising for you?

I think when a magazine's fashion editor endorses a product, it has the most benefit.

What makes your product so unique?

I think the fact that they're innovative, playful yet sophisticated, so I've got that quirky element with quality. I think Miss Bloom (the character) as the ambassador for the brand gives the product personality and a sense of fun.

When did you create Miss Bloom the character?

It was created in 1997, so she wasn't really in the initial stages of the brand, but has become a key element of the brand.

Currently, how many product lines do you produce?

There are 240 lines in our range, and we try to keep it to that, so in the next season if we launch new products, we delete older products.

Where have you expanded to internationally?

We sell to 14 different countries and 50 per cent of our sales are exported internationally. The US is our key export market along with Japan, Korea, Thailand, Asia, Singapore, Hong Kong, Philippines, New Zealand.

How did you break into the international market?

Originally the distributor contacted us. It was a positive and a negative thing because in some cases we ended up getting caught up with the wrong distributor early on, but it was all about keeping up with requests and demands, people were just so keen to get the product.

Does the business call for you to travel?

It does and I used to travel every six to eight weeks. I was always on a plane and it got really exhausting, but now the Export Manager and General Manager do most of the travelling because it's not possible for me to travel. They're constantly travelling.

How many employees do you have?

Currently 30 staff.

What do you think have been some of the highlights so far in your career?
Creating a successful brand. Originally it was just the product out there, whereas now I think we've got brand equity and that's the most rewarding for me.

Were there any major obstacles or challenges you had to overcome in the first year of operating the business?

I think in the first year it was just a matter of managing everything by yourself because you couldn't afford staff, whereas when you become more sophisticated, your obstacles and challenges become larger. I look at the challenges that I have today and what I started with, and they're bigger and more challenging.

Did you sacrifice anything besides time?

I think my biggest sacrifice was my twenties because I worked such long hours and weekends, and I was so focused and furious. I think it was fantastic and I wouldn't change it for the world; I was very motivated and excited and loved what I did.

When you're in your thirties and you've got your kids, you don't have the luxury of being able to party all night and you don't want to. But you do want to when you're in your twenties, and I think I did sacrifice a bit of time then. At that time in my life, I was probably too furious about what I needed to be, but then I wouldn't change that.

How many hours do you think you put into the business a day in the first year of business?

I probably did 12-hour days every day on average. Some days I might do a 16-hour day, and then a 10-hour day on a Friday, but it was every single minute I had, and then I would work every weekend. Sometimes both days; or just one of the days or two half days. There wasn't a weekend when I wasn't in the office.

And now, do you still work as many hours?

I put the kids to bed at 7.30 and often go back to my desk until I feed them again at 10 or 10.30 at night, so I'll do an extra two or three hours at the end of the day. But I can't do that every day because I'm wearing myself out.

On weekends when all the kids are asleep in the middle of the day, I'll go and catch up with my emails, so my hours are very ad hoc, but I'd probably be doing the equivalent of a full-time week.

In the early days, did you find it difficult dealing with men in business, for example, in manufacturing companies?

I think more than anything it was the fact that I was young and I look young and I didn't have a proven record. That's what I found to be challenging, but I never found men to be a difficulty and I still don't.

Can you tell me what your percentage increase in revenue was last year?

We were growing at 20-50 per cent every year—the business was growing at a rate that we couldn't keep up with. I suppose in the last three years it's become very focused on where and what we want to be. I suppose we've been growing at a much slower rate because of that, and we don't want to be all things to everyone, so we've sacrificed turnover for brand positioning. The last few years it's been growing between 5 and 10 per cent. Since about the 2000-2001 financial year, we've decided to change our focus and reduce our number of doors in Australia from about 1000 to 70. That's the non-department store business, so we can really focus on our department store business and make the brand have more depth in fewer doors.

We've managed to increase sales without massive reductions as we just wanted to get rid of anyone that was cherry-picking our range and make sure that whoever had it could do the brand justice and really present the brand the way we wanted to. We could have just kept growing at that rate but I was nervous about the longevity of the brand equity in the marketplace.

What percentage of your money did you initially invest into the business?

I was 22 still living at home. Whatever I earned was mine, it was really a luxury, and I had no intention of ever moving out of home at that stage. I wasn't even saving up, so basically I think I invested $2000 into that first range of greeting cards that I made, and they paid for themselves and gave me profit because I wasn't renting premises, I was working out of Mum and Dad's garage. I had absolutely no overheads at all and because of that I was able to finance the next range—the candle-making kit—and that was such a huge success from there I then had to go and get a warehouse. It was all just self-funded.

Have you ever had to obtain external funding?

No, never.

When did the business first start making a profit?

It was always a profitable business. For years I didn't have any overheads, and then when I did have overheads, I did it because I was in the situation where I could afford it. It's been a profitable business from day one.

Do you currently have a partner or investor in the business?

I'm the sole director of the business, no partners. I think there are advantages and disadvantages to having a partner. I think definitely the advantages are that you share the burden and you don't have to be the sole person in charge of everything, but I think there are complexities to having a partner—you can't just make a decision on your own; you have to have very clear boundaries as to who has decision-making power. I've thought about it at times and I think that for the time being it's not something that I would pursue.

What is your main role within the business today?

Ideally we're not quite there yet but I've really progressed significantly in the last 10 months for my role to become a purely creative one. My personal goal is to be in a position to be able to focus probably 80 per cent of my time on the creative side of the business and the brand, rather than in the business, although I still want to be involved in strategic business decisions.

On your management style, what sort of staff culture do you build within your business?

I really try to have a culture of discipline with an entrepreneurial ethic, so I don't want us to be in the situation where we're all so disciplined that we forget to be entrepreneurial, and unfortunately as you grow and get more skilled staff, which you need in the business, they can sometimes dampen the entrepreneurial spirit of the business. I'm always mindful of encouraging people to make decisions that sometimes might not fit with traditional structures, and to step out of the box occasionally and take an opportunity because it's a good opportunity, and pat that entrepreneurial mind when it's appropriate. That's an ongoing challenge. You need to set boundaries for people and people need to work within the boundaries but understand when it's appropriate to forget about everything and take on an opportunity.

How do you motivate yourself on a daily basis?

I don't know, I never have a problem with being motivated, and I think that enabled me to have stamina to keep going. I've just recently met someone in the last three months who's developing into a mentor, and I've found when my motivation level has sometimes slipped a little bit, he has just been my saviour. In fact there are two people: There's a lady who's running a huge company in Australian fashion retail, and this mentor. They've both instilled motivation back in me when I've had my moments of doubt. So by surrounding yourself with really motivated focused people, you can always stay motivated yourself.

In general, what motivates you? Is it money, sense of achievement, growth, business, recognition?

I think it's the sense of achievement and growth of business. I've never really been motivated by money although you need to be profitable to stay in business so it has to be a motivation behind, I mean the key motivation to me is the brand and the development of the product. At the end of the day that is what I'm passionate about, what I love, but you need to have some financial motivation because you need to be a profitable business to be able to do the things you love.

How do you prioritise your time?

By focusing on what will make a difference, and I define what will make a difference by making sure it fits with what our core competencies are and what we're good at.

What techniques do you use to achieve your goals?

I've recently introduced to the company a goal set where everyone in the company has to do six-monthly goal setting and then a review of the goals. My ultimate goal for the business is to sit on the top and to achieve this I need my team to help me. This technique has been a really valuable process. Personally I'm into list-setting and I've read a really fantastic statement recently that says it's not about your to-do lists, it's about your stop-doing lists.

As far as mentors, you mentioned before a lady who's a fashion retailer that's a mentor to you. Have there been any other mentors along the way?

Sally Browne, she had a fashion business which she stopped doing probably five years ago. She was quite well known in Melbourne, and I did work experience with her when I was at school still, and then coincidentally the year after she became my next-door neighbour. She was so motivational and just reassured me that what I was doing was the right thing. I think she was definitely a mentor;

I think my dad has been a mentor, and as I said, more recently those two people have become mentors for me, in particular the guy who has become like a formal mentor.

How often do you meet with him?

At the moment it's intense, and we've been meeting on a weekly basis, but on a long-term basis it will just be on an as-required basis with a monthly catch up.

Do you read any motivational books?

I love reading autobiographies about people who've been in business. There's a book on the guy who started Starbucks. I've read unusual ones—people in the fashion industry like Ralph Lauren, Calvin Klein. I've read all the pioneers of the cosmetic industry—there's an autobiography on Estee Lauder, Helena Rubenstein, Charles Revson (he started Revlon), and I find they're motivational books for me. I don't read traditional motivational books but more motivational articles, so people who I surround myself with know my thirst for reading good articles, and they'll often forward me things that are tried and tested.

What was the best advice that you were ever given with regards to your business?

Sally Browne in the very early days continuously told me to do everything with integrity, and that always rang true in my mind—don't cut corners, do things properly. Then my dad was always very focused on having good reporting in place. That was advice that was so valuable, and even though I was so busy and didn't have time, I would make time and had very structured reporting in place from day one. When I look back on what I was reporting on, it was nothing, but we have maintained those reports and evolved those reports, and I think we have to be disciplined in doing that.

It's been a good experience having the children and stepping back from the business because it makes me have a more disciplined environment.

Where does the business go from here? What are your plans for the future over next five years?

To become the leading niche cosmetic brand in Australia, and to focus on our export market with a very controlled and selective distribution strategy. And to always maintain our innovative spirit.

◆

Three key strategies for Bloom Cosmetics' success

1. Be passionate.

2. Do everything with integrity.

3. Have innovation as the key priority for the business.

Natalie's words of advice

1. To know what you're passionate about, and to be in business because you're passionate about something. I've seen so many cases of people wanting to be in business because they just want to be in business, and they don't even know what they want to do or what they're good at, so I think it's understanding what your passion is and being passionate about it and having that genuine passion. If you don't have that, then there's no point proceeding.

2. Getting the right people on board is an important tip. People know that some people put people on because they're bright and they need to—I've done it, I'm guilty of it, but it's about really focusing on getting the right people for the right jobs.

3. The Hedgehog Concept—understand what you do best and stick to it.

4. Understand what drives the profitability of your business. Understand what is profitable and what is not, and why you're doing things.

5. Be disciplined while remaining entrepreneurial.

6. Put the best people on the biggest opportunity. In the past I've put the best people on the biggest problem because they know how to manage it. But y.ou really need to be disciplined in making sure those key people aren't just doing all the problems.

KIRSTY DUNPHEY
M&M HARCOURTS REAL ESTATE

Kirsty always knew she would be in business for herself; at 15 years of age she had two small businesses and a part-time job at a real estate office while continuing to achieve excellent grades in her final years of school.

In 2001 at the age of 21, Kirsty became the youngest person to manage and own a real estate agency in Tasmania. In only four years Kirsty and her partner Tony Morrison have managed to achieve a level of success that most people could only dream of.

With her dynamic approach and determination, Kirsty soon led M&M Real Estate to become Launceston's most successful real estate agency per salesperson, smashing local sales records with its awesome service and innovative marketing strategies. The agency has sold over $165 million dollars worth of real estate in its first four years of operation.

Kirsty's talents and skills have not gone unnoticed, winning the Tasmanian and National Award as Telstra's Young Business Woman of the Year in 2002 and for being the youngest ever to win that award. She was also named Young Australian of the Year for Tasmania in 2004.

Kirsty recently released her first property investment book *Advance to Go; Collect $1 Million.*

◆

Could you give me a brief overview of your business?

I've been working in real estate for the last 10 years—ever since I was 15. It started as an after-school job for me—certainly not something I saw myself continuing on with for the rest of my life. It was really just a fill-in job I did during high school, just a way to earn money.

I then went off to university and dropped out after a bit more than a year (much to the dismay of my parents obviously). I was a bit directionless, and decided to move back home to Tasmania. I then began working in a real estate agency (the same one I'd been working in when I was 15), and started doing a broad range of different jobs within the firm—I worked in administration, property management, IT and as a PA for the managing director of the real estate agency.

When I was 19, I had a go at selling, and that's when things started to change for me.

Once I actually started selling, I realised it was fulfilling and that selling had all the criteria I'd been looking for in a job. My criteria was made up of three points; 1. I wanted my career to be fun and exciting. 2. I wanted something I could potentially make good money from and be really successful at. 3. To be in a career where I could have a profound effect on the people that I dealt with on a day-to-day basis.

At 20, I decided that if I was going to be really, really successful, I had to open my own agency so I went and acquired my manager's licence. When I was 21, I commenced the business along with two business partners. Now I have only one business partner.

We first started trading as M&M Real Estate. The M and M were the two surnames of my two business partners.

Could you tell me where you grow up?

I was born in Darwin, and then lived in country Victoria. My family moved from Victoria to Tasmania in 1988, when I was 9.

Do you come from a large family?

No, just my younger brother and I; we're 10 years apart.

Where did you complete your schooling in Tasmania?

At Scotch Oakburn College, and I left after Year 12 and went on to Monash University in Victoria. I studied a double degree in accounting and computing.

At school, were you an academic?

Yes, I was academic. The schooling system differs from state to state, but in Tassie it's a TE score. I received a fairly high score—98 out of 100, which I guess is one of the reasons that my parents were pretty disappointed when I decided that university wasn't for me.

Do you think that your childhood and your parents influenced your decision to go into business for yourself?

Yes, they both were heavily involved in small business, in investment properties. I do believe that helped me develop a good work ethic at a young age. I was always helping out and working in our family businesses. Unfortunately they had financial difficulties a lot during my teenage years, so when I got to an age when it was time for me to set out and do things for myself, I had to make a decision; I could decide that what they'd gone through was too scary and not go there, or take the view that I've had the best life education I could have on the topic, and that's what I basically chose to do.

What was your first job?

I worked in a real estate agency, just making the coffee and filing as one of my part time jobs. When I was 15, I had two part-time jobs and I also had two small businesses. One of them was importing sterling silver jewellery from Thailand and then selling it at markets and wholesaling to some local shops; the other one was creating websites with a friend of mine from school. I also worked part-time in an ice-cream store. I had only worked for two real estate agencies before I decided to go into business for myself.

When did you decide to give up your other small businesses and put all your efforts into real estate?

In my last two years of high school, and I gave up both of the small businesses when I went to university. My efforts were not really focused on real estate though until I was 20.

What's your current age?

I'm 25 years old.

Do you have a partner in life?

Yes I do—I'm engaged. My partner is not involved in the real estate business.

What led you to start your own business?

I wanted to be able to do things differently to what I'd seen other agencies do here in Launceston—to be able to use some modern marketing techniques and innovative ideas. I've always wanted to have my own business, ever since I was young. I had no idea what I wanted to do though.

When you say modern marketing techniques and innovative ideas, what did you have in mind?

I like to look at other industries, not only real estate, so one thing we consistently try to do is to take fabulous customer service and innovative marketing from any industry where we see it operating well, and then tailor it to suit our industry and our people.

For example, we realised that no-one was advertising real estate agencies on television in Launceston. So we started doing that over three years ago. There are now a couple of other firms that do this as well. Actually we've won the Real Estate Institute of Tasmania Television Awards two years in a row, for ads that are different and innovative.

We focused on branding our corporate image. Linking everything back to our website, ensuring fax headers, corporate stationery, presentation packs that go out were all congruent. We implement new ideas, like our window display, we've got 15 flat screen monitors, so our properties are all digitally put up on there, and rotate 24 hours a day. It's just doing things a little differently, in a more exciting way, and a little bit more high tech.

Launceston is almost like a big country town in some ways—it's a real community. We are still one of the newest real estate agencies to open up, and we opened four years ago. It's different to other places in the world—things move at a different pace and word of mouth is so important.

What were your first steps in setting up the business, besides getting your management licence?

It took about nine or ten months to actually get the licence. It usually takes a bit longer than that but I knew what I wanted—I wanted to get it done quickly and get through it.

We started operating from a two-bedroom apartment that one of my business partners owned for the first couple of months. We then sold a motel complex and ended up operating from there for a while, then we moved into the city for a couple of years, now we've just bought our own office building right in the CBD.

To start off with, we had no formal business plan whatsoever. We started on the first day with phone lines but no signboards and no Internet. We were running everything by the seat of our pants for a short while. But, we did have a projection of income which we wanted to earn for the first year. I think we ended up beating that within four or five months, which was great.

How did you get your name out into the marketplace?

In the beginning, I was based in the office running that side of things, being the licence holder, running the trust account, establishing the property management.

My two business partners were out there actively promoting us in the marketplace, selling on a day-to-day basis. The beauty of the two people that I started the company up with was that they already had fantastic names in the community—they'd both been in real estate for over a decade. They'd already established their names and reputations, so fortunately we were able to get listings.

It's a small town and people started talking; word of mouth was really powerful in our start-up because we didn't have any marketing budget to get out there and splash a lot of money across newspapers, television and other forms of marketing.

Do you network with any other real estate agencies?

In the last six months, I've definitely started to network more with agents in our area, but in the beginning we didn't have those relationships, which was a bit of a struggle.

I've found forming networks within other real estate agencies across the country has really been valuable. Having a couple of mentors who are with other agencies is great and they've usually 'been there, done that' when it comes to helping me out with those tricky sorts of questions that crop up day-to-day.

What was your target market initially?

Launceston isn't the type of market where you can really focus on a niche market to a great extent. People always assume because we've a young company that it will be the youth market that we target, but our clients are varied.

We do a large proportion of our sales in rural areas and we have a large demographic of clients in older age brackets as well—we also have a very strong base of investors and mainlanders.

There's no one niche market that the company specifically focuses on although different agents within our company have their preferred markets.

How many properties did you sell in 2003?

About 450 properties in 2003. *BRW* named us as the 24th fastest-growing company in Australia in October 2004 on the BRW Fast 100 list.

On average, how many properties would you sell per month in Launceston?

I think it's around 40 a month at the moment, but we're still in the process of growing our sales team.

How many employees do you have?

We have a team of about 26 at the moment and it will be growing, especially as Harcourts branches out across the state.

How many of those are in sales?

Our sales team is around 10 at present.

Can you tell me about the joint venture with Harcourts?

Over 2004 our company went gone through a bit of a change. We formed a joint venture with a group called Harcourts who have over 170 offices across Australia. We decided to join forces with them to expand our company, so we're now M&M Harcourts, rather than just M&M Real Estate. Our office actually serves as the head office for Tasmania, so part of our job within Harcourts is to open more new offices in Tasmania. We've already had great success with this and it's a real benefit to have Harcourts offices to refer to. The company name M&M Harcourts will only be around for about two years, after two years, our office will be called simply Harcourts and we'll drop the M&M. It's been a big shift for us getting involved with a franchise group and forming a joint venture. It's very exciting and a great learning curve. We feel that the strategic advantages a group like Harcourts can provide, such as training, systems and technology, will take our company to the next level.

What was your main reason behind joining Harcourts?

If you'd spoken to me six to eight months ago, and said that M&M Real Estate would be part of a franchise group I would have said you were mad, because our independence was so vitally important to us.

How it eventuated was that I had done some guest speaking for Harcourts in New Zealand and the Gold Coast. I was very impressed with their professionalism and corporate policies. Everyone I spoke to at Harcourts had a similar mindset to us—a very high emphasis on customer service, which is something that we're passionate about—and they're continually innovative.

We had all these goals to get our systems developed and our technology right, and by joining Harcourts we've been able to leapfrog ahead to where it might have taken us five to ten years to get to. We've been able to do that within a period of a couple of months.

Do you deal with properties only in the Launceston market or all of Tasmania?

We will eventually deal with the whole state but for the moment we're in the north and north east.

Does the business call for you to travel a lot yourself?

Yes. The business does call for us to travel a bit, especially with Harcourts as their head office is based in Queensland. I also tend to travel a fair bit with public speaking as well. I've been to New Zealand a couple of times this year and it's pretty common for me to be interstate at least once or twice a month on that sort of thing.

What have been some of the highlights so far in owning your own business?

Being listed 24th on the BRW Fast 100 for 2004 was pretty cool. Winning the national Telstra award in 2002, personally for me was phenomenal. I was the youngest winner ever to win the award for National Telstra Young Business Woman of the Year. The doors that have opened for me have been amazing.

In early 2004 I was named the Young Australian for Tasmania—that was great as well.

One of the biggest highlights for us is watching our staff grow. We do a lot of team building exercises. Our whole team jumped out of the back of a plane and did sky diving earlier in 2004 in Sydney while we were at a conference and we took the entire team to Melbourne for our Christmas party. Just little things like that—watching the staff grow and discover new things, and achieve their own milestones. The joint venture with Harcourts has also meant that we're able to establish a formal career path for our staff to develop and grow within the ranks. That really wasn't there when we employed our first staff member, when we were only a four-person company.

What percentage of your sales are residential sales as opposed to commercial properties?

We do very few commercial and business sales—we probably sell about 95 per cent residential.

As far as obstacles or challenges that you had to overcome in your first year of operating go, what would you say were the biggest?

Probably initial financing—we ended up financing our business on two personal loans. As I was only 21, I couldn't imagine the bank giving me a business loan to start up a real estate agency, so we took out the personal loans. We ended up paying off all our debts within the first three months. That initial fear was probably one of the scariest things. And I guess finding the right location for our business, which only happened in August 2004.

I believe that it was so difficult getting finance in the beginning that you took out loans through the bank for cars?

We did that at the beginning—we took two personal loans out for $10,000 to finance the business initially. Since then, we've taken a loan on the building we're in at the moment, but apart from that, the business operates relatively debt free.

What was your annual turnover for the business last financial year?

$2.3 million.

What's your forecast for 2005?

I'd like to see us crack $3 million.

When did the business first start making a profit?

Three months after we started and that was only because with property sold in Tasmania, we don't get paid until the property settles so there's a lag time. You have two or three weeks to market a property, and then four to six weeks for a property to settle, so there was no money coming in for the first month to six weeks or so.

As far as dealing with debtors, do you deal with that yourself internally or do you have an external company that assists you in that area?

In terms of debts to the company, most of our debts are from people who owe us commission, and with that we hold a deposit that covers our commission, so it's not been a huge area for us to worry about, and we handle it in-house.

What sort of properties do you personally invest in; commercial or residential?

I have 11 residential properties. My business partner and I own the commercial building that we're operating from now.

You mentioned that you started the business with two other partners, are they both still involved in the business?

There were three of us originally and one of them is no longer with the business. Now it's only me and one of the original partners, Tony Morrison.

What do you think are the advantages and the disadvantages of having a partner?

There are heaps of advantages if it's the right partner. Tony and I have very complementary skills and a similar mindset and attitude. We are both highly focused on customer service, looking after staff and building the company in an ethical way. I tend to be the organised one, who's in the office overseeing the staff and administration and dealing with the press. I'm the public face of the company for advertising and promoting the business, whereas Tony is the face and contact for the business with clients. His role is sales manager, and his expertise in that area is second to none.

What sort of advice could you offer to someone who may be considering going into a partnership?

I'd advise them to seriously consider going into a partnership, especially with friends or family. I've seen too many friendships and relationships ruined from partnerships gone bad. You have to have the same goals and ambitions for the company, and both be passionate about what you're doing. I think I'm exceptionally lucky to have the business partner that I have. Typically, what you find in real estate agencies is that the people who start up agencies are usually phenomenal salespeople who are at the top of their game in sales, but I have found being a phenomenal salesperson doesn't necessarily make you a great business owner or manager, yet that's where most of our business owners come from in our industry.

What staff culture do you create within your business?

A highly charged, very busy environment. That's why we try to make sure there are fun team things going on as well. It's the busiest workplace anyone here has ever worked in, but the culture is really important to us. We have a policy where we hire on the right attitude, not necessarily on experience.

What percentage of staff would you hire who were new to real estate?

Most of our staff are new to the industry. At first the only person in our office with real estate experience was my mother, who was the first staff member that we put on. This is pretty unusual for a real estate agency, but the training we have set up is quite intense (we do all our own training—the sales team do two hours every week; admin and property management do it fortnightly).

How do you prioritise your time?

I'm a list person. I always have a notepad with me and work down the list by highest priority.

Were there any sacrifices that you had to make to get the business off the ground?

None that I didn't expect. Even now, I'm in the office early in the morning, and both my business partner and I don't finish until quite late most nights. We still work six or seven days a week, but that is to be expected.

Have your personal relationships suffered from the long hours put into the business?

No, my relationships ares fantastic. I've got a really understanding partner who knows that I'm not going to be home at 5.30 every night, and he just works around it—he's fabulous. It wouldn't work with anyone who isn't flexible, and as he does shift work, we have a great understanding.

If you had to start over, would you do anything differently?

No, not really. I'm very happy with where we are at the moment. There's nothing we've done that I could pinpoint and say I wouldn't do that again.

Have you had any role models along the way?

I'm a motivational and business book junkie. I've read Richard Branson's autobiography—and I'm just fascinated by him. People like Julia Ross, Sonia Amoroso and John McGrath have inspired me and have been great role models.

Would books would you recommend to anyone wanting to start a business, you mentioned Richard Branson?

I'd definitely recommend the *Rich Dad, Poor Dad* series of books—they're phenomenal. Then there are a whole series by Jan Somers on residential property investments that are great. People could of course get my book: *Advance to Go; Collect $1 Million'* at www.kirstydunphey.com.

Do you regularly undertake training yourself?

Yes, definitely. I do courses through Harcourts and I also get to attend some of the best training in the country. When I speak at conferences I make sure I watch everyone else who's up there speaking as well—whether they're speaking on marketing, small business, or real estate, I just love seminars. Even if you pick up just one little thing, it's made it worthwhile—especially in our industry.

What's the best advice you were ever given with regard to your business?

Don't take everything personally. Say if you don't get a big deal you were hoping to close or if you have a staff member who isn't doing what you want or is perhaps leaving the company, don't take it personally because it clouds your judgment in terms of being able to learn from it. That was one of my weaknesses early on—I tended to let my emotions rule me a bit. I'm a big believer in learning from your mistakes, and if you let emotions get in the way too much, then you're not able to learn from it effectively.

Where do you go from here? What's the plan for the future over the next five years?

The next five years—I know in terms of M&M Harcourts, we'd like to have a larger Harcourts family throughout Tasmania and a growing prosperous team here in Launceston.

◆

THREE KEY STRATEGIES FOR M&M's SUCCESS

1. Self-promotion—going out and nominating myself for awards, for example, the Telstra Awards. The publicity we received from winning those awards has been incredible for the business.

2. Realising I can't do everything myself. It took me a long time to realise that delegation was actually a good thing. Finding the right team to support us.

3. Keeping an open mind to new ideas.

Kirsty's words of advice

1. Know your competitors and know what you want to do differently to them.

2. Find inspiration, someone who is amazing at what they do and find a way to approach them and ask whether they will be willing to coach you in business.

3. Trust your intuition, it's usually right.

4. Look at the people you're going into business with very carefully and make sure you have the same mindset, goals and ideas on how long you both intend to stay in the business.

5. Do a really good analysis on yourself and figure out what your strengths and weaknesses are. Complement those strengths and weaknesses by building the right team around you.

6. Make sure every client you have is a raving fan—that's the best form of marketing—to have your customers advocating you

KAY BARNEY
CORPORATE HOUSING

In 1999, Kay Barney and her husband Craig moved to Melbourne, with their one-year-old toddler. Craig had been transferred with the company he was working for at the time. They placed them in a very small one-bedroom serviced apartment that was totally unsuitable for a young family.

It was that experience that sparked an ingenious idea for Kay to start her own business from home, providing fully furnished apartments and homes for corporate executives relocating to Melbourne. Kay invested $5000 and established Corporate Housing, which now has offices in two states and a multi-million dollar turnover.

Her accommodation service takes the hard work out of every HR person's role by finding suitable furnished accommodation for their staff, without having to connect power, gas, phone and computer lines and having to employ cleaners to maintain the accommodation.

Within five years Kay's juggled raising three young children and building a steady business, providing fully serviced accommodation for large companies such as People Soft, IBM, Deloitte, Oracle, and Unisys, which temporarily relocate executives Australia-wide for projects.

In 2003, Kay and her husband Craig sold off the Melbourne operation and moved their family back home to Sydney. Since then they've successfully built the NSW operation of Corporate Housing in Sydney's highly competitive accommodation market and their plans are to expand the business Australia wide with an office in each state.

Could you give me an overview of your business?

What we essentially do is provide fully furnished apartments to executives who are relocating. Most of the people we cater for are on extended stays of a month or more, so are generally people who are either on assignments or traineeships or maybe even relocating, and the company puts them up for a couple of months at a time. We really fill the niche between full service hotels or serviced apartments and the difference between a company actually going out and renting something full time, that is, renting something under lease with a real estate agent.

So you provide everything from furniture, crockery, linen, the lot?

Exactly, so when the person moves in, it's just like what we call 'a home away from home'—they're all in private residential buildings—so they have a much more home-like feel, rather than being in a hotel or serviced apartment where all the rooms are the same, and you're walking past the reception desk every morning. Each one is individual and unique, so it's nice, especially these days when a lot of people are moving or going out on assignments and taking their families with them. They're much more suitable for long-term stays.

Can you tell me a bit about your upbringing, for example, where did you grow up?

I grew up on the Central Coast in NSW.

Do you come from a large family?

I'm the middle one of three. My parents ran small businesses, my dad is a builder and my mum did the finance and administration side of things for him. He was the brawn; she was the brains.

My parents divorced when I was seven, and my mum remarried and went into another small business with her new partner. I was always around people who were running small businesses, so I think I was destined to go in that direction. When I finished school I went to university for a couple of years, but it was never for me, I got to the point where I thought why am I heading down this path? I don't really want to work in a big company for a big corporate office.

Where did you complete your schooling?

I finished my schooling and achieved my Year 12 certificate in 1990 at Corpus Christi College, which is a private Catholic school on the Central Coast in Tuggerah.

You mentioned you went to university when you left school.

Yes, I went to Sydney University after I finished school, and I did one year of an economics degree. Then I transferred over into an SAB law course which I did for another two years. That was a part-time course, and while I was doing that I started working for a small business—a lighting company that was based in Sydney.

What sort of position did you hold in that company?

I started out working in Accounts Receivable, and slowly it overtook what I was doing at university. It was also a pretty hefty workload because I was commuting from the Central Coast, studying at night and working in this business. Eventually I stopped myself one day, after a few years of that, and thought why am I doing this? I don't really want to be a lawyer anyway and I went full-time with that company and worked for them for a couple of years. The company was Low Voltage Lighting—a boutique provider of European light fittings and for residences, offices and that sort of thing. I went from Accounts Receivable, adding on Accounts Payable until I was the office manager. That was where I really got my experience in accounts and learned how to do the books for a small business.

What age were you then?

I was 21 and married when I was still working there. I'm now 31.

Where did you go from there?

From there I went to another small business called Outdoor Sign Services. Low Voltage had made some changes internally and I was looking for something on the other side of town, and I also got to a point where there was nowhere for me to go—I'd learned as much as I could learn within that company, which was a family business, so I was looking for something else that would just give me a little bit more scope, so I sought out another small business.

Outdoor Sign Services was a production company for outdoor advertising, like for billboards. My role there was in accounts and I was also PA to the managing director. I started doing a lot of sales and took on that role. The guy I was working for was a fabulous salesperson and taught me a lot about relationship-building and about nurturing your customers; how to create long-term relationships that are the key to a small business. I really learned about customer service, about making friendships almost with your customers and how important that is to your business; and about service levels—I learned a whole lot of different things in the three years that I was there.

I left when I fell pregnant with my first child, leaving when I was 39 weeks pregnant. My husband was offered the opportunity to go to Melbourne to be the project manager for the company that he was working for. We decided it would be a good opportunity to live in another place for a year, so we went down to Melbourne and took our son who was still a baby.

Do you and your husband have any other children?
Yes, Craig and I have three children now. Ryan is our eldest—he's 6 now; Ella is 4; and Ayva is 1.

Is Craig involved in the business?

Yes, Craig works for Corporate Housing as well.

How long has Craig been with the business?

Craig joined the business about 18 months after it started—it was getting to a point where we needed another managerial-type person and that's when we decided that he would leave his role with the company he was working for and come work with me. It was a lifestyle choice really because at that time we had two small children; Craig was doing really long hours for the company he was working for, and we just saw it as a good opportunity for him to be around the house more and be around the kids, and get away from this 12 hours a day corporate lifestyle that he was leading.

How do you balance the domestics of home life with business?

The way I balance it is that we have help. We have had a full-time nanny ever since

I started Corporate Housing, and in the first year that enabled me to work from home but still have the kids in the house, which is what I chose to do initially. For the first 18 months I worked from home with Ryan who was then two, and Ella who was a baby because I was feeding for the better part of a year and that enabled me to still be at home and be around the children. I had an office set up and I just worked from home. When Ella was 18 months old, Craig came on board and we took an office in the city only because it was just getting too difficult with the children around at home. Then we put on some additional staff and that allowed me to have two days a week off to do things with the kids, and for the three days that I worked we had a nanny at home. It wouldn't work without help.

What led you into the business?

It really came from our experience when we moved to Melbourne. Craig was working for a company that was contracting to Ford Australia who were based in Melbourne, and he was working out of the Ford headquarters, so they gave his company an allowance for relocating for four to six weeks while we found ourselves a permanent home. The budget was around $700 a week, and for that we were put up in a tiny, dingy, serviced apartment in South Yarra, which was completely inadequate for our needs with a toddler around. It was a pretty poor experience for us—we had our baby yet it was only a tiny one-bedroom; there was no room for the cot so we had to put it in the lounge room and when he wanted to go to bed, we had to go to bed too at 7 o'clock! It was just a really unsatisfactory way to spend the first month when you're under such stresses anyway, looking for a new home and being in a new town not knowing anybody.

I didn't think much about it at the time but a couple of months later when I was at home twiddling my thumbs and Craig was working his 12 hours a day, I was speaking to a friend in Sydney who was in the corporate accommodation market and made a suggestion: What if we were to get a couple of apartments down here in Melbourne? Some nice modern apartments and furnish them for any corporates that are relocating? About a month after that I received a call asking me to put together three furnished apartments for some executives who were coming down to work in one of the banks in Melbourne, so I did that. I put together three of these apartments and furnished them (they were unfurnished and I arranged rental furniture), hooked up the phone, electricity, all of those sorts of things, and found a cleaner who could service them once a week. Then we rented the whole package back to this company.

That went really well—the people ended up staying for nine months rather than the initial three, so that was a nice start. Those three people were contractors and ended up going to work for PeopleSoft and they spoke to the HR manager and explained their accommodation setup they had experienced previously in Melbourne. Then PeopleSoft phoned and said we've got some people coming, would you do the same for us? And it just snowballed. Before I knew it I was running 20 apartments and I was still at home. It was very much a word-of-mouth business.

Was your next step to employ staff to assist you with all the setup?

Yes, only because it got to the point where I was going out doing everything—I was finding the apartments; I was meeting the furniture people onsite; I was setting them up for the people arriving, putting the welcome hamper in and doing everything—that at first I thought I need to get rid of some of the tasks within the business and the most obvious thing for me to outsource to someone else was the bookkeeping. The business that we run is essentially a very administrative-heavy business because that's what we really do. While we provide apartments, we're really saving the companies a lot of administration by taking all that on, so I brought in somebody to do the books—probably at the point when I was running about 20 apartments—when it was actually becoming a reasonably significant job just to do the bookkeeping. That lady came in for three days a week and was with us until we left Melbourne.

How long did it take to get those first 20 apartments?

It probably took me the first year to get to 20 apartments in Melbourne and that was in 1999.

What was your age then?

I was 26.

Did you do any market research in the early stages?

The first thing I did was get onto the Internet when I started fleshing out the business model. I bought myself a book on starting your own business and did all that sort of research just to find out the sorts of things I should be thinking about. The first thing that was pointed out to me was that I needed to do a detailed business plan, so while those first three apartments were going along, I spent a lot of time researching on the Internet and writing my business plan which was pretty thorough.

The best research that I got was from companies in America that were actually doing what I was doing which was just amazing to me—when I got on the Internet and found out that this idea that we had, people were already doing it and had been doing it for years in America.

I learned quite a lot in the first few years of our operation and I went to the States a couple of times. There's actually a corporate housing industry over there. They're so far ahead of where we're at in Australia, I've been over to their conferences a couple of times and spent a lot of time talking to people who've been running businesses like this for ten or so years, which is when the industry started over there. I actually gained a lot from those times in America because I'd learned about things that we hadn't even thought about doing.

That was probably the extent of my market research because there was really nobody else in Australia doing what we were doing with the same business model.

How often would you travel to the US now?

Every other year with travel, we maintain fairly close links with the Corporate Housing Association in the States because they are a very big industry body. It's a $3 billion industry over there in the States. They do it really well and have been doing it for a lot of years and they're really very willing to share information with us Aussies. They love telling us what they do and they realise we're not competitors to them and they're very good at sharing information and giving us tips. I've had people give me their business plans and financial spreadsheets and models and all sorts of things because they want to grow the industry and they're happy to help. It's very beneficial for us.

Did you have a particular target market that you went for in the early days?

Yes. It became pretty obvious early on that our target market would be companies who had a recurring need for extended stay accommodation, so we really defined our market as nothing less than one month because hotels and serviced apartments do that quite well, and because there's quite a lot of work in setting up an apartment, it wasn't cost-effective to be catering for really short stays.

We defined our market as stays between one and six months because from six months onwards it's more cost-effective for the company to take a long-term lease and do it themselves. So we really worked out that we wanted to fulfil the gap in the market that was created between long-term apartments that you could rent yourself and a hotel—where a hotel became not the ideal solution for something that was more than a month. The product that we wanted to provide was targeted at companies who would have a recurring need, that is, companies who had consultants working on projects that they were bringing people in from overseas for. for example, IT companies, consulting companies, anybody who had a secondment program where they perhaps rotated staff from overseas offices. They were the ones we were after, so we made a hit list.

As far as getting your name out into the marketplace, did you cold-call businesses?

Yes, I made a list of the big four accounting firms and approached them direct. I'd already had the contacts at PeopleSoft so we kept working with them. They're still a customer to this day.

When I went for companies like Oracle, it was cold-calling. Eventually people started to find out about us too and we would start to get calls. We advertised a little in the newspaper and we created a website; we just put ourselves in the places where HR people would go looking traditionally if they were trying to find a solution to some long-term accommodation.

Did you have anybody you could call or get advice from? You mentioned a girlfriend in Sydney earlier.

Yes, she was working in a company like a broker—where they would actually book hotels and things like that for companies, so she knew about corporate accommodation. There was nobody else really, except advice from my mum— just in terms of the actual business model and the financial side of things—to make sure I was on track there.

Was the original business plan followed through successfully?

Yes definitely—it's funny I wrote the original business plan in the first few months of business, about 18 months later when I went back to revise it when we were moving to offices into the city, I got out that old business model to use as a basis for writing the new one, and I kind of laughed at the projections I'd set because we had so far exceeded the expectations of what I had put in place as goals for that first 12 months of starting the business. So we have stuck to it and we revise it every year.

Do you deal with any international accommodation?

We do because the Internet is a fairly big source of enquiry for us, so in terms of the people who come in to our apartments we've worked out that about 50 per cent are domestic and 50 per cent are international and that's generally because there's a company within Australia who are bringing people in from overseas. for example, at the moment there's a big trend in bringing in Indian IT consultants, so a lot of our customers are using Indian staff and bringing them in for projects. We get a lot of international people here but the business generally comes from their local office in Australia. The international work that we get from overseas generally comes via the Internet.

In the early stages, were there any obstacles or challenges that you had to overcome?

There was always a market for the business—it seemed like companies were waiting for us to come along and do this, so the business took on a life of its own and it had a momentum of its own very early on. Probably the challenge for me personally, was to give enough time to the business and juggle what was happening in my personal life. That was probably the biggest challenge—and continues to be. The business itself is a good business and I think we are the right people to be doing it. We enjoy what it involves.

What were the sacrifices you made to get the business off the ground?

I made a sacrifice in terms of the time I've spent with my children. I think maybe any mum who works feels the same—I don't believe that you can ever have it all. You sacrifice things. I look back and think my nanny took the kids to things that maybe I wish I was at too but then on the other hand, I'm a lot better off than mums who have to go out to an office and leave at eight in the morning and get home at eight at night.

What sort of hours did you work in the first year?

The hours I worked would probably be 50 hours a week but because I was running it from home initially, what I used to do was get up really early—maybe 5—and then get a couple of hours in early before the little ones woke up, then again I could do some work at night when they went to bed. So the face-to-face contact I did during the day, and then all the extra things I did on the nights or weekends when I could get some time.

How do you compare your hours worked, from then to now-a-days?
These days I've still got an 18 month old, so I probably work around 30-40 hours a week, depending on what's happening. We do tend to have some peaks and lows in our business. for example, at Christmas time it's quieter because

companies are sending their people home; they're not bringing staff in, so I can take time off around that time of year.

How has the structure of the business changed?

When our third child was born, we decided to move back to Sydney because we'd been in Melbourne for four years. We decided to sell the Melbourne operation rather than put a manager in place because given the fact that we had three small children, we knew it wouldn't be feasible for us to travel back and forward, and we didn't feel comfortable not being there on a regular basis to keep an eye on things. We sold in March 2003 and we started from scratch in Sydney in July 2004.

The Corporate Housing brand is now jointly owned by the new Melbourne owners and ourselves—it acts like a parent company and is responsible for the joint activities of the two offices.

Being the same company as the Melbourne branch you sold off, do you take advantage of sharing marketing, advertising, etc?

Yes, definitely. What we try to do is gain the economies of scale that we can, say, for example, we put out a quarterly newsletter—we need a couple of thousand; and the Melbourne office needs a couple of thousand—the printing costs of doing them together are a lot less than if we did them individually. So we just pool our resources to get the benefits of being a larger organisation. It also improves our presence to our clients; we can actually offer the same service to Sydney and Melbourne, which are the two biggest locations for our product. It helps us win bigger accounts—this year we've started working for IBM, and I'm sure that part of that is due to the fact that we can offer a seamless service between the two states.

What percentage of your own money did you initially invest into the business?

Five thousand—my husband wrote me a cheque for it. I was lucky that it wasn't the kind of business where I actually had to outlay money—I didn't have to buy stock, so I only had to outlay money when somebody gave me a booking. for example, for the first one that I did, there were three apartments required so I needed the money for three lots of rent in advance and three bonds (because we had to pay bond on the unit), so I just needed the money to bankroll that, and then the customer paid me. Hence the need for $5000 to start with; then I had some cash flow and we built from there. So we only ever put in $5000. We've never had to source external funding.

What year did the business start making a profit?

Year 1, 1999.

Do you deal with debt and creditors yourself or do you outsource it?

We do it all ourselves. We're very fortunate because we're dealing with a purely corporate clientele, we don't have the issue of bad debts and that sort of thing.

What is your husband's role in the business?

We have separate roles and always did, right from the beginning. He runs the operational side of the business so he's out of the office five days a week organising new apartments; he coordinates the cleaners on staff; he's moving people in, checking people out; meeting people at the airport—he coordinates all of those operational things. I do everything in-house—the money side of things, the sales and marketing, the actual reservation of guests, customer service in-house.

What are the advantages or disadvantages of having your husband as a partner?

There are only advantages to be honest. It's been fantastic for ourselves personally because he's around so much. I think when he was working for another company, I sometimes didn't understand the pressures he might have been under or what was going on, but because we're now in the same business, we understand what each other's pressures are; we can support one another with things going on in the business. There's always somebody to talk to who understands what's going on and to share the highs and the lows with.

Where are the majority of your houses or apartments within Australia?

Probably about 80 per cent of what we do would be CBD or very city fringe and 80 per cent to 90 per cent would be a standard CBD apartment, but you do get the odd request for a house out in the suburbs, and that's one of our benefits and strengths in that we can take our service anywhere that the client wants to be.

What would you say have been the highlights so far in running your own business?

I think the highlight is just the fact that it's worked. That's just very rewarding—that we started something with an idea and it's grown into something that now provides us with an income and allows us to be around our family. It's fulfilling and rewarding that it's been a success. That simple fact in itself is probably the most rewarding thing of all.

What awards or recognition have you received?

Business World 2001, winner of the Young Hero Award for Business Entrepreneurs under 30. In 2004 I was a finalist of the Sydney Business Review Weekly's Business Woman of the Year Award. Corporate Housing has also been featured on ABC's *Inside Business* in 2003; we've had publication coverage in Melbourne's *The Age*, *Sydney Morning Herald*, *Management Today*, the *Sun Herald*, and *Business Travel Monthly*.

How would you describe your management style and your staff culture within the business?

Because we're such a small team, the people who work at Corporate Housing all have similar ideals about the levels of customer service and what it is that makes our company successful and what it is that people like about it. So I think we all inherently understand what it is that makes it successful, so in everything we do we try to carry that theme through.

Whether it's on the accounts side of things chasing an invoice, that we do it in a way that is mindful of the fact that there's the customer relationship behind that, or whether we send out a quotation, that we make sure it's of a high quality, that we respond to things quickly—all of those little things on a day-to-day basis that fit together to form the picture that is that we provide a certain service at a certain level that the corporate client expects.

That's what's made us successful, and that's really inherent in what we do—we all do it in a similar way and to a similar standard. We make a lot of decisions together; we work in a small office together; we talk through most things together; we decide how we're going to go about things. So we all just work together as part of a team; we each have our roles and know everything there is to know about it in terms of what we're doing or what we're trying to achieve, so there's nothing really hidden from anybody.

How do you motivate yourself on a daily basis?

I think I've always been someone who's pretty focused, and I like to do things well. I don't believe in doing things half-baked. That's probably what motivates me—the fact that I just like to do a good job and do things well, and get a good result. There are days when I think it's all too hard but I still have this thing inside me that says I have to do a good job and I have to make it work. I don't want to make one silly mistake that's going to cost me a client who's been a good customer for years. You've worked too hard to bring them on in the first place to let them go by just being a bit slack on one given day.

Generally, what motivates you? Is it the sense of achievement, money, growth of business, recognition, helping others?

I think that the reason I do this is for the same reason I started in the first place—I wanted to run a small business and I really enjoy doing that; I like the sense of achievement that comes from running a successful one. I like the fact that it provides me with the lifestyle where I can be around my children while they're still young. They're the things that really motivate me to keep going with it—because it just suits our lifestyle. Craig and I can work together; not many businesses can give you that, and I think we're really fortunate to have come across something that does.

How do you prioritise your time?

Our time is prioritised for everybody in the business towards the customer, so everything else is secondary to a customer enquiry, handling a maintenance issue or delivering. That's always number one and everyone in the business understands that and works in that way, so priority is always, if there's an enquiry for new business, that's done before anything else. It's pretty simple. You can't let any opportunities that are sitting right in front of you to drift away because you're doing bookwork or something else. So landing the sale is always number one.

What steps have you put in place to achieve new corporate business?
There's quite a long sales cycle in what we do. We can't just go and see a HR person and then tomorrow they're going to ring up and book something. Quite often they might think it's a great concept but they don't actually have anything happening for three months, so we just need to be very consistent in our sales and marketing. We have a plan that we're going to make contact with what we call 'prospects' four or five times a year, and we actually set out a schedule that

says this individual falls into this sales group and we have about four or five different sales group, and we say this person falls into group A which means that they're a prospect; they like what we're doing but haven't actually made a booking yet. Therefore they will receive our newsletter four times a year; they will also receive one sales call once a year; they will receive a phone call twice a year—so we actually have a plan for each of the different sales groups. That's how we go about our sales and marketing. If there's somebody who's a really established customer, they might still receive our newsletter, but they'll get two personal visits a year. We're quite regimented in our approach with our sales and marketing; we try not to let it just be something we do when business is slow. We market all year round—are quite consistent about what we do each quarter. That's the reason I have somebody who solely does sales and marketing.

If you ever had to start over, would you do anything differently?

No. I wouldn't do anything differently.

Have you ever felt vulnerable in business?

Yes, plenty of times, especially when we came to Sydney—we came into a much more competitive environment. There are people up here in Sydney who are doing what we're doing, maybe just on a localised basis, a certain region or a certain building, so we came into quite a competitive environment. But here in Sydney it's a little bit more cut-throat and more competitive so we've had to earn our place and be vigilant about that. That makes it a little bit tougher. I've always had complete faith in the business model.

I guess that's the one thing that's sustained me—in that never for a minute do I think that we're doing something that might fail because I know and have a great belief in this business. It's something that customers want and need and like, and it's a financially good business.

I've always had that faith that so long as we're prepared to run it, it'll always be a success.

Did you have any mentors or role models along the way?
Ultimately I think it was my mum; she ran two businesses and was the brains behind the businesses. I think that she has really taught me the importance of getting the money side of things right, and I also recognise that you can work really hard and not make a lot of money, so it's a matter of making sure that you turn away the business that is not profitable as that just drains your time and drains your resources. You should actually focus on the bits that work well, make

money and are efficient in running your business as well. She's really helped me understand that and realise how important that is within your business.

I've learned different things from different people. In terms of actual business mentors, probably the most significant influence would have come about two years down the track when we actually got ourselves a mentor through the Victorian Small Business Association, which has a mentoring program. We were fortunate to get a business mentor by the name of John Foley who had worked in a similar industry in the UK and had a lot of interest in corporate accommodation, so he was fabulous in terms of suggesting new ideas and ways to market ourselves and to position ourselves for the corporate clients.

As far as business or motivational books, are there any that you'd recommend?

The biggest life-changing one for me was *The E-Myth*, which I know a lot of people read—Michael Gerber. It had been recommended to us by somebody, and I think it was probably the most significant influence I've ever had from a book like that because it changed the way I thought about my business.

What was the best advice you were ever given?

Probably my mum's again: 'Aim for the stars and hope you reach the moon'.

Lastly, where do you go from here? What's the plan for the next five years?

The plans for the next five years are pretty lofty. What we're hoping to do now is to expand the service into the other smaller states. We're speaking with somebody in New Zealand and somebody in Brisbane so we can start the service in those areas as well. Within this partnership that I've formed with Chris Miller from Melbourne, what we're planning to do is establish offices in other locations and start offering a truly national service.

◆

Three key strategies for Corporate Housing's success

1. Do a business plan. That's essential for everybody I think. You have to do a plan to find out if there's a market out there for what you're doing, and try to take away your own personal enthusiasm about what it is you're doing—actually look at it with cold, hard numbers and facts, and decide if it could be a good business to begin with. I think it's very easy to get caught up in your own enthusiasm for your new range of handbags or whatever it might be. You've got to actually step away with that and think how competitive is it? How realistic is it that I can break into this market? What's the time frame it's going to take? Be very realistic about it and don't cloud it with your own enthusiasm.

2. I think the success of Corporate Housing has been about providing a consistent service. You have to ensure that you can deliver what it is that you've promised to your customers. I haven't found it that hard to find new customers. It's really easy to lose them though if you drop the ball. There are always businesses out there who are willing to try new things, who will give you a go, and sometimes they'll only give you one chance so don't lose that chance—make the most of it, capitalise on it, over service and really impress them.

3. The money side of things—ultimately I think if you want to create a business that is financially successful, it's really important to get the money side of things right. Make sure your margins are reasonable, make sure you do your sums properly, get some advice and make sure you're not going to be working 60 hours a week for no reward.

Kay's words of advice

1. Research the market; find out if there is an actual demand for your business, and try to find a niche. One of the things that has been really great for us is that we happened to find something that no one else was doing. We fell upon it through personal experience, but you can go looking for those sorts of things—choose a market you understand and know, and find a niche because it's going to make it a whole lot easier for

you to present your services when you can say hey, we're doing something different. I think that can be a real start.

2. Try to surround yourself with people who are going to motivate you as well, and support you. You don't want people who are going to be knocking you down. You want people who are going to ground you—who you can bounce ideas off. Surround yourself with people who actually will motivate you and encourage you.

3. Try to keep your overheads low to begin with. I think that was really important for us in those early stages until we actually came to a point where we were confident in the business model, but in the start-up phase, I think for me in my experience, it was really important to keep the overheads as low as I possibly could. I used my home PC and I worked from the spare bedroom at home. I did everything I could just to keep the overheads really low.

4. Make sure the early perception of your company is what you want it to be in the long term. Even though you may be working from the garage at home or the spare room to start off, I don't think any of my customers would ever have realised that. I think that's important—especially if you're pitching to big businesses. You need to make sure there's nothing that will let them think that you're not a big company who can handle a big order.

5. Stay true to what it is you started out to do to begin with. Don't let your customers drag you off in a direction that you inherently know is not right for your business. Don't diverse into too many areas. Pick your niche, your market and your price range and your product and stick with it. So stick true to what it is you set out to do in the first place and don't get dragged off into directions that you're not comfortable with or that aren't what you're about.

6. You have to take it seriously. It's your livelihood and it's your income and your future. You have to expect it's going to take time; expect there are going to be ups and downs. You have to make a very conscious decision to succeed and stay focused on it. Of course, you have to have your time away from the business, but expect it's going to be tough—it is.

KRISTINA KARLSSON
kikki.K

Originally from Sweden, Kristina moved to Australia in 1996 when she was 22. After twelve months of travelling around Australia she settled in Melbourne and worked as a travel agent until deciding to start her own business.

The business idea came to her while setting up her home office, she couldn't find any stylish stationery products that inspired or appealed to her. It was then that the idea was born, to create a distinctive Scandinavian range of stationery and storage products.

After months of researching the market and what people wanted she started manufacturing a range of innovative stylish home and office stationery products, launching them originally through focus groups, where she sold her products to over 400 people who participated in the focus groups.

Two years later Kristina opened her first kikki.K concept store in the fashionable Melbourne Central retail shopping centre. With the success of that store she opened two other stores in Chadstone Melbourne and Bondi Junction in Sydney.

Kikki.K distributes to over 120 stores in Australia and New Zealand, and exports globally through their website. Receiving numerous accolades such as winning the Channel 9 Small Business Show's—Brother Website Awards in 2001 and the Lord Mayor's Retail Innovation Awards in 2002, as well as winning the My Business Magazine Young Gun Award and a finalist for the Telstra Business Women's Award in 2002 and 2003.

◆

Could you give a brief overview of your business?

We are a stationery retail business—we have three stores. Our focus is on Swedish design, we manufacture beautiful things for the home and office market. Most of our customers are people who just love stationery. The business model is mainly retail but we also distribute to about 120 stores around Australia and New Zealand.

We also sell to Sweden but our main target is the Australian market at present. We also offer workshops to our customers providing advice on how they can get organised with a touch of style. They are conducted by a professional organiser who runs the workshop at night in our stores.

Where did you grow up?

In Falkenberg, on the west coast of Sweden, on a dairy farm.

Do you come from a large family?

I have two brothers and a sister. They're all located in Sweden.

Did you complete your schooling in Sweden?

Yes. I did the equivalent of a Year 12 certificate.

Did you do additional studies such as university or college?

No. I went to America and I spent a year travelling around—I worked as a nanny and waitress in different places.

At school, did you have any great achievements? Were you academically inclined or artistic?

I was a little above average as a student. I was very driven to work outside of school and had been working various jobs since I was 13. I always wanted to buy nice things and knew the only way I could do that was to earn money! Throughout my later school years between the ages of 16 and 18, I worked as a tour guide taking Swedish people over to Germany and Austria. So academically I didn't really do anything special.

What influenced your decision to come to Australia?

An Australian man! I met him in a ski resort in Austria, while I was working there for a season. I decided to come to Australia on a year working holiday—when I was 22 years old. When I came out here, I didn't initially intend to stay longer than a year. After 12 months of travel around Australia, working a bit here and there, I eventually decided to stay.

Do you believe your parents influenced your decision to go into business?

My parents had a business, where they contracted out new equipment and staff to assist the smaller farmers in the area. They worked so hard, 24/7, so I guess that's where I got my drive from. I can't say they had a direct impact on my decision though.

So when you left school, is it clear to say your ambition was to travel?

Yes. I worked in America, and Germany for a year in a wine district, and I was a tour guide there—taking people around the winery. Then I studied German and French as languages are another passion of mine—and then I worked a ski season in Austria. That's where I met Paul, my partner.

When I came to Australia, I worked in the travel industry after finishing my travels around the countryside.

What is your current age?

I'm 31 years.

Is Paul involved in the business?

Yes, but only the last three years. He previously worked for Rip Curl in marketing, so he had a good understanding about manufacturing, selling, retail— the whole bit. After a while, when he saw the idea develop and really start to happen he decided to join me. So he is now a shareholder in the business.

How do you balance work and home—working together, being in a relationship?

We work incredibly long hours so I'm far off from being balanced, but we absolutely love what we are doing. I just employed another three people in the office, so soon we will be starting to see a difference, whereas in the past I'd thought I could do everything and we probably were working 80 hours a week, so in terms of balancing home, I guess we really only have Sundays to switch off at the moment.

What led you to create designer stationery?

When I decided to stay in Australia, I started researching different business ideas that would give me the opportunity to regularly travel home to Sweden.

I'd always had a big interest in design, and especially Swedish design, and I also wanted to make at least $500 a week.

So with my list of business ideas I thought *I need to set up my office, get myself organised and get myself into the right frame of mind,* so I started to look for stationery for my office and I realised that there was nothing really stylish—nothing I would like to bu except for traditional stationery, but that reminded me of the corporate world. So that's really when I thought there's not really a lot out here and I guess that, coming from Sweden, I was very used to having great stationery. We're very good in Sweden with design but here there was nothing so I saw an opportunity and a gap in the market.

Where did you go from there?

I asked all my friends what they thought and got their input. Then I did some research trips to London, New York and Japan to see what was available, I already knew what we had in Sweden.

Initially I thought I could import, so I looked at all different opportunities of importing. I did that for two years. At the same time I researched Australia in terms of manufacturing my own products by basically looking under 's' for stationery in the Yellow Pages. I went to everyone from printers, book binders, paper merchants—everyone—because I had no idea of how to even put together a notebook. Through that process I found suppliers, and two of those main suppliers are still with me today.

After you found the supplies, what came next?

More research, I went and asked over 100 people on the street—in Chapel Street, Melbourne—what they thought of the concept—and if I opened a store where should it be—should it be in the city, should it be in Chapel Street? I had all these questions and people answered them. That was amazing and quite difficult—I could never do that again. So if someone asks me things now, I always make sure I stop and answer research!

I then got together a focus group and I had some samples done, and I said what would you pay this and what would you spend on that? And everyone was very enthusiastic. But that was all easy to say when you don't have to put up your money yourself. So then I borrowed $3000 from Paul and I decided to make up some more samples of each product, and then I called my friends to come over. I had about 400 people in total made up of 10 people per group.

How did you find these 10 people for each group?

One friend of mine would bring nine friends and so on. Even now when I work in the store, people come in and say, 'I went to one of your first focus groups'. That's really fantastic.

So did you only do focus groups to build up enough capital to open a store?

No, I then went to RG Madden (that's a stylish homeware shop) also Orson & Blake, and I started to wholesale to them in August 1999. That was the first step towards getting our brand into the marketplace. I guess because I had something unique and different, I got loads of publicity.

In 2001 we set up an Internet site, and that would have been the time when e-commerce had just started. It was really hard—I didn't have any money, and I wanted a really slick website from the outset for the customer to look at and buy products offering the convenience of on-line shopping by using a credit card facility over the net. One of Paul's friends helped us set up the website www.kikki-k.com.au.

In December 2001 we actually won an award for that website, from over 650 other websites around Australia, which was incredible. It was called the Channel Nine Small Business Brother Web Site award. With that award we won $10,000 cash and a multi function fax/scanner/photocopier, and computers, as well as a one year free phone bill. So it started to roll from there; we then secured a store site in Melbourne Central, opening the first kikki.Kconcept store in 2001.

After six months of trading we won two awards—one the Lord Mayor's Most Innovative Retail in Melbourne, and also one for Customer Service in 2001.

What year did you start the focus groups?

Between November 1998 to February 1999.

With all the research you conducted did you come up with a specific target market?

Yes, people who want to create stylish and organised working environments, and anyone who loves stationery! It's amazing when people come in the store, they get so excited. It's like a lolly shop for grown-ups—something special.

In the early days, did you advertise to get your name into the marketplace?

I never did advertising—it was really through word of mouth, and I guess because I had a unique concept and something different, I got a lot of publicity. We won three awards within six months and that helped a great deal, as a result of winning the awards there were editorials in the newspapers and television press coverage.

Did you network with any other businesses in the early stages?

I am a natural networker, but I didn't know anyone so I went to see a lot of people speak at functions, especially business women through the Australian Businesswomen's Network, one of my mentors has been Gillian Franklin from the Heat Group—she won the Telstra Business Woman of the Year a few years ago. I approached her after a function and asked for her business card and then asked if I could catch up with her to ask her some questions about business. She's been my mentor ever since, so she's been an amazing support. Recently we set up a board of advisers, a mentor group. We meet with these amazing four people bi-monthly and just do a quick presentation about our businesses and our issues at the time. They all have their input, giving tremendous support.

When you started, did you have a business plan in place?

Yes, we developed a very detailed one and it's still evolving. We've achieved everything and beyond, and the business plan gets updated all the time, and it's a working document we change regularly.

What would you say were the biggest obstacles or challenges in the first 12 months?

There were a few: no formal business training, the language barrier as English was my second language, lack of capital and definitely limited resources. I would also have to say decision-making was a hard thing for me—hundreds have to be made a week or the business stands still; and no family support network here has proved difficult—but that was also a good thing.

As far as sacrifices to get the business off the ground, what was your biggest sacrifice do you think?

Not having time for other things—time with friends, leisure time, and a normal calm life.

How many hours did you work per week in the first 12 months of operation?

Up to 80 hours, 7 days a week. You can imagine too, working with my partner we'd even work at home; but I'm very passionate about what I do and it's fun.

You now take Sundays off?

Yes. I'm quite strict now, trying to find a balance between the two.

In the early days, did you find it difficult dealing with men in business, for example, with manufacturing, sales, finance institutions?

I've never had a problem with working with men. I think it really has to do with attitude.

What's your annual percentage increase each year?

We basically double each year, it's really growing steadily.

In the start did you invest a lot of your own savings into the business?

Everything I had. We sold our house when we were about to open in Melbourne Central, and that's when September 11 happened. My friends were worried and wondered if I knew what I was doing? That was really scary.

Did you also source any external funding?

Yes, but it was very hard. Because I didn't have anything else, it was not a good move to sell the house. We didn't have anything to borrow against so I guess in the beginning we were really only working with credit. We worked with our suppliers to get better terms, for example, we made an arrangement with our shop fitter to pay him off over time. It's been tough but we've been able to do it.

When did the business first start making a profit?

In 2002. It took a long time to see results—I started in 1998.

As far as debtors and creditors, do you deal with that internally?

Yes, we have a bookkeeper and an accountant.

Paul Lacy—your partner, what's his role in the business?

He's the general manager.

Can you tell me what the advantages or disadvantages are of having a personal partner involved in the business?

I think for me there are only advantages. If you have the right partner, it's a definite advantage because two heads are better than one—when one person is down, the other one carries you through.

How many product lines do you currently produce?

Over 800 products.

Are all your products made here in Australia?

No, we make about 90 per cent in Melbourne. We also make things in Europe and Asia.

How many stores do you distribute to Australia-wide?

Approximately 120.

What sort of retail stores are they?

Good quality specialty stores, like gift and design stores.

How do you make your decision about store locations?

We have our own method of working out where our customers would shop, but so far we've been really fortunate, for example, we were invited to open in

Chadstone and Bondi, because we offer something so different.

Do you currently distribute internationally?

Yes—Sweden, and we sell all over the world through the Internet—on our website.

Does the business call for you to travel regularly?

I travel interstate regularly and take a couple of trips a year around the world—New York, London, Copenhagen, Stockholm. We have Swedish designers who are located all over the world, but we manufacture here.

Do you design products yourself?

I design only a little bit these days, but most is done by Swedish designers from all over the world and we now have one Swedish designer who is based in our Melbourne office working on designs full-time.

How many employees do you currently have?

We currently have 35 staff members.

What would you say have been some of the highlights in running your own business?

The first thing would be when we opened up the first retail store. Every day is a highlight for me—when I drive to work, I think how fortunate I am. I'm very happy and love everything I'm doing. Another highlight is seeing some of our staff really develop—we have one girl, Amy, who's been with me since day one. She's now our retail manager and looks after all the stores.

Also, winning the awards and being invited to open stores in the three shopping centres that we're based in was fantastic too.

On a day-to-day basis, what's your main role in the business now?

I am the managing director so I oversee the whole business especially the creative design side of the business, I look after all the product development to make sure it gets publicised and that it's also marketed right and selling.

How did you come up with the name kikki.K?

Kikki is my nickname and K is for Karlsson. The night I decided on kikki.K, I sat with the creative director for Quiksilver, and he asked me if I'd thought about a logo. I said yes, and wrote it on a serviette. He then put it on the computer and it's never been changed since.

How would you describe your staff culture within the business?

I would say everyone has their role, but with product development I get all the staff involved. They're all really passionate about stationery and design, so even our book-keeper gets involved in the process. I always get everyone's input and feedback. We encourage teamwork, decision-making and if there are mistakes, we encourage them to look back and see how they can learn from them. We also give them lots of responsibility.

How do you motivate yourself on a daily basis?

I absolutely love what I'm doing and I'm generally very self motivated. But, my friends also really motivate me—to meet up with a friend, talk to my mentors, talk to other business owners. I read loads of books—inspirational books, and that really motivates me.

So what motivates you most, is it money, sense of achievement, growth, creativity, recognition, helping others?

To produce beautiful products. One of my visions is to have kikki.K in every classy office around Australia. It's never been about money. Growth of business is partly a motivator because when you grow, you make new products.

How do you achieve your goals?
I find using vision as number one—I know where I have to get to and it's clear in my mind. It's so easy to get sidetracked, so I set small goals daily that lead to big goals.

If you ever had to start over, would you do anything differently?

One thing I would probably do is set up a structure and a management team earlier. What I know now is that you can't do it all on your own. If I had to do it again, I would do that much earlier.

As far as mentors, who have you had along the way?

Gillian Franklin from the Heat Group; my old boss Phillip Weinman who pwned the corporate travel services that I worked for. I have a mentor called Peter Daddo who set up 60 stores called Ooh La La. He is my mentor but he also now works four days a month for us; Laura Castel Anderson is another one. They've all been absolutely amazing.

What motivational books would you recommend to anyone who wants to start a business?

E.Myths by Michael Gerber, and *You Inc* by John McGrath—I loved that too. Also *What Colour is your Parachute*—a book about timing, your career. I give it to a lot people who don't know what they're going to do. It looks at your skills but also your passions and your interests—combining those two.

Do you undertake any training to update your management skills?

Yes. I've done retail training with the Freedman Group and I'm just about to do a course at the Australian Institute of Management AIM for leadership.

What was the best advice you've ever been given?

To do what you love to do. That was the best advice I ever had in terms of my personal life and business, and that was given by Paul my partner. He really made me think about what I want, rather than what I could do. I wouldn't have done this if I didn't have that frame of mind.

Over the next five years, where do you see the business?

My plans are to have a world class retail chain of stores globally. We have started to look overseas—New York, London, Stockholm, Copenhagen—and continue to expand in Australia. We will continue to wholesale but our focus will be on developing our own retail concept.

◆

Three key strategies for kikki.K's success

1. Clear vision—I found it so important. More and more I understand the importance of it because if you don't know where you're going, on those tough days you can really lose sight of where you're going.

2. To do something I loved and was passionate about.

3. To build a good team. You can't do it on your own.

Kristina's words of advice

1. Make sure what you're doing is your passion, and that your team shares the same passion.

2. Don't be scared to ask questions. It's amazing what you can learn from doing that.

3. Networks—go listen to speakers, and you meet a lot of people who are like-minded.

4. Take risks and make decisions—even if they're not always the right ones, as long as you learn from them.

5. To progress is more important, than focusing on perfection. With running a business it's almost impossible to get everything perfect from day one.

6. Do lots of research and understand your customer.

SHELLEY BARRETT
MODELCO

ModelCo has been in operation for only three years, yet the innovative beauty company is booming with phenomenal success. ModelCo was established by Shelley Barrett and launched in 2002 at the Australian Fashion Week with Kylie Minogue and Elle MacPherson.

Shelley was no newcomer to business, having previously founded magazine houses, production companies, and advertising agencies within Australia and internationally.

Shelley saw a niche in the market with enormous potential and began producing a range of unique innovative beauty products packaged in hot pink, branding it ModelCo. The company's annual turnover is over $6 million and growing steadily.

Today, ModelCo distributes to David Jones and Myer stores, over 150 independent stores in Australia and exports to the UK, Japan, Dubai, France, Berlin, Denmark, Sweden, Norway, Germany, Spain, NZ, United Arab Emirates and the USA.

Shelley's won numerous awards including the NSW Telstra Business Women's Awards 2004 and 2004 Westpac Group Business Owner Awards. She was also the winner of the American Express Award for the Fastest Growing Small Business in 2004 and ModelCo products won Cleo's 2004 Best of the Beauty Awards and New Woman Beauty Awards 2004.

◆

Where did you grow up?

I grew up in the eastern suburbs of Sydney. I'm a single child. I completed schooling at St Claire's College at Waverley and Brigidine College, Randwick. I went on to do a business management course and a Diploma of Psychology by correspondence. I feel that having business management and psychology gives you good insight into not only how to run a business but how to deal with people.

At school did you excel in any particular subjects?

I was always a people person at school, and enjoyed debating and public speaking.

Do you believe that your parents and childhood environment influenced your decision to go into business for yourself?

Yes, my mother has always had her own business. She's actually ModelCo's financial controller and she's been with me from the very beginning. She's got a bookkeeping background and she's a dance teacher as well. I was brought up in a culture of dancing, public speaking and advertising. I also come from an advertising agency background, so I think that the personalities around me did influence me as a young person.

When you left school, what was your ambition?

I always wanted to run my own business, but when I left school I wasn't 100 per cent sure of what I wanted to do. I started by working as a receptionist in a modelling agency, and because the models and I were of a similar age, I was in touch with what they wanted and what they were missing in the Australian modelling industry. Knowing it was going to cost a lot of money to open an agency, I started at the age of 18 with a small business. It was called Elite Productions; I was putting together fashion shows and model search competitions for some magazines and reputable model agencies in Australia. It was from there that I saved and earned money to start the business; to this day the business is still self-funded.

Where was your first job as a receptionist?

I worked at Gordon Charles Model Agency. From there I started Elite Productions to self-fund and start a modelling agency. At the age of 21 I opened the modelling agency which was based at Woollahra NSW.

Shelley, I believe you are 31 and married?

Yes—my husband and I are expecting our first child at the end of 2005. So for the moment we are savouring our time together as a newly married couple. That said, we are both very excited about the prospect of becoming parents.

Is your husband involved in the business?

Yes, Damien is involved in the ModelCo business. He's my business partner and he runs the import/export department of the business—basically the global distribution side.

How do you balance work and home life, especially working together?

We have a good balance between work and personal life. I have a good business plan and organisational chart as well as good business practices, which allow me to have an even split.

Shelley, tell me about ModelCo.

ModelCo is an innovative beauty company that has been in existence since May 2002. I had a modelling agency for 10 years that I launched when I was 21 years of age. As a model agent for 8 years, I found that models from all over the world were always on the lookout for innovative beauty products in their make-up cases and the luxury brands just weren't providing them. So that inspired me to create the first ever, heated lash wand as I had a number of young girls always complaining that they wished they could keep their eyelashes intact without being ripped out by the old-fashioned eyelash crimp curlers.

We launched Lash Wand in conjunction with Australian Fashion Week in 2002, and we were lucky enough to have Kylie Minogue and Elle McPherson rave about the product, which in turn generated a lot of press for this one particular item. It became the best-selling product in Myer and best-selling product in various premium department stores around the world, such as Space & K in London, Collette in Paris, and The Bay in Canada. After the great success of that product, and the research we did on it, as well as our unique ability to have contacts with all the magazine beauty editors, we decided that there was room in the marketplace for a young, fresh fashion forward, beauty company. The point of difference between ModelCo and other cosmetic companies in the world is that we're from the fashion business, not from the beauty business, so all other cosmetic companies are make-up-artist inspired and we're fashion inspired. Having the modelling agency gave us the unique ability to look down the porthole of fashion to see what fashions were coming through, be in touch with fashion, models and celebrities and influential beauty critics.

We set about creating the brand essence of Wow and The Perfect Way to Model Skin so with that in mind, we created an organisational chart and business plan, and we then set about painting the world pink.

You've basically told me what led you into your own business, so exactly what steps did you take to start ModelCo?

My strategy was to launch one innovation into the marketplace first and see how the global beauty market accepted it. So you could say it was a bit of market research and trial and because the lash wand was embraced in such an amazing way with phenomenal sales worldwide, it was really proof for me that there was a niche in the market for innovative beauty products.

Where did you go from there, to start manufacturing products?

Damien and I hopped on a plane and went over to Asia and sourced a reputable manufacturing plant in South Korea that manufactured the moulds that we own today, as well as all the IP of our products and formulations.

And now what percentage of your products are made in Australia?

Eighty per cent of our product is Australian made and 20 per cent is made offshore.

And where are the products made in Australia?

Sydney and Melbourne.

When did you start Shelley's Model Management?

I started Shelley's Model Management when I was 21. Shelley's Model Management is the name of the company and we have three agencies underneath—Face Models for fashion models; Commercial Faces for actors; and Lollipops Children Model Management. There are over 1200 people on our books that we managed.

And where is the model agency work predominately sourced from?

Our models worked both nationally and internationally, we service the major advertising industry, magazine houses, casting agencies, production companies in Australia and all over the world.

What's your target market for ModelCo?

Our target market is 18 to 39, but in saying that, our products have a broader appeal. We have die-hard fans who are in their 40s, 50s and and 60s using some of our products. Essentially, our innovative beauty products speak to a range of women who are looking for quick-fix beauty tricks, and who are style conscious and beauty/fashion savvy. I'd like to think in some cases that the brand has an ageless voice.

Besides Fashion Week in 2002, how did you get your name out into the marketplace in the early days?

We have a great network, we don't advertise. It was my close ties with the beauty and fashion media that was the stepping stone. Things really started to kick off for ModelCo when we branded it with our signature pink, and we launched the world's first ever TAN Airbrush in a Can. That was where we reached global stardom with the press and media all around the world.

Do you still do regular press releases?

Yes absolutely—it's imperative to keep media informed of new products released, marketing, sponsorships, brand alliances, and interesting company developments and achievements. We have an in-house public relations manager who generates all the press for Australia, and we have appointed PR companies in various markets around the world where the brand is represented, to spread the word and keep press always informed in each market. In terms of ModelCo's marketing, we have a marketing director who develops and manages the global marketing strategy for Australia and all other markets.

With the modelling agency, did you originally set up a business plan?

Yes. We had business plans for both businesses.

How formal are they?

They are quite structured business plans that we follow to a tee, and we re-address them every three months. We have one-year goals and five-year goals, not to mention bigger picture dreams and goals that we constantly work towards.

How did you break into the international market with both businesses?

I jumped on a plane, first with the agency, once we established a good pool of models.

I met with agencies in New York, London and Paris, and marketed them over there and placed them with agencies in different parts of the world. With ModelCo, as soon as Lash Wand went on sale (I'm talking within a couple of weeks), and the PR started to roll out, I did the same and jumped on a plane and went around the world to Europe and the USA meeting with buyers and presenting the concept. With the products being sold in premium stores, like Space NK and Colette—everyone wants a piece of you. And that's been it, we're actually turning away distributors every week. Since the launch of the brand in top-end department stores and apothecaries we've never had to propose business to anyone. People just keep knocking on the door.

Do you do a lot of editorial press with beauty editors of magazines?

Yes, we've been fortunate enough to receive fabulous support from press all around the world—and I think that's testament to the innovation and premium quality of the products. From international editions of high-end fashion magazines like *Vogue*, *Harper's Bazaar*, *Marie Claire*, *Cosmopolitan* and *InStyle*, to weekly celebrity driven magazines, business magazines, trade journals and lifestyle colour supplements.

Were there any major obstacles or challenges along the way with either of the businesses?

My youth. Not so much now, but when I was younger. Being young, people think you're going to be a bit fly-by-night and therefore don't give you the time.

What would you say was your biggest sacrifice with owning your own business?

I think devoting your time to a business, I probably didn't have a massive social life and I didn't do the 'trip around the world for 12 months' most young people do. Of course I've travelled, but I've never really had that time in my life, but I don't think it's hindered me one bit. I think I've had the best of both worlds. I had a lot of responsibility at a young age.

Wat sort of hours per week would you put into the business?

I usually do 50 to 60 hours over 5 or 6 days a week.

What was your annual turnover last year?

Last year it was $5 million for both businesses.

What are you forecasting for 2005?

I'm in the process of selling the agency, so we estimate the turnover for ModelCo alone next year to be $6 million.

What influenced your decision to sell the agency?

I've had the agency 10 years and I feel that I've built the business to a certain level and that my focus in the future is in the cosmetics industry. We have now merged the modelling agency with another, and I will take an advisory board role as I'll still have an interest in the business, but in general my future is taking ModelCo to newer and bigger heights in the international world of beauty.

What percentage of your own money did you put into the businesses?

One hundred per cent. I've never had finance—I don't deal with banks. I self-funded both businesses.

When did the businesses first start making a profit?

I think the agency in its second year, and the beauty product company from day one.

How do you deal with debts and creditors?

We use external accountants and we have a financial controller.

What do you think are the advantages and disadvantages of having Damien your husband as a partner?

Surprisingly enough, we don't spend a lot of time together during the day. Damien's off at our external warehouse and managing the distribution globally of our products. The advantages are that he understands the business and knows the growth of the business—what you go through day to day, the ups and downs of running a business. The disadvantage is that sometimes all you do is talk about work, so we've got a new rule—come 7 o'clock no work.

How long has Damien actually been involved in the business?

Two years—basically since ModelCo, and he's come in to do all the importing and exporting.

How many product lines do you currently have?

We have 72 products in the range. We'll be expanding to 85 in 2005, and producing a line of innovative colour cosmetics in 2006.

Currently, what countries do you export to?

The UK, Japan, Dubai, France, Berlin, Denmark, Iceland, Sweden, Norway, Germany, Spain, NZ, United Arab Emirates and the USA.

How many staff do you employ?

With the agency it used to be 1200 talent on the books, and 5 staff at the agency along with 12 staff at ModelCo. Having now sold the agency I employ only the 12 ModelCo staff.

How often do you travel with the business?

I travel quite often, I would say 20 per cent of the year, mainly to Europe, Asia and the States.

Do you currently network with other businesses, in similar industries?

Yes, fashion industry, manufacturers, retailers and other Australian companies exporting luxury goods overseas.

What would you say have been the highlights so far in running your own business?

Seeing a product sell out in the retail world; seeing beauty editors embrace your product and in turn being given fabulous editorial. Hearing from delighted consumers who love our products, and seeing what was once a dream turn into reality.

What recognition have you received so far?

Various awards—I've been a finalist in so many things—Cleo Best of Beauty Awards, FHM Beauty Awards, New Woman Beauty Awards both here and in the UK; and I was a finalist in the Telstra Business Woman of the Year.

Now, on a day-to-day basis, what's your main role in the business?

I'm the CEO of the company. My time is split between research and development and running the business.

Could you describe a typical day's activities?

I wake up in the morning; try to fit some exercise in before work. I like breakfast—always a cup of coffee as I'm running up the street. Sometimes I make calls to America early in the morning because of their time. Throughout the day I focus on the Australian market. There are several meetings scheduled throughout the week with different key staff members. Then come 6 o'clock, Europe opens, so every night my time between say 6 and 9pm is focused on servicing the European side of the business. I always try to cook a home-cooked dinner but sometimes it's impossible.

So, every night between 6 and 9pm you work your Europe section?

Yes, and in between 7.30 and 9 am, I work the USA.

Can your describe your management style? What sort of culture do you like to create within your business?

It's a relaxed culture, and all of my staff work quite autonomously. They have a responsibility in their role, but we also work together as a close-knit team. While people officially work for me, I work with them, we all work together on the same playing fields. It doesn't matter whether you're a key player, senior staff member or somebody who's relatively new in the business, we all work together. People working with me, not for me, is the type of culture we have. Our business is quite systemised, but there is a relaxed atmosphere and the freedom to speak.

How do you motivate yourself on a daily basis?

I am a self motived person—everyday I use my products and am constantly on the look out for new beauty innovations and products that don't exist on the market and make looking beautiful just that little bit easier. I never switch off. I'm very passionate about what I do, and my sources of inspiration are varied. Plus, I'm constantly motivated by my vision for the company—it's my driving force.

What motivates you generally—money, sense of achievement, growth of business, recognition, helping others, creating?

Growth of business, recognition, creation of our products. My ambition is to create the most innovative cosmetic brand in the world and to be recognised as an Australian brand. That's what I aim to do. It's not about the money for me—at this stage. I'm not motivated by money; I'm motivated by success.

How do you prioritise your time?

I write a very efficient diary. I think if you run a business, stick to a business plan and have key staff, then you can have an even split between personal life and business life.

What tools do you use to achieve your goals?

I engage a company called BTS (Business Thinking Systems), and they help you write your business plan. They help you stick to the goals that you are trying to achieve. I consult them three or four times a year.

How do you relax and unwind when you get some time away from the businesses?

Exercise—walking, running and tennis; travel; catching up with friends is always very grounding; travelling to places of relaxation; socialising I think is always healthy for the soul.

Have you had any mentors along the way?

Yes, my godfather—his name is Ian Elliott, and he's the former CEO of George Patterson Bates Advertising Agency. He's always been a good mentor throughout my life, my husband Damien is a wonderful support; also my mother.

Do you read motivational books, and if so is there anything that you would recommend?

How to Win Friends and Influence People is a good book as far as people management skills. It's very general but it's a good book. *The Power of Cult Branding* is also a great book that gives you an insight into some of the world's biggest brands and how they achieved their success.

What was the best advice you were ever given?

Work hard; be honest—everyone gave me that advice; understand the business you're going into and research what it is.

Where do you go from here with ModelCo—over the next five years?

To position ModelCo as a premium cosmetic brand and the most innovative cosmetic company in the world; to expand our distribution channels with key outlets worldwide, and to paint the world pink.

Three key strategies for ModelCo's success

1. To continually educate myself as a businesswoman.

2. Self-improvement within the business area.

3. Taking risks—setting goals, being ambitious and trusting my instinct.

Shelley's words of advice

1. Understand the business you're going into, and all facets around it. (In my case, beauty is one thing—knowing cosmetics, but it's understanding the world of retail).

2. Be passionate.

3. Have a good network and the support of people around you.

4. Have a brilliant business plan and stick to it.

5. Understand the financial outlay.

6. Take one step at a time.

KATRINA ALLEN
DE JOUR SANITARY PRODUCTS

At 32 years of age Katrina Allen followed the advice from her father to create a recession-proof business, and within eighteen months De Jour Sanitary Products emerged into the marketplace. Katrina launched the business at the beginning of 1998, after leaving the security of a high powered position of 10 years as senior art director at M&C Saatchi, one of Sydney's largest advertising agencies.

Katrina invested her savings and ventured out on her own with a burning desire and vision to make it happen. Her eye for detail and expertise in advertising, packaging and marketing proved to be an advantage. Katrina was able to develop a unique, simple and discreet package for her range of tampons using clever zip lock resealable plastic purse packs in subtle grey, instead of the bright flimsy cardboard boxes, that fell apart in your handbag that we were all used to seeing in our Australian supermarkets and pharmacies.

Not only has this enterprising woman been the only female in the world who has solely founded a tampon business, Katrina has triumphantly secured 8 per cent share of the $80 million tampon market in Australian supermarkets and is planning to expand into the US market.

Katrina also campaigned for Australian women against the government's proposed introduction of GST on tampons in the year 2000.

◆

Where did you grow up?

I grew up in Brighton, Melbourne.

Are you from a large family?

I'm the eldest of three children.

Did you complete your Year 12 certificate or go on to university or college?

Yes—we called Grade 12 the HSC back then and I went to college and received a degree in graphic design at Swinburne Institute. After that I went into advertising and I became an art director, I had finished my schooling on the Friday and was employed on the Monday. I'd already organised a job to go to before leaving school.

At school were you creative?

I did art, but I wouldn't say I was unbelievably creative. I was very analytical and I did quite unusual subjects, such as English obviously; and I did pure and applied maths because I was very good at maths; then I did physical education because it actually became a group A subject so it was equivalent to English.

I suppose I did the physical education side because I really enjoyed the biomechanics and the human body (because I'm very physical and was very sporty) and I did maths because I loved it. Then I did art because I was creative.

Do you believe that your childhood and your parents, influenced your decision to go into business? Were your parents in business for themselves?

Yes, my father is a lawyer and has always had his own business and always dabbled in lots of other businesses outside of law; he's more a lawyer/entrepreneur.

When you left school, you became an art director?

Yes, I started working as an art director in the creative department of an advertising agency. In the creative department there are art directors and copy writers. The writer does the words; the art director does the pics, but it's not that clear cut. You work as a team, so I always worked with a copy writer and we would sit down and come up with ideas for television, radio, press ads, magazine ads—for a campaign. for example, I did the Vodafone campaign with Kramer so my copy writer and I were briefed on the proposition about Vodafone—we came up with the creative idea to use Kramer. We wrote all the scripts. Effectively I was in charge of pictures and he was in charge of words. But it's never that clear cut because a lot of copy writers can say how they think something should look, and a lot of art directors will say why don't you do this, change this and that, but that's basically the principle behind it. It's very much a team collaboration when you work as a pair in an advertising agency.

How long were you there?

I worked in advertising agencies for 10 years—in four different ones. M&C Saatchi was my last one.

When did you start researching going into business for yourself?

While I was working in advertising at M&C Saatchi in Sydney, I started developing De Jour tampons in my spare time, and then basically I took a sick day and I presented it to Coles at that time, and they said they would take it and also get it into BiLo. Then I quit my job and sold it to all the others—Woolworths, Priceline, Independent supermarkets and pharmacies.

How old were you when you started the business?

I was 32 when I started, I'm now 37.

Is your husband involved in the business?

No, it's just me.

Do you have you any children?

Yes, I have two, a 2-year old and a 6-month old.

How do you balance work and home with the kids? Do you have outside help?

I've got really good family help in that respect, and also I'm very organised.

What led you to start your business?

Basically in advertising what happens is, as a creative person, you might write maybe a thousand different ads, and when I think about it, only about 2 per cent of it gets made. So it's a very frustrating job because what happens is a client comes in and, because it's a client thing, they think they know what they want and they suddenly start changing your whole idea and nothing ends up the way you want it to. I'm not speaking out of school, every creative has the same problem.

So you just get very frustrated, and what I wanted to do was create a company where I had complete and utter creative control. That was one of the main reasons behind it, and the other main reason behind it was because I'd always been encouraged to have my own business by my father, and I knew one day I'd be married (I wasn't married at this stage, hadn't even met my husband) but I knew one day I'd be married and have children, and that I'd still want to be able to work.

I really wanted to have my own independence and earn my own money, and not have to be confined to being at work from 9 till 5.

I just didn't want to have to answer to anybody and I wanted to be able to do what I wanted to do when I wanted to do it, so that was one of the reasons I went off to do my own business. But it had to be a business that was going to generate a pretty good income for me because I was earning very big money where I was, so it would have to be a big idea—it couldn't just be some backyard hobby.

What were the first steps you took in starting the business?

The idea, my father actually gave me the idea and straightaway I could see all this packaging. It's a long story, but he was doing a legal case for a company that was owed money by a tampon company and said he thought there would be money in tampons. And I just thought I hate tampon packaging—gaudy and bright and colourful.

I'd never worked on tampons, actually I'd never done anything in the sanitary area, and I never worked at an agency that had them in their business. But I just knew straight away that there was a real opportunity to Calvin Klein that market.

Then I went off and read these business books on how to write a business plan and stuff. I was working in Sydney and reading all these books, and it was all very complicated. I remember going to Melbourne and speaking to Dad about it, saying I'd read all these books and he said chuck all that out the window and just do it. Stop messing around about having to write this and that—just do it! So I thought okay, I will just do it. Basically what I did was throw all that out the window and treated it all like a pitch, like when we get them at the ad agency, for example,; here's the brief—the client wants to launch a new brand of tampon. What are you going to do? So I tried that and I asked lots of questions, went and saw people who had businesses and dealt with supermarkets, found out lots of things, and at the same time put together a presentation at the other end.

What year did you start the process?

In 1996, I spent 18 months working on the process and launched the business at the beginning of 1990.

Did you do any market research yourself?

Yes, I did lots of market research to find out what the opportunity was in the market, and the opportunity was that there was a huge opportunity to provide the consumer with discreet packaging that sealed better, so I thought, if I could come up with a tampon box that was discreet-looking and sealed better instead of those little clumsy boxes, then there was a market out there looking for it. Then I tried to do some research on packaging, but in the end I threw that out the window because I thought what am I doing? This is ridiculous—I know what I want. In the end I just threw everything the research groups said out the window and said this is what I like and this is what I'm going with.

What was your target market initially—did you have an age bracket or not?

Target markets are always a funny thing. My target market, I think, is someone who's 24. I use this principle when I worked on fashion: When you're 18 you want to be 24, when you're 35 you want to be 24 or 25. That's where your prime age is. I'm 37 and still think I'm 25. So I aimed right at that market, but I aimed it more at someone who wanted discreet packing. I aimed at a market of women who were concerned about what they carried in their handbag and who were image conscious. That doesn't necessarily go across an age group—that goes across the geographic group.

How did you get your name out into the marketplace?

We did television, a little bit of magazine, radio, cinema, and then lots and lots of PR.

What sort of advertising do you do today?

I haven't done any advertising for a while, probably about 18 months, except for PR and sampling.

How did you initially break into the supermarkets?

I found out the best way to go about it was with a supermarket broker, who is somebody with a team of merchandisers who can go around and make sure your product has actually been put on the shelves in the supermarket, and merchandise your product to make sure it's always there and the right tickets are displayed; they look after it at store level. So I went in with a company that did that, and they already had established relationships with people in Coles, so I went with them and did my presentation. But at the end of the day it was the zip lock bag and the discreet packaging that was the thing the buyer looked at and said. 'Wow this is different.'

And you said you didn't have a business plan, you threw that out the window and you just went for it?

Yes, it's pretty simple. I tried to overcomplicate it, and when my father said just do it, I suddenly said wait a minute, he's right. I've just made it too complicated, so basically what I did was employ a student straight out of college, and I had him work at my apartment when I was living in Sydney. He was working there three days a week and I was going to the office at M&C Saatchi, but they didn't know at the office that I had someone else working for me at home. He was designing my tampon idea plus two other ideas I had. I actually had three ideas on the go at once, the tampon one just happened to be the one that came off. Once I got the packaging worked out and I worked on a presentation and did all my costings and that sort of thing, it really wasn't that difficult.

What were the other ideas you had?

There was a thing with Christmas bonbons and another way of getting advertising into changing rooms.

Did you have many contacts in those early days that you networked with to get the business off the ground, besides your dad?

No. I'd worked on so many pieces of business as an art director; I've worked on everything from Qantas to Vodafone to National Australia Bank to SPC to CUB, and I understood the business pretty well. I've been brought up in a business environment. My brother has the packing company that packs all my products for me, so between him and my dad (my brother's a lawyer as well), I've just been brought up very business-minded.

How many product lines do you currently have?

I just produce the De Jour tampons in regular, super, and then there's the combo packs of slim, regular and super sizes.

How many distribution outlets do you have in Australia?

I have all Coles, Bi-Lo, Woolworths, Priceline, all reputable pharmacies and independent supermarkets chains such as Action and Richies.

How did you come up with the clever zip lock idea?

That came about because I was trying to do a cardboard box that locked better, and I couldn't come up with a machine that would be able to fold it and then put the tampons in it, so I actually went up and down the aisles in the supermarket and saw Gladbags. They can seal and reseal again and it was actually in the last two months of the whole 18 month process that I came up with that idea, which is actually the whole selling concept.

Are you looking at selling outside of Australia in the future?

I have been into New Zealand and it wasn't successful, and I'm in talks with people in other countries at the moment.

What process did you go through to find a manufacturer to make the tampons?

That's not too difficult; I went to the German consulate and found companies that manufacture.

Does the business call for you to travel regularly?

Not too much actually. I just do the presentations to my Woolworth's people, and travel a little bit interstate to check up on stores, but not a huge amount, no.

How many employees do you currently have?

We have five staff.

Do you currently network with any other businesses in the same industry?

No—they're all owned by multinationals. I have nothing to do with them.

What have been some of the highlights for you in running your own business?

Being nominated twice for the Telstra Business Women's Award, in both 2003 and 2004 I was a finalist. In 2000 I was inducted into the Australian Businesswomen's Hall of Fame.

Also getting front page coverage for the 'no to GST on tampons' that I leaked to *The Age*. It was pretty good to know that I created that entire debate across the whole of Australia because I'm the one who wrote the paper, submitted it to the government and sent it to *The Age* and then they ran the story.

Winning my first lot of private label work, I also packed quite a lot of private labels for supermarkets in other products, I don't just do tampons. I suppose a high was just getting into Coles in the first place, when they said in the meeting that they would stock them, I remember walking out of the meeting and turning to the broker and saying that was easy and he was nearly white and said I've never seen a meeting go so well. I suppose that was probably my greatest thrill.

Were there any major obstacles or challenges that you had to overcome in your first year operating the business?

I think probably the greatest challenge I had to overcome in the first year was getting used to working on my own. When I started the business, it was just me and I had to do everything. That was probably the hardest, coming from working in an advertising agency to working by myself out of my old bedroom.

What sacrifices do you think were the biggest ones you made to get the business off the ground?

I sacrificed every weekend.

How many hours per week did you work in the first year?
Maybe I was doing about 11-hour days.

And now, do you still work those hours?

Now I don't. Now I just do 9 to 5.

Did you source funding to start the business or was it your own savings?

Yes, I had bank help and my own savings.

As far as debts and creditors, do you control that internally?

We do all our own accounting and invoicing.

Do you currently have a partner or investor in the business?

No, it's totally my business.

What's your main role in the business?

Everything. I know everything that's going on. Every email that comes into the business comes via my computer, then it's directed to the appropriate people.

What's your management style and what sort of staff culture do you build within your business?

I expect people to be very thorough. I'm big into time management so I don't care if you take two hours for lunch, as long as the work is done. It's important to me that all the people are very organised and thorough and that they follow through with things. If I ask someone to follow through with something, I like it done within that day. Between myself and my PA, we have a communication diary, so everything goes in that diary. So there's no question about what needs to be done because we can always flick back to it. We can check back and say that was meant to happen, or what happened with that, so I very much follow through with things like that.

How do you motivate yourself on a daily basis?

If I felt really flat in the early days, I used to go and read a book on another entrepreneur to spark my energies. But I'm a really motivated person and enjoy coming to work. I plan what I'm doing every day—for example, today I will set aside 15 minutes to plan what I'm going to do tomorrow. I never have to think what am I going to do because I've already planned it. I've got everything locked in, so I'm always planning ahead. But I've always been very energetic, full of ideas, that's the way I've always been.

In general, what motivates you?

Sense of achievement and growth. There are a whole lot of different things, but there's nothing nicer than when you meet people and someone asks you what do you do, and I say I own the De Jour tampon company and they say, 'I use them, I love them. Do you own them?' That's wonderful, it makes me feel great, to think I've created something and people know it.

With achieving your goals, do you set monthly goals, quarterly goals?

Yes I do, but I'm not structured. We have family meetings and I have private meetings with my father every six or seven weeks, and I'll have a list of goals. There are things that you're looking ahead to try and do. As I do them, they get ticked off, then something else might come up.

So your father is still very much involved in the business?

Yes—he's my mentor.

If you had to start over, would you do anything differently?

The only thing I would have done differently is that I wouldn't have called myself initially The Woman's Room. I would have called myself De Jour Sanitary Products. The only other thing I would have done differently is that I would have got a PR company involved when I did the 'no GST on tampons' as I missed a huge PR opportunity there. They're about the only things I would have done differently.

What do you do to relax?

I exercise three or four times a week. This morning I've been up running since 6 am. At night, I'm home by 5 and I bathe and feed the kids and all that. Then I watch television, I love television it's the best relaxation. I can spend hours just glued to it, I'm shocking. Half of the time my husband will talk to me and I'll ask him about 5 minutes later, 'What was it you said?' There is nothing better if I'm feeling tired than to jump in bed at about 7.30 and watch *CSI* or something. I've always been like that, my whole life. I can get rejuvenated from two nights at home watching television.

As far as mentors, has there been anyone else besides your father?

Just him really, then outside of that, people who've been successful like Ray Kroc, Howard Schultz or even Lance Armstrong and Richard Branson. Even though I don't personally know them, I read books on those people and take away ideas, even if one bit of advice that helps you can run your business better. You can always learn something because each of them has a strength. McDonald's, for example,, is all about systems. To know you can go anywhere in the world and have the same cheeseburger. And the whole place is run by kids, kids from all over the world who all speak different languages can give me the same cheeseburger. That's called a system. Howard Schultz never gave up pushing to get StarBucks happening. He just kept on and on to these guys about launching it and doing it, pushing it and never giving up.

Do you personally undertake any training?

No, I don't do any of that sort of thing. But I read books and go and listen to inspirational speakers such as Janine Allis who's a contemporary and has Boost Juice, through to Gerber who wrote *The E-Myth*. If Richard Branson came, I'd like to listen to him talk.

What's the best advice you were ever given with regards to your business?

There have been so many different pieces of advice. I work by saying. 'There are many ways to skin a cat'. You can always find a solution—it's just a matter of re-looking at a problem. I've always been like that. That was my job as an art director. for example, suddenly a client will say, 'We don't like that campaign. You have to go back and write a new one.' There's always another way to write an ad. You can give the same brief on how to sell a car to 20 different creators and they'll all give you 20 different ads. Five of them might be absolutely brilliant, and there might be no difference between the five of them—they're all great ads individually, but they're all quite completely and utterly different. So again, because I've come from that background I know there are many ways of skinning a cat—I've had to do it.

Probably the greatest advice is to face the problem, sit down and don't react straightaway, think about it first. I'm a great one to react straightaway and I've learned that sometimes it's better to sit down and digest, think about it overnight, talk about it with your mentor, talk about it with the people whose opinions you respect, get a few ideas about and then tackle it.

Where do you go from here, what are your plans for the next 5 years?

Get into the US market. Expanding my business into other areas, that's one of the things I'm looking at. Concentrating on the private label business, with completely different products outside of tampons for supermarkets.

What sort of private labels are you talking about?

Toothbrushes, toothpaste, soaps, bandaids or house-cleaning products. Home branded products that come from a supplier; it's a big market.

Three key strategies for De Jour's success

1. There are many ways to skin a cat, that is, there are many ways and angles to look at a problem. If one way doesn't work, try another way.

2. Never give up, be like a dog with a bone. Sometimes I'll get frustrated if something's not working or I'm not having success, and I might give up for a couple of months, but then I'll come back to it.

3. Under-promise and over-deliver, you will win every single time. If I say to somebody that I'm going to do something by Friday, I try to have it to them by Thursday. I pride myself on being really thorough and over-delivering and being really competent.

Katrina's words of advice

1. Find out what are your strengths, what are your weaknesses and accept them, and employ people to cover your weaknesses. I think that's really important.

2. Be smart with your time, manage it by your highest priorities.

3. There's this great line which is very deep and very true: 'A body will continue in the same direction unless impacted by an outside force'. Look at books, you can learn so much from just reading books on how other people are doing businesses. When I sometimes want inspiration, I might just go to Myer to look at all the beautiful packaging in the perfumery department. Or just go to a beautiful shop that imports the most beautiful perfumes and all those sorts of smelly lotions and potions from all around the world. I think it's important to have outside forces to make you really look at what you're doing.

4. Know when you are you at your peak: is it in the morning or in the evening? Plan around your peak performance time. I'm a great morning person—a fantastic morning person; if I've got a huge day, I'll be up at 5.30, ready and in the office at 7 o'clock. I hate working past 5 o'clock. I always recognise that I'm a morning person, so if I had to do a presentation when we were in advertising or anything like that, I would prefer to finish my day at 5, go home, have a shower, relax, make a few notes— just have a nice evening, then get up at 5am.

5. Nobody has the monopoly on right and wrong, everyone has a lot to contribute. I am always happy to listen to a better suggestion. If someone can show me a better way to do what we're currently doing that would save time and is better, I'm all for it. Keep an open mind. If you can find a better way of doing my system, go for it.

6. Not everybody should start their own business. Some people make wonderful employees and some people make great bosses, and some people make great thinkers—there are all different types. I think some people try to start their own business thinking that it's going to be really easy and it's not that easy. Think carefully about taking the plunge.

SUZI DAFNIS
POW WOW EVENTS

Suzi and her partner Peter Johnston have come a long way from their humble beginnings, starting their business from the spare room in their home. Their vision was to create an educational company that would provide events for anyone wanting to improve their business, finance and personal growth.

Pow Wow Events was founded in 1994. Within 10 years the company has evolved with offices based in Sydney and Arizona in the USA. Pow Wow Events represents and promotes 10 internationally renowned speakers such as Robert Kiyosaki, author of bestselling *Rich Dad, Poor Dad*, John Burley and Dr Fred Grosse.

Pow Wow Events publishes their own books and training material, and they also distribute and export a range of over 100 products including tapes, videos and books, which they sell globally through their website.

Over the past 10 years Suzi has grown Pow Wow Events data base to over 200,000 people. The company provides educational events throughout Australia, United Kingdom, America and New Zealand, hosting workshop and seminars for groups as small as 20 people to conventions of 6500 people.

Suzis combines Pow Wow's International Enterprise with her commitments as General Manager of the Australian Businesswomen's Network, an organisation that supports and services 10,000 women throughout Australia, with networking events, seminars and publications. Suzi was a finalist for the Telstra Business

Women's Awards in 2001 and also the Ernst & Young Entrepreneur of the Year award in 2003.

Where did you grow up?

I grew up in south western Sydney. I'm first generation Greek–Australian, my parents migrated here in the mid 60s with a view to giving their children a better life than they had enjoyed themselves, having grown up in small villages in Greece.

Do you come from a large family?

I'm the first of three. I have two younger brothers.

Did you complete your schooling in Sydney?

I went to Kingsgrove North High School, which was a co-educational school in the south–western suburbs. I finished in 1984.

Did you go onto university or college?

No—all my additional studies have been through either reading books or attending private courses, I've travelled to the UK, Canada, America, New Zealand to participate in training seminars, I'm very much self-taught.

Do you believe your childhood or your parents influenced your decision to go into business?

My parents are self-employed and always have been—my dad's a builder. Mum didn't work a lot when we were growing up, but as soon as we were old enough to be in school, she would work from home—she was a seamstress. I can remember at one point she had an Avon business. They were self-reliant, and I think I took that on—just wanting to be my own master and not having to have someone else determine my income or put a ceiling on what I could or couldn't do. Yes, it was definitely genetic.

When you left school, what was your ambition?

My ambition was to never go to school again. I wanted to stay in education but I hated school so it was kind of a contradiction, in the end I've ended up in education but in a very different environment.

When I finished high school and needed money, I started work as a receptionist and learnt basic administration skills, but I really felt that I'd done myself a bad turn in that if I didn't go to university, I'd never amount to anything. Even culturally within the Greek community, it was very normal (just like a lot of communities I guess) to want to go to university. I remember having cousins and family friends who were all going and they just couldn't understand how I had dropped out of school because how could I ever do anything with my life without that tertiary education. As we know now in retrospect, there are actually a lot of successful business people who have never finished school, and the academic studies part, while important and relevant, are not the only key to having a successful business.

Your first job?

I finished school in 1984 and my first job was working in a sandwich store, while still at school. I was 14 and 9 months and started working at Roseland Shopping Centre because, again, I just wanted my freedom.

After your first full-time position as a receptionist where did you go?

I went into promotions. It was something I was always interested in. I worked in the promotions department in a very small fashion house. I then did temping for two years while I travelled, so it wasn't until I landed a job at Virgin in 1990 that I actually became serious about my career. I came across Virgin when I was in the UK and thought it was a great organisation, and being a 21-year-old working in the music industry, it was fantastic.

Where did you go from Virgin?

I was at Virgin for three years. In actual fact I didn't have a lot of years working for an employer—maybe 8 years in different careers in between travelling and that sort of thing. In 1991 I did a personal development seminar and it absolutely changed my life. The seminar company that put it on is no longer around, but that company had an affiliation with Robert Kiyosaki, who's the author of *Rich Dad, Poor Dad*. When I reflect, I think the purpose of going to that course was to meet Robert Kiyosaki and learn about him and his work because that's been very much a part of my life for the past 10 years.

Where are you based now?

In Arizona and Sydney. For the last four years we've been going back and forth, and we've managed to maintain a base in both countries. Currently, I spend more of my time in the US.

What led you to start your own business?

I wanted to work for myself—I didn't want someone else determining my future. PJ and I started the business because we had a passion for education, but not traditional education. We set out to create a boutique operation where we would represent authors and individual speakers exclusively through our marketplace.

So what were your first steps in starting the business?

We had some savings and set up our office in our home at Mosman. We literally set up the spare room with a couple of desks, a filing cabinet, a phone and a fax machine. That was it. We had 'call waiting' so that was our two phone lines. We worked out of home for the first two years before we could afford what was then an astronomical amount of $400 a month in rent for an office. Now we have 1800 square metres and our own building in Rosebery.

Did you have a business plan?

We didn't have a business plan until we had to get an overdraft, and then we went to our accountant for advice and he helped us devise a business plan with a more predictable cash flow.

What market research did you do with regards to searching for potential speakers?

Part of it was through referrals. Then we hit on the vein of personal finance education, which has been a big part of our curriculum, and although we have speakers on all sorts of business subjects, the area that's been the most popular has been investing—particularly real estate investing. To start with we tested the market with subjects; we'd do maybe a three hour program and see how many people showed up. If that was successful, we'd do something bigger and then something bigger again. At some of our early events on the subject of finance, we'd have 120 people. The biggest event we've done to date has been 6500 participants, but that's taken a number of years to build up to that.

So really it's been a lot of testing and making mistakes. One of the most wonderful tools of market research for us has been email because the response time is so quick, so when you put a message out, people either respond or they don't, but you know within about five days, and it's a very low-cost way to test something. So technology has been a wonderful tool for us doing our market research.

How did you get your name out into the marketplace—before e-commerce really took off?

In 1994, emailing wasn't really big. It was probably a year and a half before we had our website and email, which again was very early compared to the uptake from other companies.

We started to build relationships with other organisations, whether they were an AIM bookstore or anyone else who had contacts with people who were interested in education, personal development, and we'd ask if we could re-sell their product to our customers in exchange for a commission, and slowly people would refer other people, so it was very gradual. One of the things we did very early on to get our name out there was to print a newsletter; it was an 8-page newsletter, and none of our competitors were doing it.

What was your target market?

It was mainly self-employed people, because in our experience they were probably the most hungry to learn. That is a bit of a generalisation, but there were a lot of skills that they did not have, just as we did not have, that they were searching for—whether it be sales and marketing or Internet marketing, or what to do with cash flow once they had it. Today, 10 years later, our demographic is still mainly people who are self-employed or investors, self-directed individuals.

How did you initially recruit motivational speakers?

In the beginning, again it was by referral. A couple of people whose events we'd been students at, we started to represent as their promoters. With Robert Kiyosaki, asking to represent him exclusively in our marketplace was obviously one of our better moves in business.

So did you cold-call a lot of them to get them on board?

Mostly, existing speakers, yes, and then they would recommend others. They're quite a tight-knit community. for example, Robert had recommended another couple of our speakers, and they in turn have recommended others. And because our business is not just events—it's publishing and marketing—we'd look for someone whose message we could package a number of different ways. They had to have good content to work as a book; secondly they had to have another range of products that we could sell, so even when they weren't in the country, we could continue to maintain cash flow.

How did you break into the international market?

We started here in Australia, and then went to New Zealand. The Internet opened up a lot of avenues for us, with interest in ordering books and tapes online from all over the world.

In 2000, at the invitation of the 'Rich Dad' company in the US, we were invited to produce some events like Robert Kiyosaki.'s. That was the perfect opportunity to get our foot in the door with the US market. Initially we thought we'd go for a couple of years, take a look at this opportunity, then come on back, but it's already been four years. The wonderful thing about being in the US is that you can do so much more market research—and bring things back to Australia that have not yet reached us. So it's been great, I always wanted to have an international company, and even though we don't do events everywhere in the world, it looks like we'll do something in the UK next year.

How often would you travel?

I travel all the time—I'm on planes at least twice a month, most months.

Where do you operate events in the US?

New York, LA, San Francisco, Dallas, Chicago—all over the US. It's not only a big country by land mass, but there are many big cities ideal for us to work and we're also looking at doing some events in the UK in 2005.

How many events do you conduct a year?

Probably between 100 and 120, some years have been busier than others and they range from 3-hour events to 3-day programs. We've done fewer events in the US this year, but all of them have had between 2000 and 3000 people—so fewer events but bigger numbers of attendees. The majority of events are in Australia.

What percentage of your business would you say is processed through your website? for example, tickets sales, motivational books and tapes?

We sell at least 30 per cent of everything through the website, although this varies based on the campaign and the price point. People seem to feel better paying for smaller amounts online and larger amounts over the phone. In fact, we try to direct most of the traffic to the website, rather than people calling us where possible. Yet the phone is still the most used medium for placing orders.

How many employees do you have now?

We currently have 22 full-time staff. We've had as many as 8 and as few as 2 in the US; it fluctuates a little bit based on demand.

Do you currently network with other event companies?

Not a lot—not as much as we used to when we were smaller, but we network more with distributors of other products or the media. We don't do a lot of cross-promotion with other event companies.

So you started the business in 1994. What was your age then?

I was 26, I'm now 38.

Do you have a partner in life?

Peter Johnston—PJ and I are in business together, but we're also in a relationship. I can't imagine it any other way. We worked together before we were in a relationship, and we had our 12th anniversary in October 2004.

For the partnership to work so well you obviously have the same goals?

Yes, which is great and I can't imagine coming home and saying. 'What did you do today, honey?' Our vision and goals in our development have been parallel. I think a lot of couples would hate it—spending that much time together—but for us, we are a really good team, we have very complementary and different skills.

How do you manage work and home life to find that balance?

The challenge has been that ability to switch off—when your partner is also in the same business, it's very easy to sit and chat business over dinner, breakfast and so on. For probably the first six years of business, we worked seven days a week. Now we try to take a couple of days off a week—it's not always on weekends because often our events are on weekends, but we do manage that a whole lot better now.

Do you have any other partners within the business besides Peter Johnston?

We had a business partner for most of the years that we've been operating in the USA. This has been an important factor for us—knowing that there is someone with a financial interest in the company running it. We have a number of strategic partners for various projects.

Besides PJ, we have a CEO who is a minor shareholder, and that's only occurred in the last couple of years because we were moving to the US and we needed someone who had an interest in the business to be part of its management team. Her name is Sue Price.

What do you think are the advantages and disadvantages of having a partner?

Firstly I wouldn't want to be in business myself—I don't know how people do it to be honest. I love being part of a team. The only thing about having a business partner is being accountable to another person. When it was just PJ and I, we'd make decisions quickly, and now there's another person to consider, which can be challenging at times. There are definitely pros and cons. But again, the three of us have very different skills, and Sue's very much involved in the day-to-day running of the team so there's a unique skill that she has that is important.

What advice would you give to someone who wanted to take on a partner in business?

The relationship is really very important. It's important that your partners have needed skills, but even more important that you have common values—about life and business. You'll be spending a lot of time together.

We knew Sue for seven years before she came on as a partner. She had been a client, she'd been a friend and an acquaintance. I don't recommend you get into business with a stranger, and if you do, then make sure you've got really good out-clauses. Even with us with our great relationship, we still have things in place in case it all goes to pod, and how we're going to get out of it.

What would you say has been the highlight so far in running your own business?

The highlights have definitely been the personal growth—for PJ and I, as well as our staff. A number of our staff has used the information they have learnt to start their own businesses or invest in property, which has been great for them.

Financially it's been very rewarding because we've done pretty well over the last 10 years and that has allowed us to have a quality of life that we had aspired to, so that's been great.

Another highlight has been the number of people, especially in the Australian marketplace, who've been positively impacted by the work that we do, and not only the individual who reads the book, or the bookstores that sell those books, but also the people that attend the seminars and learn valuable lessons that empower their entire families.

We've sold 1.2 million books, and that's a lot of books sold in a marketplace of 20 million people. When we started out we knew nothing about publishing, now we're probably one of the most successful small publishers in the country and because we didn't know how to publish and we didn't know that most publishers only promote a book for a six to eight week cycle, we found when it's your book and you're responsible for the bottom line, you'll promote that book for seven years like we have done for *Rich Dad, Poor Dad*. It's a different level of interest.

Other highlights have also been, putting on events for 6500 people at the Sydney Convention Centre, doing an event at Madison Square Garden in New York, and having seven No.1 best-selling books; there have been so many highlights.

Wow, seven No.1 bestsellers—were they all for Robert Kiyosaki?

Not all of them, but many. One of them is a Rich Dad title. Others were also in the personal finance area—one by Dolf de Roos (Dr Ruth)—a real estate writer, and another gentleman John Burley, who's also out of Arizona—he wrote a personal finance book called *Money Secrets of the Rich*. We have three totally different titles coming out in 2005—we're very excited about that, and it's in the personal finance area, but then that's definitely been our best subject overall.

Have you received any awards for yourself or the business?

Yes. I was a finalist in the Telstra Business Woman of the Year awards, and the Young Entrepreneur of the Year Awards in 2003, I've been listed in BRW's Young Rich issue for the last two years as well. As for the business, we haven't actually entered Pow Wow Events into any small business awards, as we are just too busy running the business.

What led you to take on the role of General Manager of the Australian Businesswomen's Network?

I fell into it a little bit. It was when we were bringing one of our American speakers out here to Australia, who was in the area of sales, and we were looking at other databases to market to, that I came across the Australian Businesswomen's Network which had been founded in Victoria, and they had quite a significant database. We did some work on the network and met with the woman who founded it, and she said you sound like you're really switched on. Would you like to start the Sydney branch? That was in 1995, and I was very new into business and I thought I don't think so; I don't think I can do that. I'm so busy with my business and actually PJ was the champion of it. He said go on, do it, you don't know who you'll meet, and that was almost 10 years ago.

There have been times when, because it's a voluntary position, I thought I can't do this, but I've stuck with it because I meet the most amazing women, who have been great role models and mentors. It's wonderful—I love it. If I decide to close down Pow Wow Events tomorrow, that is still something I would do because it's just so close to my heart—I love supporting other women in business.

What would you say was the biggest sacrifice to get the business off the ground?

Personal time—it probably took us six years to really build the business and start to see a lot of the financial rewards that we'd been working so hard towards. So the sacrifice was social time, personal time and time with family— that sort of thing.

What sort of hours a week were you working back in the first two years?

It's not that much better now, but I'd have to say 70 to 80 hours a week.

What would you say were the major obstacles or challenges that you had to overcome in the first year of operating the business?

We didn't have a lot of systems to start with, and in fact our systems didn't really develop until we had to leave the country to set up in the US.

Other challenges were hiring staff, hiring the right staff and knowing how to remunerate them; knowing how to reward them; how to show appreciation— staffing is a huge job in itself.

What was your annual turnover for the business in 2003?

About $9.2 million. That's for Australia, then combined, we probably had our best year about 2 years ago. Between the two countries, it was $18.3 million.

What's your forecast for 2005?

$10 million.

What percentage of your own money did you invest into the business?

We started with PJ's savings of $30,000, which we ate up, then we lost another $40,000 in the first year. Then we had an overdraft for about six months and we've never had an overdraft again. Since then we've always managed on cash flow.

How did you obtain the external funding with the overdraft?

We went to the Westpac Bank in 1995.

When was the first year that you made a profit?

That was 1996.

Does the business deal with debts and creditors itself?

In our business people pay in advance, which is a great type of business to have so we don't have to be chasing up money much. We're usually paid before we deliver a service, which is fantastic from a cash flow perspective.

What's your main role within the business now?

Marketing strategies, and concentrating business growth.

Can you describe a typical day?

I do a lot of email communication, mainly because often I'm not at a desk in my office; I could be anywhere. A typical day would be the strategic planning around a marketing campaign, meeting with key personnel. External meetings with possible suppliers, possible speakers—things that are more working on the business than in the business. I do a lot of writing—even to this day I do a lot of the writing for our marketing. And I would spend a couple of hours a day working on the Australian Businesswomen's Network, whether it's co-ordinating the Board or looking at events or possible sponsors.

How would you describe your management style?

I'm pretty clear about what I want and I'm very happy to have input from people, though I don't suffer gossip or fools lightly. I really believe that the workplace is for being productive and producing results and I want people to be happy at the same time, but in the end, if the company's not making money, then we're all going to be out of a job. Somewhere in there is a balance.

What generally motivates you the most?

Helping others is a big part of it for me. I feel like one of my personal missions is to empower the human spirit—as fluffy as that might sound, I think that's what I'm here to do. And financial rewards really do motivate me. I didn't think they did, but we've done things where we've lost money and it's much nicer to make money. Also for me, just having an outlet for my own creativity—to be able to create a PR campaign, marketing campaign or a staff initiative is motivating and rewarding.

What techniques do you use to achieve your goals?

I set goals all the time. I start 1 January—PJ and I sit down and we do our personal goals—for our health, relationship, investing—all there is in our lives. I'm very goal-oriented and I'm always setting targets for things like the number of sales we want to have in a week or the number of memberships we want for the business. I believe very much in intention and being very clear about what you want and what you don't want, and just never giving up. Something might take a long time to happen, but if I really want it, I just won't give up.

As a female, have you ever felt vulnerable in business?

I did in the beginning—I thought that people would want to talk to PJ rather than me over business deals, and it did occur that way a number of times where we'd be in a meeting and people would be directing their conversation more to him. But part of it was psychological, and until I felt that I had the credibility and I had the personal power to communicate better or present an argument, then it all changed, so it was all centred around my own self-worth.

If you had to start over, would you do anything differently?

I would recruit management staff sooner. When we started in the US, the first person we recruited was an operations manager, and that business runs far more independently because we have this senior person who watches our back like you wouldn't believe—she watches every dollar as if it were her own. Yet when we started with Pow Wow Events, for the first four or five years we managed every single staff member ourselves. I also didn't have a PA for the first six or seven years, and I'd probably do that differently because my time is worth more than I gave it credit for.

Have you had any mentors along the way?

Not at a close distance—I've never had anyone mentor me directly. For the past two years we've had a Board at Pow Wow Events. We meet once a month—they're external people, and come in with their own experience and they have mentored us with managing our cash flow better or making different staff decisions.

Also through the Businesswomen's Network, I've met a lot of entrepreneurs who through sharing their story I've learnt lots of things. I think in general you can really learn from anybody, there's always something to learn—even from your most junior staff member if you're willing to listen.

What motivational books would you recommend for someone wanting to go into a business?

There are a couple of key books—for me these have been the books that have been most inspiring. *Rich Dad, Poor Dad* certainly—because it's been the key for me and for our business. One of the things I learned very early on is that a lot of money could go through my hands, having my own business, and at the end of the day, I could be very tired and burnt out and have nothing to show for it. So one of the things that PJ and I started to do in 1997 is to buy our first investment property, which was in the far western suburbs of Sydney. It was a $53,000 house, and now you can say that it was no risk, but at the time it was a huge risk. What if we don't have a tenant? What if we lose money? After that one little property, we bought another one, then another one, then another one, and soon we had enough assets that if we decided to close the business tomorrow, we would be fine. So the reason I mentioned that book is not because we promote Robert Kiyosaki, but because it was a turning point for me.

As was his book *Cash Flow Quadrant*. It talks about the difference between an employee, someone in small business, big business and investors, and it talks about the psychology of what differentiates those four types of people—not only where they earn their money, but their psychology. To me it was a real eye-opener because here I thought I was going to build this big business but my thinking was very 'self-employed' thinking. It was a very important book for me when I read it about five years ago. I loved *Losing my Virginity* by Richard Branson, and *Good to Great* by Jim Collins—phenomenal.

I would suggest people getting into business read *The E-Myth* immediately. It's fundamental because it teaches you how to create a systematic business that doesn't rely on your input. There's another book called 'Influence—the Psychology of Persuasion', it's one of the best sales marketing books and deals with the psychology of the customer. Again it's very good for any small business owner. But there are hundreds of books. My thing is just personal education— just read, learn and go to seminars. As I said, PJ and I have travelled all over the world to learn from who might be the best expert in any one area, and it's one of those things that when you're ready to learn something, it appears. I was in Canada in I think 1998, and met a guy who was in Internet marketing. It was very new then and we bought him out to Australia. We did so well because no-one else was doing that, but it also catapulted our business and our marketing to a whole new level.

I'm such a believer in education—that's why I'm in this business—because I think the only way that people can be set free to have the life they want is through learning new things—it is education I think that will differentiate a successful business person from one that isn't.

How often do you personally undertake training for yourself?

I'm always reading a book. I probably attend seminars, apart from our own, at least once a year. Recently I saw Donald Trump in New York City, he was fabulous—just like he is on the show—really blunt and very wise in his very unique way.. I was able to hear him speak for about an hour on his strategies for success. Do you think I learned something? Absolutely. The fact that I had to go to New York—I didn't care. There are worse places to spend money and time.

What was the best advice you were ever given about being in business?

To invest for the future.

Where does the business go from here? What are your plans for the next five years?

For the next five years, I think we're going to be doing a lot more publishing, working with local talent. Another thing we're looking at is distributing new product lines from the US.

The difference is, if I look at it five years from now, firstly that I won't be as involved in the day-to-day, the curriculum—I think we're about to go into a new area of personal development, health and well-being which I'm hoping will be bigger than the financial education. In five years we will be definitely more advanced in technology, even now we're implementing a new CRM system that will allow us to deal with our customers needs and wants much easier—with more infrastructure for reporting and reaching more people. The idea in our industry of web seminars has been talked about for a long time. I think the next five years will see how much of a reality that will be, and whether the market accepts it.

Three Key strategies for Pow Wow Events' success

1. Finding out what we were really good at. Part of our success was being really good at the production and promotion of personal development education events. So whatever that unique thing is, it's finding what's different about you.

2. Building relationships. It's so important. We don't always do it perfectly, but building relationships (not only with your customers but with strategic alliances). One of the ways we grew was by grabbing onto the fin of a bigger fish and swimming alongside it.

3. Integrity is the essence of everything. First up when you make a mistake, be honest—have that level of integrity in your organisation. That's why I mentioned the thing about gossip—it doesn't support the team. Integrity is the essence of everything, and I would hope that even though we're not perfect, Pow Wow Events would be known for its honesty, delivering goods and value information.

Suzi's words of advice

1. Start getting educated.

2. Seek out role models.

3. Get financially literate. That goes back to education but there are a lot of things to learn about business; understand money. A lot of small businesses think that their business income is their personal income and it's not—they're two very different things.

4. Never, ever give up.

5. Marketing. If you can't market and can't sell, then it's really hard to be successful because you're always marketing, and selling your business or your service or even yourself. Build up yours skills in this area.

6. Personal development. It's really all about you, and the more you can know who you are and what you're good at and what you're not good at, then the more successful you can be.

LISA MCGUIGAN
TEMPUS TWO

For years Lisa McGuigan wanted to step out of her father's shadow and avoided the wine industry. Her father Brian McGuigan is known for building wine companies such as Wyndham Estate and McGuigan Simeon Wines. Instead Lisa opted for a career in hospitality. Lisa spent 10 years of working in five-star hotels in Sydney, taking on a variety of roles including food and beverage manager, and sales and marketing.

Eventually her father convinced her to move back to the Hunter Valley to work in the family business by offering her the opportunity to redevelop one of the Hunter Valley vineyards and cellars. Within a year Lisa had developed her own boutique brand wine, after recognising a niche in the marketplace for an upmarket premium wine label. As a result, in 1997 she launched one of Australia's most dynamic, innovative and successful wine brands this decade, naming it Tempus Two.

These days she's following the family tradition as a fourth generation McGuigan to produce wine, and her label Tempus Two is now in its seventh year, is producing in excess of 200,000 cases of wine a year and exports to the United Kingdom, Philippines and New Zealand.

Tempus Two also boasts its own cellar door in Pokolbin; the boutique winery offers cellar door, Oishii Japanese restaurant and amphitheatre, and provides regular concerts and programs.

◆

Can you tell me a little about Tempus Two?

Yes, about seven years ago my objective was to create something that had appeal to a niche market. My idea was that I would have some packaging combined with wines that I'd selected from the regions all around Australia that grow the particular grape varieties the best, then source that fruit from those regions, and put that into a product that would come out in two different ranges of wine and appeal to the premium end of the market.

Could you tell me about your upbringing?

I grew up in the Hunter Valley, two hours north of Sydney. I had a sister who died about 10 years ago of cancer.

Did you complete your schooling in the Hunter Valley?

I went to an all-girls school called St Joseph's College Lochinvar, which is a boarding school but I lived fairly close to the school—half an hour away—so I was able to be a day student there, until Year 12.

Where did you go from there?

I decided that I wanted to study visual arts and I applied to get into that course. I then decided to put the course on hold and take a year off, and I went overseas and studied French and cooking. The intention was to do just a short 3-month course while I thought about what I wanted to do. I loved the course so much that I ended up completing it and then staying on there for a year. I spent some time in Switzerland studying, and then when I came back, I had the hotel management bug; at the time (1985 when I was overseas), everyone was studying hotel management. It was the craze in Europe. It was one of the top courses you could do and one of the most popular courses at the time.

When I came back, I decided that what I really wanted to do was enrol in the Ryde School of TAFE Hotel Management course. They ran the only course in Australia for hotel management at the time—before working in hotels was regarded as a profession. We're talking 20 years ago. So when I came back from overseas, I went back to the Hunter, and for the first year in the Hunter Valley in Newcastle—at Hamilton Food School in the Hunter Valley, they were running the course for the first time. I decided to apply for the course and I got quite a shock when I went to apply because they said you have to sit an exam and there are 300 other applicants and we're only taking 15. I really wanted to do it, and because I spent some time overseas and I had an understanding of cooking, that really helped me and I managed to get in. I spent the next four years studying completing a Diploma in Hotel Management.

As soon as I finished my course, I moved to Sydney and took a job at the Renaissance Hotel. I'd worked in hotels in the Hunter Valley while I was doing my training and I really had my eye on working in a five-star hotel, so I started as a waitress in one of the restaurants at the hotel and 12 months later I was managing the restaurant.

A year after that, I was promoted to a position where I ran three restaurants in the hotel. I started in 1990 at the hotel, in 1991 I was running the restaurant, in 1992 I was running three restaurants, then two years after that I moved into a role where I was in charge of all the marketing for the food and beverage department.

I loved doing all of that, and I spent another two years in that role. My goal was to be the first five-star female general manager in Sydney. I was extremely motivated and really wanted that job. But I realised that in the hotel industry, I would eventually have to work overseas and I didn't really want to go and work all around the world in hotels, and that my goals in life had changed. I suppose having lost my sister a few years before, I needed to be near my family. The positions I was being offered overseas were fantastic for my career, but other things became more important to me.

My father had his wine company, called McGuigan Wines, and for many years he had wanted me to work for the company, and he really wanted me to go and study wine marketing when I left school. He wanted me to have the best opportunities, but I'm a bit stubborn, a bit like him—headstrong, and I like to make my own decisions. I suppose over the years when he had offered me various positions, they were great, but I never really wanted to do what my dad did. I wanted to be my own person, and not 'the daughter of', and I suppose doing all those other things that I did really helped me to become my own person. If I had been in his shadow, I might not have had the confidence that I have now.

The contacts I made in the hotel industry I still have and that's great, particularly because working in the wine industry is very closely related to the hospitality industry.

So one particular day, I think I'd done about five back-to-back shifts that week, and my dad asked me to lunch. So I met with him and he said, 'I've got a great position for you. I think this time you'll love it.' I'd always said to him, 'If you offer me the right position, I'll take it.' He offered me a position, which involved moving to the Hunter and opening a new cellar door outlet that he'd taken the lease of. It was the old Hungerford Hill in the Hunter Valley, that many people even back in the 70s knew because there was a great children's playground. It was an underground cellar, and it had one of the first restaurants in the Hunter attached to it. Anyway, Dad offered me the job as the Cellar Door Manager, and so I thought about it for a couple of weeks, went and had a look, and I saw it was a complete mess and a great opportunity, so I agreed to take the position. It was hard for me to leave the hotel industry, but it was right up my alley because it was a management role and I'd been trained as a manager, and I felt that I could really contribute as a manager. I also made an agreement with him that he had to let me do it my way, that he couldn't come in and say no, this is how you do it. He gave me complete autonomy for 12 months, and if I didn't deliver the budget that he had given me, then sure he could intervene, but that was the deal and was the condition that I took the position on.

So what happened then?

A year went by and I really loved what I was doing, and saw that there was a really great opportunity in the market for the people that I had been looking after at the cellar door—there were opportunities for a really groovy boutique wine brand to come onto the market. I suppose I call myself a marketer, and I think marketers like to see opportunities. When I was running the cellar door, it was a job that I loved, but I also loved looking into the possibilities of things I could come up with that might be earth shattering.

Our company is run by a board of directors (because it's public), and I had to come to the Board of Directors this particular day and fill them in on my results for the first year's trading of the cellar door. We'd absolutely doubled our budget, so I was in a good position, and at the same time thinking of these ideas I had. The Board thought I was great and I'd achieved my budget and that was a good thing. I remember going to my father and saying, 'I've got this great idea. I want to start a boutique wine brand.' He said, 'Go and tell the Board about your great idea.' And I did, and the Board said, 'What do you need? We'll back you.'

My idea came about by me working in that retail outlet and having had that experience in hotels where I could see that there were some great wines on the market, like Vasse Felix and some of the Western Australian brands that were starting to build a really good name, but I just felt that I had this idea and could see the opportunity. Nothing could hold me back. I built that up over 12 months, reached the targets and budgets that I had to achieve, went to the Board and approached them with my idea of Tempus Two, a boutique wine label. They were all very positive and backed me all the way.

Did you do a marketing plan in the beginning?

I did a very basic business plan and incorporated a marketing plan and a sales plan, and probably the first thing I worked out was the name of the brand. The next thing would have been the philosophy of the brand, so the name of the brand wasn't Tempus Two when I started (that's a bit of a story). The original name was Hermitage Road. I made the decision on the name, then I made the decision on the philosophy of the brand, which would be that we would source fruit from vineyards around Australia and we would develop two ranges of wines—one being quite premium, and the other being the everyday 'drink as much as you can, as much as you like wine'—just good value—and identifying the regions that grow the grape varieties the best. I had two ways of selecting the fruit. I wasn't just limited to the public company vineyards. When I started, the Board said you I had to be absolutely independent. They allowed me the working capital of $50,000; and I had to remain in the black, not in the red at any time, or the brand won't exist any more or they'd just use it as another small brand that they'd sell overseas or something.

I hired a contract winemaker, which meant I only needed that person's services for approximately three months of that year to release my first vintage. I employed one salesperson and I moved back to Sydney because I felt that was where I had to be—that's where the market was. I rented a little apartment in Glebe. From there I started the brand.

What year was it that you established Hermitage Road?

That was 1997, I was 30 and I'm now 37.

What was your initial target market?

Well, I thought I had two markets really: the boutique market where, I suppose, if you look at Sydney you'd probably target the Eastern suburbs, and a person who was looking for some packaging that was innovative and someone who would spend maybe around $25 for a bottle of wine, and someone who was educated in wine. The other range, which is the varietal range—that would appeal to someone looking for wine that was about $12, someone going to a BYO restaurant or someone who was in a restaurant wanting to take advantage of the wine of the month offer or wine by the glass.

I wanted to make sure that I didn't put myself too high up there and think I was some elitist wine person. I actually put myself right in the middle of that market, so if I went to a bottle shop and was looking for a nice wine to take to a dinner party that was $25 and looked good, and after trying it, I knew was a quality wine product then I'd become confident with that product. But also I might be going for a quick entrée somewhere and want a $12 bottle of wine to pick up at the bottle shop across the road from the restaurant (a BYO) because I don't want to spend $25 every night but I want a good quality wine that has been produced from a particular region and I know which regions I like. There is a part of the market that I felt would be attracted to that, particularly if it's good value.

How did you get your name out into the marketplace in the early days?

I pounded that pavement big time. I positioned myself in a sales role and I took on a territory, and the other person that joined me took on the other half of Sydney, we basically split it in half. We went into every area. The strategy was that we would go to one restaurant, one bottle shop and one hotel in every suburb, and the reason we chose to do that was because we knew in every suburb if we could go into a bottle shop and say you'd be the only bottle shop that has it, it gave me some sort of opportunity and it was attractive to the retailer because you have to have some point of difference to get them to take your product on. The fact that they would be the only ones in the area to have it meant there would be some exclusivity about it.

I gave most of my clients exclusivity in their area for 12 months, and that was part of the plan because my first year's budget was 6000 cases.

We also concentrated on Sydney and I went to see some of my contacts in the five-star hotels. By that stage, a lot of the people I'd worked with were moving into running restaurants, so I had quite a few connections there where I was able to go in and get into some of the top restaurants in Sydney, which is great for your brand and for your image, particularly in your first 12 months.

Did you do any additional advertising, for example, newspapers and magazines?

None at all. I didn't have any money to spend on that sort of advertising, but what I did do, was I put any money I had into a range of products that would back up my wines. I prepared a little presentation kit that had a photograph of each product and a tasting note on the back. The only money I would have spent in advertising and marketing was all spent on the presentation box and kit. That was something I'd leave behind with retailers and restaurateurs.

What do you do now to build the brand and the concept today?

I do a little bit of advertising today, but in the first couple of years, because I didn't have any money to spend on advertising except for the point-of-sale stuff I took every opportunity I could, I'd get a lot of enquiries from charities, in particular, who were looking for wines for their events, and so a great way of advertising was to put your wines in front of an eclectic group of people from all parts of the community, and through the charities I realised that after doing a couple of functions, it was a really great forum for me to promote the wine, and a way to help those people who are trying to raise money for worthwhile causes.

We've all been to functions where the wine's bad, and I think that it's a responsibility as a wine person to try to ensure that we can provide the best wines to the community. When they don't have a budget, I suppose I don't see it as a business opportunity. I see it as an opportunity to get your name out there and help people in the meantime.

Why did you change the name from Hermitage Road to Tempus Two?

This was a situation that probably was a turning point in my life. The name Hermitage Road was something I came up with because the winery I was renting from my father was located on a road called Hermitage Road in the Hunter, and I thought that was a logical name; people would be able to find it. At the time when I was setting the brand up, I had a list as long as my arm of things I had to do, and the name was one thing I put to bed. I registered it, and one year later I received a letter from the French Government, stating that I could no longer use the name Hermitage Road because it's a French regional name. As you may know, you're not allowed to use 'champagne' any more for Australian sparkling wines, so the same rules apply to French regional names like Hermitage, Champagne, Chablis, Burgundy—they're all styles of wine and they originate from France.

The French decided that they didn't want anyone using those names any more. In the 70s, everyone used Burgundy—there's Houghton's White Burgundy, for example. All those brands that were established in Australia in the 70s adopted French names because they were the leaders in the world at the time in wine production.

As from 2002 we could no longer use French regional names. So you can imagine what kind of shock I was in—I knew about this whole issue, but because it was Hermitage Road, I thought of it as an address—it's already somewhere physically in Australia and they wouldn't have an issue with that because we're not calling the wine Hermitage; we're just calling it Hermitage Road. I never thought it would be a problem, even though I knew there was this ruling coming in.

After 12 months, as I said before, my first year's budget was to sell 6000 cases, and I'd just finished off that first year at 10,000 cases (nearly doubling my budget). You could imagine how disappointing it was when my first year had gone so well, and then all the work I'd done on marketing and getting the name out there and people familiar with the name,—just wiped out totally.

I felt like I'd just wasted a whole year creating something that had gone exceptionally well. I was in the black, not the red. I'd over-sold and spent all those hours in the retail outlets just building the brand and getting the name out there. The French Government gave me four weeks to come up with my new name. I'd already had some of my next vintage packaged with the label on it, so it was quite a dilemma.

Once I came to terms with what was needed to be done, I came up with the name 'Tempus Two' which means 'second time'.

How hard was it for you to go back to all the restaurants and bars to re-sell them the new branding?

Well, it was amazing the support that I got from my customers at the time. I also had support from a couple of journalists as well. One of them was Huon Hooke, and he is somebody I really respected. When I went out and told people they were so supportive that probably within 12 months, I'd never looked back again on those times.

It was extraordinary support, so I think it all came from building the relationships with these people. It's not often you get the person behind the brand out there selling as well. There was nothing that could stop me. I suppose having gone through that experience of having the identity crisis with the name, it's probably made me a lot stronger. I don't really get too bothered by obstacles any more—I work out ways to get around them or climb over them. I would never have learned that if something like that didn't happen.

Do you export?

Yes. Two years ago I started selling into the UK. I went there two years ago to promote Tempus Two, and I struck a deal with a chain called Tesco. They now buy 100,000 cases a year from me.

I sell into New Zealand and the Philippines, and I've just come to an arrangement for selling wine into the USA, and I've found a distributor who's going to take all the wines and I'll probably in the first year sell them about 50,000 cases. I've had incredible growth since year five, and that was all part of my plan anyway.

How many distributors do you have in Australia?

What I have now is a situation where because we sell 100,000 cases here domestically, I needed to put on a whole load of sales reps. With 50,000 cases I made the decision that I could no longer sustain my sales by having a small sales team, and to put on a large sales team that were just selling one brand wasn't an economically viable position.

What I did to ensure that the brand continued its growth was to go to the public company of McGuigan Simeon. In Australia, McGuigan Wines has a distribution arm called 'Icon Brands', and Icon Brands distributes for all the McGuigan products and quite a few other companies that they have an agency arrangement with, so it's really a whole sales division that looks after all the company's products plus takes on some agency arrangements.

I went to the public company and was able to take on 45 sales reps for the brand who sold McGuigan products as well, but also took on my portfolio. That's how I took it from 50,000 cases two years ago which is where we were at. Two years ago we were coming into the end of my five year plan, and my five year plan was to build the brand to a point where everyone knew the name, to reach 50,000 cases within five years, and to sell nationally in Australia plus have my own full-time wine maker and not just a contract winemaker.

Now at year 7, we will sell 200,000 cases this year and we now sell nationally. We sell into the UK and I have my own winemaker, which is fantastic. We even have our own winery and cellar door facility in the Hunter Valley now. Before, because I rented a corner of my dad's winery, a lot of my retailers would say we're going to the Hunter. Can we come up to your winery? and I'd have to say no, we're cleaning it this weekend. What about another time? Because I couldn't take them into a winery that was just a corner with a few tanks. So it was about time—I had to get to a certain point before we could afford to invest money in a winery—that was year 5 into the business. We started building it in year 5 and it's been open for just under two years actually. The cellar door is called Tempus Two.

How many employees do you have in total now?

I guess I can't count the 45 sales people because they're not totally Tempus Two, but if I looked at my immediate employees, I'd have around 15 full-time people. If you take into account the fact that I use the sales reps of the public company, there's another 40 odd people there. That includes the winery and the cellar as well.

Does the business call for you to travel regularly?

Yes it does. Now that I've got the sales in hand in Australia and I have people looking after the loyal customers who I've established relationships with in the early days, I don't spend as much time on the road as I did. I used to be on the road all day every day. I now visit my clients nationally on a regular basis, but it gives me time to go and do the export side, I travel overseas at least once or twice a year, and I go to every state to spend time with our sales reps at least twice a year.

When I'm in those states, I put on a cocktail party for consumers and retailers, and I show them all the new wines, have finger food and a bit of fun, and keep trying to build the brand in that way. In the early days when I started, there was no way I could probably even get a cocktail party together because I only had a few customers. These days I've got a lot more, it's great when you can get 50 or 60 people and spend a couple of hours with them. I do a series of those around the country.

What would you say have been the highlights so far for you in running your own business?

The first highlight was exceeding my first year's budget. Another highlight would be completing the cellar door and having a facility like that to represent the brand when I could have given up all those years ago in year 1, but I'm glad I didn't. To have that is a highlight to me. The other highlight is knowing that I'm going to achieve my 10 year plan. It's year 7 and I'm really optimistic about achieving that, and that keeps me really motivated.

Has Tempus Two received any award recognition?

Yes—we've received medals and trophies and stuff, but I'll just tell you the trophies: We've received 87 major trophies over the years. Four of them in the last two years, and three of them in the first year. The other really exciting award was the National Packaging Award I won two years ago for my lines. You would understand why that's important to me knowing that all I wanted to be was an artist, to win the National Packaging Award—I look back and think I've actually been able to achieve in my life what I wanted in the beginning, but by doing it a different way. It took a long time, but that was probably one of the biggest highlights for me—winning that award.

Then this year I received a gold medal in the prestigious Wine and Spirit International Design Awards in London. Only 11 gold medals were awarded from over 220 entries including liqueurs, malt whiskey, wine and beer. The judges said Tempus Two was among 'the crème de la crème when it comes to design, packaging and branding.' We are now in the running for a major trophy in a field of only five finalists.

What would you say was the biggest sacrifice for you to get the business off the ground?

I think probably the time that I had to put into the business, and the time I didn't spend with friends and family.

How many hours per week would you have worked in the first year?

Approximately 60 and now probably 50 per week.

Are you married?

No, I'm single at the moment—no children, just a Border Collie.

In the early days, did you ever find it difficult dealing with men in business?

Not really. I think a lot of my customers were men—publicans and retail, and I think in the wine industry that there are so many men, when they see a female coming along, they get quite excited. They like dealing with females, particularly those people I was dealing with. I suppose when I was purchasing or talking to manufacturing-type people, it might have been a bit different. They might have thought, 'Who's this chick?' But I think it takes a matter of time in any relationship—to build confidence, whether it's with females or males.

What was your turnover last financial year?

It was $9 million.

What would you say will be your turnover for 2005?

My prediction is $14 million.

Was your first profit year, the year you launched?

No, I just made a dollar, but I did stay in the black. I wanted to re-invest money I was making into it, and I really needed to at the time.

Does the business deal with debts and creditors itself etc?

I used to manage it until two years ago—I did all of that myself at night. I'd send all the bills out, chase debtors, did all the paperwork. It was at that point that I mentioned before when I realised I had to let the baby go. I let it go externally to McGuigans because their sales reps turn the sales in so we just use the same system that we have for the public company.

Do you currently have a partner in the business?

I sort of do have a partner in the business—not a financial partner. Sarah-Kate Dineen is my winemaker, and I have a partnership with her as far as the creativity of the brand because she creates my wines and she has to have an absolute understanding for what kind of wines I want in the market, and the image I'm trying to create for the brand. I suppose it's great having someone like that because for many years I didn't—I did it on my own—but to have someone who is in that creative field is someone I would regard as a bit of a partner because we're moving together with a combination of our ideas.

What's your main role in the business now?

I still run the business and drive the business, but my role is probably to drive it through the sales reps, and to continue the relationships I've got with my clients, to inspire the sales reps so that they are saying the right things out there to manage those people to make them feel part of the team.

How would you describe your management style and culture?

I like to lead by example. I like to listen to people. I think the input from the people at the coalface is really important, and that that allows me to see opportunities because even though I've set up the brand and know it all, it doesn't mean I know what's going to happen in the future and what future trends will be.

What motivates you in general?

I think it's predominantly the fact that I'm inspired by being creative, but also a sense of achievement gives me inspiration.

How would you prioritise your time?

I always look at the components of the business and look at what is important. It does change from time to time, but I suppose it's being clear about how the business has come about. I look at where we're going when I prioritise, and what's important for us in the future.

What techniques do you use to achieve your goals?

I set my goals annually. I also have a long-term plan, and I guess I'd prefer to call my plan a vision because if you don't know where you're going and where you're heading, you're never going to get there. If you don't identify where you want to be, you just never know what you want to achieve; it's really important for me to continue to reset those goals.

I think when you set 5-year and 10-year plans, those plans are fairly loose anyway, but my plans are fairly specific with targets and with image, and with branding. When I say those plans are loose, they're not pages and pages—they're a page each. When you start putting crosses against things, that's one way to de-motivate yourself, but if you put things in there that are realistic and that you can achieve but are a little bit 'out there' as well. I think you've got to go out there a bit, particularly when you're setting plans like that, and make it challenging.

If you had to start over, would you do anything differently?

I'd probably start off with the name Tempus Two—that would save me a lot of heartache, but no, I don't think I would actually.

Have you had any mentors or role models along the way?

I have actually, there's a couple. One mentor is Fay McGuigan, my mum, who established a large export department for Wyndham Estate when my parents had that company many years ago, and was one of the first females to export wine back in the 80s. I've learned a lot from her.

A couple of other ones are Jancis Robinson who's a female marketer of wine from the UK. She led the way for females in the wine industry because a master of wine is a fairly high level of achievement and she's one of the most respected wine journalists in the world. I don't know her, but I look to her and think about what she's done for the industry and think about how I'd like to be able to learn from her and do things for the industry as well.

There's another person—his name is David Clark, and he's the chairman of the Macquarie Board and he's the chairman of the McGuigan Board. He's someone who's always been so supportive of me and listens to my ideas and trusts them. At the times when I needed Board approval to do things, he was the one who made it happen for me.

Do you read motivational books?

Yes. One day I hope to write a motivational book, but some of my favourites are the John McGrath books—*You Don't Have to Be Born Brilliant*—is one of my favourite books. A book written by Rudy Guiliani, who I happened to meet at a wine dinner, called *Emperor of the City*—I found that very motivating. And all the Edward DeBono books—I'm a big fan of his and read a lot of his books when I was studying hotel management, so they impacted on me at an earlier time in my life.

As far as continuing to develop your skills, do you regularly undertake any training?

Yes I do. Something that I did recently was a course at NIDA because my job involves a lot of public speaking. I suppose everyone feels nervous at some point about it, and I because I'd done it so much, I wasn't exactly nervous but I knew I could be better. NIDA runs courses called 'Corporate Performance', and they're designed to help business people who want a bit of polish. They train you as they would actors, and the course did so much for me and my presentation skills because it's so confronting—the things you have to do. It's not like any public speaking course that I've ever heard of. That was one of the most valuable courses that I've ever undertaken.

I try to ensure that I attend a lot of wine-related functions and there's a lot of industry stuff that goes on, and I'm always involved in that. I think you should always continue to learn.

What was the best advice you were ever given with regards to your business?

When I was starting the business, I was probably a bit too stubborn to listen to other people's advice, and I don't think I had heaps of advice—it was just do it, go out and sell; make it work was the advice my father gave me.

Where does the business go from here and what are you plans for the next five years?

By year 10, which is 3 years time, I would like to be producing half a million cases and I'd like to be selling the wines in the UK and the USA, and of course Australia, and building the image and reputation of the brand. I think my next job is to start producing wines that will be recognised in the industry and send wines into the shows, where before we hadn't focused on that—we'd just been focused on the consumers and getting the wine to the consumers.

I'd like to now start to compete in wine shows and get some recognition for the product. I'm hoping to have my wine entered in some packaging awards around the world. You never know—I love those packaging awards so that's on my list of things to do. But I suppose building the brand a lot more strongly in those three markets I mentioned, and to establish within those markets.

Three key strategies for Tempus Two's success

1. Planning and researching the market.

2. Getting the right people and resources.

3. Having a clear, strong vision that incorporates a realistic plan.

Lisa's words of Advice

1. Always set your own standards and don't measure yourself by others.

2. Believe in yourself and have the confidence to build your business on foundations you set rather than relying on others. Listening to advice is very important, and if you are selective and instinctive about the advice, use it to build your confidence and ensure all decisions are your own.

3. Work with people who share your vision. The strength of a business is only as strong as the team behind it. All of my team have a sense of ownership over their role in the business, and it shows in the soul and the personality of the brand, which are major factors behind our success.

Amy Lyden
Bow Wow Meow

In 1994 Amy Lyden went in search for a collar and pet identification tag for her new kitten, and was surprised that there weren't any fun, durable and quality tags on the market.

This sparked an idea, and Amy began researching the pet industry with the idea of creating a range of 80 different styles of identification tags under two brands: Bow Wow Meow and Never Lost Pet Tags.

Amy launched Bow Wow Meow in 1995, producing fun, functional identification tags. For a number of years the business grew at an increase rate of 50 per cent per year. Over 10 years Amy has built a strong business that distributes identification tags to more than 1500 vets and pet shops throughout Australia.

Amy has expanded internationally exporting to pet stores in Singapore, Malaysia and New Zealand.

With her forward thinking she cleverly established a website that gives Bow Wow Meow worldwide exposure. Her pet tags are sold online through www.pet-tags.com, shipping globally to over 50 countries, and offering free worldwide delivery. Bow Wow Meow also donates $0.25US per tag sold to the World Wide Fund for Nature (WWF).

At Pet Expo in 1995 Bow Wow Meow won the award for 'Best New Product', and in 2002 it was named National winner for the 'Telstra Small Business Awards'.

Amy was named the national recipient of the 2004 Leading Women Entrepreneurs of the World Grant, a $10,000US grant to help her grow her business.

Where did you grow up?

I was born and raised in Las Vegas in the States.

Do you come from a large family?

Not really. I have one brother, a stepbrother and stepsister. My parents got divorced when I was 9, so for a while it was just my mother, my brother and I. My mum remarried when I was 12 to a wonderful man and they are still happily married today. My dad has also been remarried for a long time as well.

Where did you do your schooling?

I went to school briefly at the University of Nevada Las Vegas (UNLV). I was really eager to get out into the workforce so I studied part-time and then ended up moving to San Francisco with a job offer; as a result I didn't complete university studies. Yet, I've always done courses, it's always been one of my core values—to grow and learn, and whether it's doing tango or marketing classes, whatever it might be, I'm always doing something. In terms of academic studies, I attended Monash University in Melbourne for about a year, doing a marketing course, but I didn't actually finish it because I started my business instead.

At school, did you have any great schooling achievements?

I always found school pretty easy, I was very good at maths and science when I was growing up. When I started high school, I enjoyed literature and English, and excelled in that.

Do you believe that your childhood, your parents and your upbringing influenced your decision to go into business?

Yes, I think so. My mum always encouraged me—maybe not necessarily to start my own business, but to be career-minded, and get a good education. I think she felt that way because she had my brother when she was only 20 years old and felt she missed out on having a career until later in life. I believe we are all products of our environment in one way or another, so I believe her influence on me was particularly very strong.

What was your ambition when you left school?

When I left school, I really wanted to just see the world. I wanted to travel and get out of Las Vegas. I knew that from my first trip when I went to California when I was about 9 years old, I saw the ocean and just thought this is fantastic. I'd always had that real adventurous spirit and curiosity, I wanted to go out and see the world, and what it had to offer.

What brought you to Australia?

I worked for a travel wholesaler in Las Vegas, then went to San Francisco to manage an office for the same company. I left that job and worked for an Australian travel company in San Francisco, then to Vancouver in Canada to run an office up there for them. I then ended up meeting and falling in love with a man from Melbourne who worked for the same company so I moved to Australia in 1992. I always say I first fell in love with an Australian, then I fell in love with Australia. And that's why I'm still here. I lived in Melbourne for three years, and have been in Sydney for seven.

Do you get home to the States very often?

Yes. Usually once, or sometimes twice a year. I'm pretty close to my family so that's probably the hardest thing about being in Australia—I really miss them and I go through periods where I just have to go home and visit my family.

What brought you to Sydney and was it after you started the business?

I was starting my business in Melbourne, and my partner at the time got a job in Sydney, and as my business was just beginning, it didn't really matter where I was, so I came up to Sydney and have been here ever since.

So you established the business in 1995, what was your age then?

I was 28.

Is your partner in life involved in the business?

No, it's just my business.

Do you have any children?

No, just two cats—feline children.

Could you give me a brief overview of your business?

We make name tags for cats and dogs, we have two brands—Bow Wow Meow, and also Never Lost pet tags. We've designed and made over 80 different styles and combinations of colours, materials, shapes and sizes. Each identification tag is actually customised, so it has the pet's name, address, phone number and whatever other information they might want on the tag.

How did you come up with the idea of making pet tags?

It purely came out of a need for my own cats. When I arrived in Australia about 12 years ago, I got two kittens as I've always had animals in my life, and went to the local pet shop to buy some products for them. I was shocked and appalled at the lack of quality pet products, particularly in the way of identification. It was something that I've always felt was so important, identification particularly— because you don't want to lose your babies.

I found there just wasn't a good selection, there were only daggy, aluminum tags that rubbed out very quickly, and I wanted good quality that was person- alised and nice to look at, and so I thought surely there are other pet owners out there who want a good quality product.

That started the idea going, and I'd always wanted to start a business since I was a little girl, so I suppose that was the catalyst to get it going. After the initial idea, I went out and did some market research and came up with a business plan.

After you came up with the concept, how did you go about manufacturing them?

I knew in my head what I wanted but I had no experience in the pet industry, and I had no experience more importantly in the manufacturing industry. So in the beginning it was really a matter of getting the Yellow Pages out. I rang people and I asked questions and I probably made a big fool of myself because I didn't know what things were called and I would phone people and try to describe little bits of things that I didn't even know what they were, little pieces of hardware.

They laughed at me quite often, but I just kept persisting. I had to design my own systems and program the software to make the tags. It was frustrating in the beginning trying to get it right, there would be a lot of days when I was trying to cut out tags on a machine and the machine would stop because all the plastic had melted onto the cutter—it was a mess!

How many machines would you run now?

I outsource a lot of the production now, just because of the volume we have—I didn't want to take that route originally. But it's easier for us to outsource it and then we do all the finishing in-house—meaning we do all the engraving.

The process is, when a customer goes to a pet/vet store, they see our counter display. They order what they want and that order either gets faxed or emailed to us unless they order online. Then we get the order and personally make it up for them. We pride ourselves on getting all orders out within 24 hours, sending it directly to the customer, so they receive a completely customised and personalized service. They choose what colour, what shape and what size they want, they can have whatever details they want on the tag.

How did you get your first retailer?

When I originally completed the research and business plan, I did some market research.

I went out and interviewed pet shop owners, vets and people who had pets to see what they thought of the concept. I thought that people would like the idea, but felt maybe the only objection to it would be that people didn't want to wait for something. What was interesting was that I found out that wasn't an objection at all. People were happy to wait a few days if they had something that was customised. I think it's a really important part of the business—to do market research—and to have a plan.

I also think it's very important to do the numbers. I've had a lot of business ideas over the years and I know a lot of people who have as well, but when you do the numbers they sometimes don't actually stack up, for example,; is there a market there, and can you actually be profitable with the business? In terms of actually getting started—I spent a good four months before I launched, making the product and getting it right, with the whole manufacturing process, and then I went to market.

With the market research, you mentioned that you interviewed shops how did you go about doing that?

I phoned them or just popped into their stores with some samples of what I wanted to do. I showed them the concept, and basically anybody who had a pet I would ask what they thought of this, if they would buy one, and suggestions for different shapes and colours that they wanted. I tried to get as much information as possible.

Did you have a particular target market when you started?

We went into pet shops initially, so really concentrated on that. Then there was a trade show shortly after and that was where the business was launched, and we actually won the Best New Product of the Year award at the show. After starting off in pet shops we then moved into vet clinics in Australia. We then expanded to New Zealand, and now we're operating in Singapore and Malaysia as well. We also have our online sales as well.

Selling to over 50 different countries, we mainly went online to reach other markets that we don't have a presence in, so we do a lot of online sales to America, the UK—really from all over the world. Our first order was from Portugal, and we've sold to Iceland, Fiji, British Virgin Islands—just about everywhere.

With getting your brand name out into the marketplace in the early days, did you consider advertising?

I think the key to any product-based business is distribution. You can have the best product in the world and have the best marketing strategy, but if you don't have the distribution, you're not going to go anywhere. It's important to do whatever it takes—marketing, advertising, or door knocking to make this happen.

Did you have any contacts that you networked with in the early days in a similar industry?

Not really, one of the things I found really difficult when I first started was just the sense of isolation. I went from working for a fairly large organization where I was constantly around people, and I had a big network of people within this organization. To go from that to just working for myself at home, with the exception of having somebody helping me two days a week, I found that really difficult, so I joined the Australian Businesswomen's Network and I'm still a member to this day. Now I'm on the Board of Advisers and I would have to say that was probably my saving grace when I started my business—just having access to other women in business, who'd started their own companies and had gone through or were going through what I was going through—I found that tremendously helpful.

Was your original business plan really detailed?

It was a pretty extensive business plan for the first three years, I think it's important to have something—even if you just do the numbers part of it. Some people say you don't really need it but for me, I did—I needed something in writing. I do think though that you also need to be flexible. Now it's harder to plan that far in advance, instead I do an annual plan and I have a quarterly plan that I work to. Things change all the time for example,; when I started my business, the Internet did not exist as a way to do business, and that's become a huge part of my business. Then there are opportunities that come along the way that you just can't plan for.

What was the biggest obstacle or challenge you had starting out?

For me personally I would say it would be the sense of isolation—until I built up a network of associates through the Australian Businesswomen's Network. For me it was really hard working from home on my own. Also just feeling that complete responsibility all the time was draining at times. I can remember one time when it was late at night and I was working away. The light bulb blew out. I was at my wit's end and didn't have a spare light bulb, and I just started crying because I was thinking, I have to do this; I have to go to the store and get a light bulb. I had days like that when I found it really frustrating—in the beginning when I was doing everything—I found that very difficult—even from a support perspective.

If I was starting out again, there'd be a lot of things I'd do differently—have a support network in place, and one of the things that I have now is a board of advisers—because while I'm the sole owner of my company, quarterly meetings with my Board of Advisors helps give me support and advice that I need.. While they don't have a financial stake in my business, they give support and feedback, and I pay them for their time. It's easy to lose perspective and become myopic when you're working in the business all the time, so it's nice to have that outside advice and another viewpoint.

Were there any sacrifices you made setting up the business?

Yes, from a point of view of time. I put everything into the business, so certainly in those early years I didn't focus on anything else. I had a relationship at the time that did not survive—I also didn't have time to see my friends and visit my family. When I say I didn't have time, I was trying to build my business, and that was what I was choosing to do.

I do believe that in the beginning, particularly if you're under resourced (I didn't have a team of people working for me and didn't have a lot of cash flow to hire anyone to do that)—so that was the sacrifice for me—that everything else in my life went by the wayside for at least the first three or four years. I lived a Bow Wow Meow life completely.

How many hours would you have put into your week back then?

I worked every day, and I worked from home so I worked from say 8 am—have lunch or whatever at home—but then work till about 4 pm; have a bit of a break (I was living in Bondi so I'd go for a walk down to the beach or the cliff tops just to clear my head)—then I'd come back and work into the night. It's hard to say—probably 70 or 80 hours a week.

And now?

Now it's more reasonable. I'd probably do between 50 and 60 hours, depending on what's happening. If I'm working on a project it would be more like 60. I think I reached a point in the business when I thought I'm not going to work on Sundays any more and I got there, then I said I'm only going to work on Saturdays twice a month. So I put those boundaries in place once the business started to get going. Nowadays I try not to work a lot on the weekends but sometimes I have to.

In the early days, did you find it difficult dealing with men in business, for example, finance institutions or manufacturing?

Yes. I would come across it occasionally, but I think more from the perspective of being underestimated. It used to really bother me, now it's funny—it doesn't happen so much any more—maybe because I've got more wrinkles, but when I was younger it used to happen a lot (even before I started my business). I think it's a really good thing to be underestimated. It's a great thing actually, because you can go on to surprise them and that's the best comeback of all.

What sort of annual percentage increase do you have each year?

We've been in business almost 10 years, In the beginning we obviously had really strong growth rate where we were growing 50 per cent, but recently because we are more established, it's a slower growth rate, at about a 15 to 20 per cent increase each year.

What percentage of your own money did you invest into the business to start with?

One hundred per cent, I didn't borrow any money.

Have you ever had to source external funding?

The only thing we have is a $20,000 overdraft just in case. Everything is re-invested back into the business, so we re-invest from our growth. We recently went in a competition for a grant that was put on by the Leading Women Entrepreneurs of the World Organisation. That's an American-based organisation, but it's global, and they help women who own businesses. We actually won this $10,000 US grant in 2004. We have also utilised the business growth grants available through the NSW Department of State and Regional Development. They match funds up to a certain amount to help you grow your business.

What year was it that the business started making a profit?

It was about 1998—about three years in. The first two years we lost money.

I would imagine it would have been a matter of establishing the brand name too?

Yes, I think that's the hardest thing. In the beginning it's really difficult because some people don't even want to talk to you—especially if you're new. They've seen a lot of people come and go; it's almost like a test—they want to see if you're going to be around for a while, so it's almost like a waiting game. One particular chain of pet shops here in Australia took three years to take my products, and I know why—because everyone selling a new product approaches them. I'd probably be the same way. They want to be sure they're dealing with somebody who's going to be around.

What do you think are the disadvantages of not having a partner?

The disadvantages are that it ultimately comes down to just yourself who is ultimately responsible for the business. Even if you have a great team around you, you are the only owner. I think that can be hard sometimes times, and that's why it's important to me to have my board of advisers and my friends who are in businesses and support me with that.

I think having a partner can be good if it's the right person with complementary skills, as long as things are really clear about what each person does; and that it's all in writing and agreed on—because I've seen a lot of people go through bad situations because there weren't clear roles or strategies.

How many identification tags do you currently produce?

We have over 80 different styles of tags. Essentially all pet tags, but we have many different styles, shapes and sizes and colours.

How many retailers or distributors do you sell to in Australia?

Australia-wide 1500.

Are all your tags made in Australia?

Yes, they are.

How often do you travel with the business?

Usually four times a year. Within Australia, mainly Melbourne and Brisbane, also New Zealand and Singapore.

Currently, how many employees do you have?

We have six at the moment.

How many people are on your board of advisers?

There are four, including me. I met two of those people through the ABN and the other one was through a mutual friend.

What have been some of the highlights so far in running your own business?

Probably in the beginning when I was working really hard, I'll never forget I was out going for a walk in a park in Melbourne and I saw a dog with a Bow Wow Meow tag—it was only about a month since we'd launched. Just seeing the product out there was a fantastic feeling—I'll never forget that day. Just the thought that this is something I created from my idea and now it's part of people's lives. Another pretty big highlight for me personally was winning the National Telstra Award in 2002, I wasn't expecting it at all. We won the NSW award first and that was a surprise, but actually going to the nationals and winning that was amazing. Just being acknowledged for all the hard work was nice, and it just adds to the credibility of the company with customers and suppliers.

On a day-to-day basis, what's your main role?

Developing the marketing and the growth of the business. I look after the web marketing, alliances and business development. With web marketing, we run four different websites, so there's a lot of work involved in keeping those up to date and making sure that we're still getting a lot of traffic to them.

One of our sites, www.bowwow.com.au, is actually the first website of its kind online, and it helps people find a name for their pet. We've have a huge database with thousands of names and it's quite interactive. People can go and search for a name by category or they can pull up the most unusual names.

We built these websites to create the community for the pet lovers, and then hopefully they'll buy a tag from us when they need to. We don't actively promote our tags. We've got a link that goes to our e-commerce site so if they do want to buy a tag they can, but it's on a different site. The e-commerce site was launched in 2000, and it's quite good for people to order from all over the world, and from our perspective it's fantastic because the system is completely automated. It actually dumps straight into the database and we get the money upfront. It's in our bank and boom—it's a great way for us to do business. But it's a lot of work making sure that the website ranks high in the search engines. It's a continual process

Do you have a support team that you work with on the websites?

Yes. But not in-house—I've got two programmers that I've had for many years, but they don't work for me, yet I consider them to be part of my team. They support the websites and also an internal database where we process all of our orders for the tags, and that's being updated constantly. We've always heavily invested into technology and systems. I'm a real stickler for having an easy system and doing what it takes to make that easier and systemised, with customised programs. We are always upgrading to the latest software, hardware and whatever it takes to make sure we're cutting-edge and more time efficient.

Where are the tags distributed from?

Here at our offices in Bondi Junction.

How would you describe your management style within the business?

I really believe in just letting people rise to their own abilities—giving them parameters of what's expected, and letting them run with it. We don't have any sort of pyramid structure here. It's very flat, very friendly, but we all have a common goal—it's a production house basically, and the bottom line is we get the product out every day on time, so that's the driving force. Most people know what they need to do and make that happen.

I have a lot of faith that people can work on their own if they have the right training, the right structure in place and the right systems.

What motivates you on a daily basis?

I think it tends to be who's around me. I get inspired by people. If I do have an off day and am feeling a bit down or frustrated with something, I have key people I can call and they just get me on track again. They refuel my tank and I'm off again.

Personally, what motivates you most—money, sense of achievement, creativity, growth of the business, recognition?

I think all of those, but I do like the sense of achievement of having a plan and then making it happen. To me that's very fulfilling—to actually carry it through, have a goal and actually achieve that. Having a successful business in turn allows me to do other things as well. It helps me to be able to give more, whether monetarily or my time to other people who may need it. I see business as more of a tool to be able to go on and do other things as well. Through my business I'm also involved with the Australian Businesswomen's Network and the Small Business Council of the Federal Government, and some of these other things that are purely voluntary. If my business wasn't a success, I wouldn't be able to do it, and for me that's very important. That's also what motivates me as well.

How do you prioritise your time daily?

It's hard sometimes. My best time is in the morning, and I always try to work on the most important thing first. Sometimes it gets a bit hectic where you end up working on urgent things that aren't necessarily good for the business but you have to do them because they're in your face—you need to deal with it. I try as much as possible to schedule time to work on projects that I know will further my business.

Have you ever felt vulnerable in business?

Yes, definitely—certainly in the beginning, trying to get the product out. I'm the eternal optimist, saying it'll work, it'll happen but there was a point where we were losing money and my accountant said to me 18 months into my business, 'It's not going to work unless you put more money into it.' I didn't have more money to put into it, and he gave me a deadline of March. It was October at that time and he'd said I was going to run out of money, and that scared me. I felt totally vulnerable and angry as well.

I'd put so much time and money into this business and I didn't want it to fail. That's when I went hard selling my product, so I think vulnerability can be a good thing. It certainly drives me into action, and I think it's a healthy emotion to feel.

How do you relax and unwind when you take time out?

I love nature so I go to the beach, have a walk or go up to the mountains. I find I need to get out of the city every so often. It's good for my soul. My cats also totally keep me grounded.

Have you had any mentors along the way?

Yes, my mother definitely. She always taught me to be independent and be the best I could be—go out there and see the world. She's a very strong woman

Are there any books that you would recommend to somebody wanting to go into business?

One of them is *The E-Myth* by Michael Gerber, which is about the importance of systemising your business. That really transformed the way I do business. The other one that really shifted me was *Rich Dad, Poor Dad* by Robert Kyosaki —It really changed the way I thought about doing business and creating wealth for myself. I highly recommend that book. It turns a lot of conventional ideas on their head about what an asset is, what a liability is and how to create more cash flow for yourself.

Do you personally undertake any training sessions or seminars?

Yes, all the time. I value education and learning, and am always doing something—whether it's a computer course or a leadership course.

What is the best advice you were ever given with regards to your business?

Probably to systemise my business. I've heard it from a variety of people—to really get it in a state where it doesn't need you. The most successful businesses—whether you have a franchise or whatever—they all have to go through that process. I don't believe you can really grow until you have really good systems in place.

Where do you go from here? What's your plan for the next five years?

I want to continue to take the business to other world markets, because it's worked well in Australia, New Zealand and South-East Asia. Also to really keep focused on the core business. We've tried a number of different kinds of products and we keep coming back to our core business of pet tags because that's what we're good at.

Three key strategies for Bow Wow Meow's success

1. Persistence—it's so important to not give up.

2. Create a support group; whether it's a board of advisers, your own leadership circle or a goals group, whatever—it doesn't matter—just have a group of people that you can rely on, who will be there to help you, and also who you can help as well. It goes both ways and it's very rewarding.

3. Systemising—particularly for me it's been so important in manufacturing products, it's been a critical factor. We've been able to produce thousands and thousands of tags, and we wouldn't have been able to do that without the system.

Amy's words of advice

1. If just starting out, get a support group or a board of advisers. A board of advisers is pretty critical and it's directly related to your business.

2. Invest in technology: I really believe that's important—hardware, software, website—whatever it may be.

3. Always say yes to the press. If somebody wants to do an interview with you in five minutes, you say yes. If they're doing a story in the paper about something—always be available. I've built relationships with journalists to the point where they ring me when they want to know something about pets or about women in business. A lot of people run from that; they're scared. We've had so much free publicity and that's been quite a key success factor for us.

4. Enter awards. We've always done this. If you win you get great publicity; if you don't win, it's a great exercise in communicating about your business because you usually have to do submissions. I highly recommend it.

5. Goals group or leadership circle, where you meet at least fortnightly, preferably weekly. In my first three years of business, I met with a goals group every week. It was just phenomenal at the time. It really guided me through the process in the early stages of my business.

6. Be generous as much as possible. Try to help people out. I get a lot of calls from women who are starting business and they want to chat about something or need advice, and I always try to give them time. I think it's important for us to help each other. We all remember what it was like starting off. People who are starting off will remember for life who has helped them. I remember people who helped me and I'll be forever grateful to them.

Sonia Amorosa

Barb De Corti

Janine Allis

Lorna Jane Clarkson

Natalie Bloom

Kirsty Dunphey

Kay Barney

Kristina Karlsson

Shelley Barrett

Katrina Allen

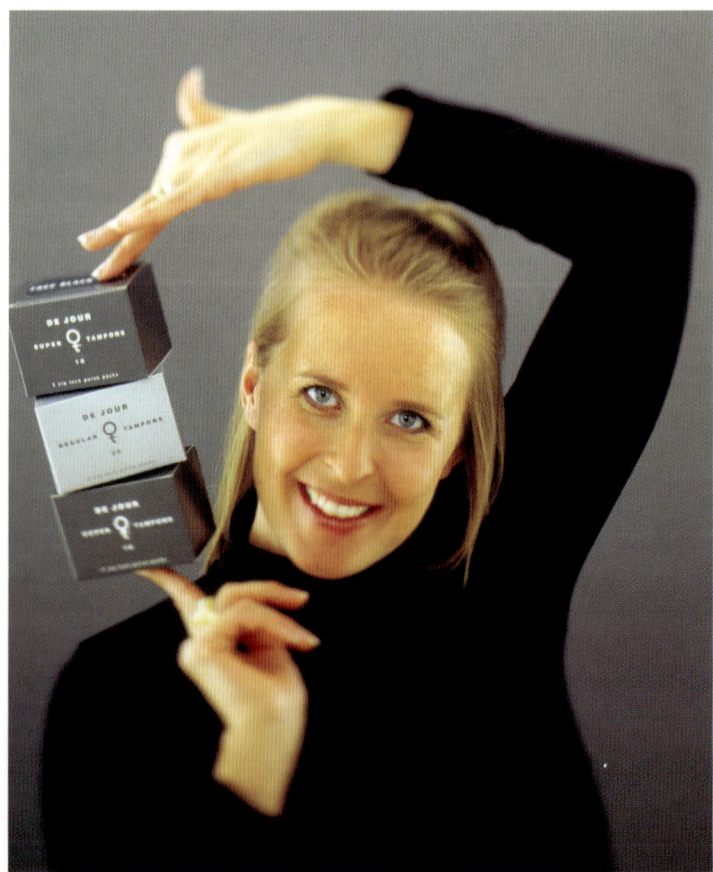

Suzi Dafnis

Lisa McGuigan

Amy Lyden

Helen Jarman

Sandra Skelton   Christine Taylor

Simone Babic and Kristina Noble

Kris Freeman

Ivanka Belic

Linda Lowndes

HELEN JARMAN
INFOACTIV LOGISTICS SOLUTIONS

At the age of 27 this determined young woman decided to take on the incredibly male-dominated Australian transport industry. In 1999, Helen founded her logistics business, starting out with a strong vision, but with no capital or clients. Within only six years she has managed to build a business that today has an annual turnover of over $4.5 million, that operates in Australia, New Zealand and the Asia Pacific region, with clients such as Hewlett Packard, IBM, Cisco Systems and Bell Potter Securities.

Her business, Infoactiv Logistics Solutions Pty Ltd, allows her clients to outsource their supply chain management and physical logistics by managing their total operations on a day-to-day basis. Infoactiv offers all its customers' one IT solution, one help desk, and one relationship for all their logistics activities, from point of manufacture through to a product's end of life.

Numerous offshore companies network through Helen to allow them to import, manage, warehouse and distribute their product all over the globe without actually having to set up any infrastructure in Australia themselves, allowing their businesses to work more effectively and efficiently.

Infoactiv is currently working in New Zealand, Malaysia, Vietnam, Philippines, Singapore, Hong Kong, South Korea, Thailand, China, Indonesia, India, Japan and the USA. Helen's future plans are to expand into areas of mining, aerospace, automotive, pharmaceutical, and medical industries; the sky seems to be the limit for this amazing woman.

Helen, where did you grow up?

We arrived in Australia from England when I was four; I grew up in Melbourne with my mum and my two older brothers. We travelled light. As a single parent, my mother worked two jobs over fifteen years to put us all through school.

Where did you complete your schooling?

Genazzano, a private Catholic Girls School.

Did you complete your Year 12 certificate?

Yes, and I didn't even think twice about going to university. It just seemed the thing you do, so I went straight into Economics at Monash University.

Do you think your childhood and your upbringing influenced your decision to go into business for yourself?

Definitely; watching my mum struggle so much—she's a great survivor, an incredibly strong personality—and the way she raised us, and raised me in particular. She instilled in me that there is nothing that you can't achieve.

She encouraged me to apply for jobs at university that were, in my opinion, well and truly beyond my skill set, but she would question this and say Why not? Why can't you get that job? Why can't you do that task? She would walk me through the process of applying and how to structure my responses to key selection criteria— applying my skills and capabilities—and so I became very creative in my approach and attitude to life. It was really the way mum raised me—to be independent.

When you left school or university, what was your ambition?

I needed some time to think about it, so after I left university, I went to Italy and lived there for a year and a half. I worked for an English language private school for the British Council. Actually, the school was in a lot of trouble.

They didn't have any structure for classes; they didn't have any written texts; a curriculum or any resources, so I wrote them all. I wrote the teacher and student books, I wrote the curriculum and I held examinations. I threw everything into it and gave it a bit more life.

When I arrived, the school was on its last legs and in a bit of financial trouble. I helped bring the school back to life, to renew the students' confidence and as a result, attendances went up. It was very rewarding.

You can work throughout your life, and it doesn't matter what job you're doing, what position you hold, you can pick up fundamental skills that have broad application and you can enhance and develop strengths for the future.

My next job was in insurance. NRMA at that time was launching in Victoria, so it was a new set-up and the department we were in was also a new department within the NRMA structure. I've always been placed in situations where everything is new, or being established—building something from nothing, developing the procedures, the processes, starting from scratch.

It was here that I got my basic business training—how to write processes, how to employ people, how to interview, how to conduct performance reviews, how to start selling something that's new, how to put the infrastructure in where it doesn't exist, so in many ways it was a great training ground from which to start my business.

What was the role in NRMA to start with before you started moving into all those other areas?

It was an outbound marketing role. I was a finalist for Retail Employee of the Year and I was flown to NSW. I was the only Victorian candidate.

What led you to start your own business in such a male-dominated industry?

When I moved into this industry, I started with Australian Air Express. I didn't have a background in freight or logistics and when I got there, I was surprised it was so different from the corporate culture I was used to. For example, it was common in the industry then for CEOs to have no tertiary education. The industry had so many gaps; there were so many aspects about modern business practice that were lacking.

I started managing about 300 customer accounts together with responsibility for a sales budget. The first thing I did was visit all of those clients on that list, many of whom had not been represented by an account manager for some time. Given the sheer volume of work, I would schedule up to 8 or 10 appointments in a day. I spoke to each manager about their business, their supply activity, what the market wasn't providing, while at the same time searching for new and additional business.

I managed every account in a way that made each of those customers feel like they were my only customer—I had a great ability to be able to manage their business in every aspect. I would handle their issues in operations, in sales, in accounts. I became an all-rounder for them, and when I looked across at the rest of their business (they had business with other transport companies), I noticed that while I had a great relationship with them, it would have been great to provide all things to them. I became very frustrated just providing for one part of their needs, and not being able to manage their entire logistics profile.

That was where I believed a gap existed—to manage the whole business and offer one relationship, overcoming the gaps that existed between international and domestic providers and providing a flexible model that satisfied all of their requirements.

I was dealing with a couple of brokers in the industry at the time, and one of them offered me a job more than once. I knocked them back a few times but eventually I decided to take the opportunity if it came up again. It did, and I took it.

The broker provided logistics solutions for small companies—for air, road, and international—but after a while I became frustrated by the limitations of the company's reach, and they weren't taking it further. So, I thought right, that's it. Day one—no money, no capital, no assets, no nothing, no customers, I started a business.

So did you quit your job straight way and start on your business idea?

Yes, I woke up the next day and I said to Mum, 'How about I do it on my own?' And she didn't laugh. When I saw that she didn't flinch, I thought right, if I can convince Mum, then that's saying something.

So she really gave me the confidence and I was absolutely determined. I had the vision in mind. I knew what I wanted the concept to be, and I believed in it 1000 per cent. If you don't have that sort of passion, you will falter later—you really will. Nothing can replace that drive to succeed.

Where did you go from there?

Because of my upbringing I have a very strong sense of ethics that extends to the way I conduct myself in business. So I didn't approach any of my previous clients. I felt it would be unfair and unethical to do that, even though a lot of people do in fact start that way. My approach was to target new customers. I approached Hewlett Packard because I knew some of the staff there and I understood their business requirements.

My second appointment was Coles Myer. I walked into Coles Myer and gave them my business card that I'd just printed up a couple of days before. The guy from Coles Myer sat down and asked—so what garage are you working out of? I told him my garage was in Rosanna, when in fact that was my home address. I fortunately knew a lot about the Coles Myer business, and I knew details. He was impressed by how much data and information I had collated—I was quoting facts to him that the average person in the industry would not know, so he had enough respect to listen.

When I came out of that meeting, I decided I had to get an office, so I went straight out and got one because I think it's important to have that presence straight away—that business location. I know a lot of people start from home, but that wasn't really going to cut it when I was approaching some of the customers that I wanted to target. So I set up the office; I struggled to get finance for a photocopier and a fax. Getting the phones was nearly impossible, and in the end Telstra helped me out, because for a business line you need to put up guarantees and have credit and financial history that I didn't have, so it was a real battle. Once we got the phone system in, that was it, I had an office—and was up and running.

It took another year to get the Hewlett-Packard account. When you start out, it's always 'about to start' and then a year goes by! It certainly wasn't quick. I went through a tender process with nine other well-established companies, and none of them put any new ideas into their tenders. Our tender submission was the most creative—it was all about new solutions for HP; it was outside the box; it was very much geared to the customer and the solutions that fit around the customer. All the other submissions were these are our services; you fit into this and that is not what HP were looking for. So they took a risk on us.

That was a year after we were established. During that year we were doing odd jobs to keep ourselves going—ad hoc work—the odd transport movement, the odd trade show, whatever—just to help pay the bills.

Did you do any market research?

Absolutely, my market research came directly from talking to service users and service providers. As I've mentioned, for three years my market research was my customer base. You can't get any better research collection than at the coalface. I knew a lot about the industry at that point and who the players were, what the politics were like, where the gaps were, where the complacency existed, what the customers wanted, what their logistics set-up was like—all that sort of thing—that was all my market research. I lived it really.

Did you have a particular target market?

Our solutions are better suited to multinational companies because of the complexity of their supply chain. If you're a trader who sends out five cartons from A to B and that's all you do, a value-added solution like ours may not be necessary. Unless we can produce a really competitive rate for them and provide straight cost saving, there's not a lot of value for both parties. They can get a rate from any broker, but I wanted my business to be in a completely different class.

The corporates are our market. Because of the complexity of their business, the different sorts of products, the extent of their supply chain, the fact that they are managing multiple vendors—that market is a better target for us. That's where we provide the greatest value. Instead of managing a whole host of different transport companies, and relationships, they can deal with one person who can manage all those relationships—for them there's a cost saving associated with that. I think we're better suited to those sorts of environments, but we do have companies that require strictly a 'vanilla style' transportation model.

In the early days, how did you get your name out into the marketplace? You mentioned that you approached HP and you approached Coles Myer. Did you actually go cold-calling in a sense to get these guys on board?

Yes I did—I went cold-calling and did a lot of sales, sales, sales; it was push, push, push. Even today, I believe that marketing is still our greatest challenge. The business grew mainly through referrals—once we operate in a customer supply chain, we interface with other companies that also have their own logistic needs, so moving through a customer's supply chain we meet other companies with supply chain needs. In dealing with them on behalf of our client these other companies develop a confidence in what we're doing and an understanding of our concept. The business grows in that way.

Last year, when I won the Telstra Business Women's Awards, was the first time that we had had any sort of exposure. We've had never run a marketing campaign, had limited advertising, but the Telstra awards were fantastic for that. This year, we went to the Supply Chain Summit in Queensland. We went the year before and no one knew us, but this year it was completely different. They had read about us in some articles; the delegates had heard of us, they'd looked at our website, and they'd come to the Supply Chain summit, not only knowing who we were, but how we could help them. It was great.

When you first started, did you network with any other businesses to help you get through?

Unfortunately I did it harder than I really should have. I didn't invest in any networking; I didn't go to any networking associations; I didn't do any advertising; I didn't go out and get any funding. Because of my background, I was so used to doing it for myself, I didn't ask for help. I was completely on my own.

I wish I'd heard about the YEO (Young Entrepreneurs Organisation) back then, now I'm a part of it and I think it's fantastic as a networking group, and there's a lot I get out of YEO that has an advantage over other networking organisations. If I were to go back and start again, I'd make my life a lot easier by leveraging as much from other organisations and networking groups as possible.

Did you have a business plan when you started out?

Yes. On day one of the business I wrote everything; I wrote all of the procedures; I wrote the company's organisational structure, the business plan; I wrote what the systems solutions were, customer features and benefits—all that sort of thing, even though it was in its infancy. It was all out of my vision for the company. It is very important to write that from the start. In fact, the organisational chart and the business units and all those things I wrote back then are still very relevant today.

Were you realistic in your business plan and of what you forecasted?

Yes, although my timing was a little out. It 'took off' a year later. I guess for me, the company's kick start was when we got the HP contract; but it wasn't all smooth sailing. There was a downturn in the IT industry that affected us badly. It got to a point where the business was really hurting, so I made the decision that if it didn't improve within three months, I would have to take drastic action regarding the business. In that three month period, I completely turned the business around. I turned it around from a situation where we were making barely any money to massive profits. It was great—an excellent year.

It's interesting when you set yourself up with a goal and you put it in a timeframe—it's a powerful incentive.

So, you contract out all your transporting?

Yes. What we do is we offer a plug-and-play environment, so if a customer uses say five different carriers, we're plugged into all of those carriers. We've got all of their information; we're integrated with them and so forth. If a customer changes provider, we simply unplug and plug into the new provider, so for them it's a flexible model. Our investment is in our technology, people and processes—that's our IP.

As far as challenges and major obstacles that you had to overcome in the first year of operating, what would you say were the biggest ones?

The first was the attitude of the industry. We were not welcome. Any third party provider was blocked by the transportation carriers, and even today, it's still a tenuous situation. There's a misunderstanding and a dislike towards third-party providers.

There's also a lot of complacency in the industry. The attitude, the approach and the professionalism of a lot of transportation carriers is not at the level that a customer expects. Often you've got a customer flying at 30,000 miles and the transport companies are still petering out at 5000 miles.

How do you overcome that?

It's just something that you consistently work at—building up a reputation for unprecedented customer service.

The first thing we do for our customers is we take everything that's happening in their supply chain and make it visible—so they know exactly where their product is, what stage it is at, who's handling it—all that sort of thing. We operate real-time exception management software that flags when certain 'milestones' haven't been achieved and the helpdesk actions this.

Then what we do is make it measurable—we measure all of the providers that we manage today for the customer so that we know where the break points are. If there are any patterns we take corrective action; we put in new procedures, new processes; we train their people, and in many ways we try to take the difficult stuff away from them and leave them with a very simple process that fits into their existing structure and network. Operationally, we are so involved in the customer's business day-to-day, we're holding it together—we're the glue, managing all the activity on a real-time basis.

But we still encounter poor attitudes from some carriers, we still find them blocking, and engaging in power plays and all those sorts of issues. The most important thing obviously is to have the customer's mandate. Without that, we've got nothing. If the customer isn't 100 per cent behind our solution, then the carriers are capable of pulling it to pieces.

As far as personal sacrifices you made, what do you think you made to get the business off the ground?

In the early stages when it was really hard, there were times when I had a massive bill and I had no firm plan how I was going to find the money to pay it. There were times when I'd go to use my credit card and the credit card company would block me on the very day I was going to satisfy all these payments. The stress completely changed me—from who I was to who I am today. It was so life-changing—mind-altering. In the first five years, I found it difficult to be able to detach myself from the business and conduct a normal life; relationships took a back seat. But now I'm engaged at 34, so I eventually found some balance!

My friendships have always been rock solid though because women relate differently with each other. In the early stages, the hours were long and the stress factor was really high. A lot of time I spent on my own. My family and friends were still there and I spent as much time as I could with them, but I couldn't share the business with them.

What hours a week did you work in the early days?

Probably twelve hours a day—probably six days a week, maybe seven. I lived and breathed the business. There were times when I'd still be at the business at three in the morning. There were times when I'd sleep at the office—on a horrible couch. Then I'd wake up with a headache and hot, to the sound of roaring trucks going by, on busy High Street. These days I'd probably work from say 9.30 till 6. I might do a couple of hours in the evening; I might do some work on the weekend, but then take some days off during the week. I'm quite flexible with it now—I work the hours I need to and go with where my energy flows.

When you were doing business in the early days, how did you find it dealing with men—did they take you seriously?

When I was dealing with transport companies, they didn't want to know us because we were an intermediary or a third party. The fact that I was a woman did not play a part at that point. Those that didn't take me seriously did so because I was a new business and they had been burned in the past with start-up operators. Being a female managing director was definitely a differentiator and perhaps a positive one in that I offered a different sort of business ethic and approach that I believe they appreciated.

When it came to new or potential customers, they would be expecting a male managing director at customer meetings. They got the managing firector, but when they saw me walk in, they look confused at first, perhaps uncomfortable. I remember one occasion where the customer actually leaned over physically, to see who else would be walking in the room behind me. They were looking for a man, or at least a more mature female, not someone who was 27. In fact, in the first year and a half, I'd walk into meetings and I'd look for it; I'd look to see the reaction in their faces and it'd be there—almost every single time.

However, when I got down to business and I started talking about solutions, the ice melted a little bit because they understood that I had some brains and I do understand the industry and their company's requirements.

Only in my fourth year did I appoint a general manager for the first time, so I'm no longer on my own. Our GM is an experience guy in his mid-50s and he has the right profile. He's our front man sometimes because reality is that men prefer to deal with men—and I'm okay with that. As long as I still win the account, I'm happy to work on that basis, if required.

What was your annual turnover for business last year?

Last year was $4.1 million. This year, we will be over $5 million, so we're getting there. This year is an important growth year for us. At the moment we're trading at $6 million, but with seasonality, that will even out closer to $5 million. The Christmas/January period is down in retail, but our overheads are still high.

In the early days, did you invest all the money back into the business or did you draw a wage?

I didn't take a salary for the first two years. I lived on $400 a month. Although I didn't have to pay rent because I moved back home. That was the one advantage I had—I lived with mum during the company's infancy.

Did you ever have to go and source external funding?

No, we never had an overdraft. After the first year and a half, we were able to get a loan from the bank, based on our history at that point. We paid that loan off within a short period and it was the only loan we've ever had. We've never operated an overdraft and today we still don't. The company today has no debt.

When was the first year you started making a profit?

In year two, because in year one we had to buy a lot of equipment and we had a lot of capital injection right at the end of the financial year, but the revenue for that came in the financial year after that, so not until year two—year 2000/2001.

As far as debtors and creditors, do you deal with that internally or do you use external companies?

No, everything is internal. My commercial manager has guided me down a path of providing him with more control, as I was holding onto the purse strings very tightly, which is understandable. I've had many colleagues have issues with theft, loss of money from all sorts of fraudulent activity, and I'm gun-shy, so I still have a very tight control over that.

Do you currently have a partner in the business in any form or an investor?

No.

How many employees do you have?

We have fifteen at the moment; two staff are in NSW, on site with a customer. We often provide in-client personnel.

How often do you travel with business?

I travel every two weeks, and it's mainly domestic; Sydney, Adelaide, Brisbane and Perth. If I travel internationally, it's usually twice a year to Hong Kong, Singapore and China.

What would you say have been the highlights so far in owning your own business?

As an entrepreneur you're so flat out moving forward and comparing yourself to where you were at last month, you never feel successful. Yet in saying that, a highlight was winning the Telstra Award and having organisations like Telstra and Westpac who sponsored my category, acknowledge me. I won the Telstra/Westpac Business Owner's Award Category in October 2003. They were definitely highlights.

Was your age a barrier in the early stages?

Yes, definitely. I'm 34 now and I started the business when I was 27. When I turned 30, I was so relieved because I felt I needed the credibility. Crazy isn't it? In years to come, I will wish I was 27 again.

What is your main role in the business now that you have a general manager?

The general manager does a lot of the operational activity that I used to do. My role is sales, marketing and financial control and IT systems—I'm still designing systems. I designed all our systems and created the systems brief for them. I didn't program them—I stopped at that point and gave it to a programmer.

How would you describe your management style in your team? What sort of culture do you build?

Very open, focused on each individual person's contribution and effort. Every person is valued; every person is actively involved. We find the team takes personal responsibility and has a lot of personal commitment to the company that you wouldn't traditionally find.

I take an interest in each of the staff and their lives. Whenever we're out talking to customers—existing or new customers, we always keep staff up to date so that they feel part of our direction and strategy. We don't have formal meetings as often as we should, but the company's small enough that every time we stop and talk we're having mini meetings because we pull the group in. Ideas are always bounced off the group. They get a lot of feedback on the job they're doing and comments from customers.

How did you motivate yourself on a daily basis in those early days?

Back then, when you're starting with nothing, you have everything to gain and nothing to lose, and the passion absolutely drives you. Motivating myself today is takes more work than in the early days, not because of a lack of passion for the solutions we provide, more so due to the length of the sales cycle today, compared to three years ago. The best motivator is the relationships we have with our customers and the positive feedback they provide each and every day.

I am happiest when I am extremely busy, building solutions, inventing new technology, creating new ways to provide value back to customers and lift the industry standard.

Generally, what motivates you—is it money, being creative, sense of achievement, growth of business, recognition, helping others?

It's definitely the growth of the business. For me, I want Infoactiv to become a brand name in the market. I want it to become a name that when spoken, it means confidence—it means a guarantee, a safety net, and a surety.

Money is important and cashflow is critical. Personally, I have other investments that are taking care of themselves, so long term I have a plan. Money is important to a degree but it's not a driving force. The rest is really about getting the company to realise itself, its potential and actually creating opportunities for staff that have been so committed—returning to them all the opportunities that they look for in life.

How do your prioritise your time?

Sometimes, if there's been an escalation, I'll fix something on the spot if required and push aside projects where time permits. I delegate everything I can to others while still ensuring that objectives are being achieved. Luckily, I'm able to work on several things at one time so I can manage enormous volume and multiple projects, and generally work faster that most.

To achieve goals, do you actually write a list of goals regularly that you work through?

Not for personal goals. But for business goals we document and talk about amongst the management team every day.

If you ever started over again, would you do anything differently?

Yes, I would—I'd go out and get that funding. I'd seek a mentor; I'd establish those networks—all the things I didn't do.

My belief back then was if I wanted something, I'd have to do it myself and that was not the best approach. I would have enlisted the support and expertise of other organisations rather than do it all myself. I put myself through very tough times—I did it all on my own, when I didn't need to.

As far as mentors, role models, who have you had along the way?

Mentors came in the form of close relationships with individuals in supplier and customer organisations, but formed later in my business life. For instance, a mentor of mine was a customer and is now my GM.

Mentors for me have almost always been male, probably because I sought a male perspective on this type of industry and as a good balance to my own strengths, weaknesses and gender perspective.

We all want to be mentored by someone who has been more successful than ourselves, who has a base of experience that exceeds your own. And these people change as you grow.

What was the best advice you were ever given with regards to going into business?

I think the best advice I had in life came from my legal studies teacher when I was leaving school in Year 12. She said to me, 'Go out there and make a name for yourself. It doesn't matter what you do; it doesn't matter if you're the most crooked lawyer; it doesn't matter if it's positive or negative, go out and make a name for yourself.' I remember that.

Any other advice came from my mum who's a big source of strength for me. No-one gave me advice on the business during infancy and growth phase. Now I utilise my fellow YEO forum members as a pseudo 'board' and their advice is highly valuable.

Where does the business go from here and what are the plans for the next five years?

The plans are focused very specifically on Asia Pacific. A lot more decision-making is happening at a regional level, so we need to make our presence known across the Asia-Pacific Region. There is a potential to set up in China, then after that the US. We need to grow from a regional plan to a global plan. I look forward to that. It's really expanding our field of influence and our presence—to become a global player which is very much the branding I was talking about.

THREE kEy STRATEGiES fOR INfOACTiv'S SUCCESS

1. Honesty and ethics. In anything I've ever done, in any deal I've ever made, any relationship I've ever built, honesty, ethics are at the core. The integrity that you display to everyone you work with—staff, suppliers and customers—is very important because it defines the relationship.

2. Financial stability. When you start from zero, you remember it like it was yesterday. The memory is forever fresh in your mind. So what I focus on is to ensure our debt is low, that we have cash reserves, that we're financially sound, and that our credit rating is perfect.

3. Never take a customer's business for granted. For me, every day is a good day, and each day is an opportunity to prove your worth to the customer.

Helen's words of advice

1. When you're starting your business, start it in small steps so you don't fall into any trouble. Take one step at a time, keep yourself small and secure your base at each step.

   Even today, when we're approaching customers and growing our business, we make sure we deliver on our promise that we don't grow for growth's sake that all infrastructure and resource are in place and so on.

2. You need to decide on your image very early. I wish I'd established a clear brand very early on. So be consistent with the message you communicate to staff, suppliers and customers. Every document, every image, every interaction should convey the same message about your brand.

3. Don't take on too many commitments—don't rely on overdrafts, make sure your structure is right from day one. Get as much advice as you can, obviously from your accountant.

4. Establish an exit strategy early on. Put it in writing if you go into business with partners. Make sure that you've got your shareholders agreement, your partner's agreement—all clarified with an exit strategy.

5. Be a natural networker. If you're not, become one—quickly.

6. Employ staff who can add value to the business. Always hire above you, greater than you, better than you. Employ people who have better skills than you do and who can bring a lot into the company that you simply can't do yourself. Know your limitations and resolve the gap.

SANDRA SKELTON
SKELTON TRAVEL

Sandra Skelton, a single mother of one, founded Skelton Travel in February 1999 after working in the travel industry for over 10 years. Sandra was determined to challenge the existing competitive travel market, by opening an independent travel company focusing on exceptional customer service to the corporate and leisure travellers.

Her clients consist mainly of small to medium corporate accounts based not just in Queensland, but all over Australia and also has some based in the USA, Canada and Europe. Sandra's successful move into her own business has resulted in an annual turnover of $4.42 million with a 43.73 per cent annual growth in the 2003/2004 year.

Sandra attributes much of her success to her passion and exceptional knowledge of travel and focusing on providing a personalised, professional service to her customers. She says her business is all about relationships. Her team are available, 24 hours a day, seven days per week with approximately 80 per cent of her new clients being referrals from existing customers.

Her consistency of growth and high standards of service have not gone unnoticed, resulting in numerous awards. Most noticeably is the inclusion in the Business Review Weekly Fast 100 List of Companies. Sandra was listed as the only Australian Travel Company in each of the three years listed. Sandra was also a finalist for the Business Achievers Awards in 2003, for exceptional customer service.

◆

Sandra, can you give me a brief summary of Skelton Travel?

We deal in corporate and leisure travel, though our focus and speciality is the corporate business market. Most of the business we've done has been through referrals over the last four years.
Our clients are based all over Australia, we also have clients based in the US, Europe and Asia we do business with as well.

Can you tell me about your childhood, where did you grow up?

Northside of Brisbane—my parents lived one house apart from each other in Shorncliffe. My childhood days were at Boondall, but I have always loved Shorncliffe and I live there now actually.

Do you come from a large family?

I'm the youngest of three.

Where did you do your schooling?

Boondall State School and then Sandgate State High school up to Year 12.

Did you go to university or TAFE or college?

After I got into the travel industry I did a TAFE course on fares and ticketing. That's basically it.

Do you believe that your childhood and parents influenced your decision to go into business?

Not really. My dad was in small business himself—he was extremely talented at what he did but on the business side should have had a manager and he could have been the artist, so to speak. The influence that I had to go into small business was more from my ex-husband, he told me I could do it very easily. To be fair to him, he gave me the inspiration. He pushed me, inspired me to believe in myself.

So what was your ambition when you left school?

To be honest, I didn't really have one. I didn't have any great ambitions as to what I wanted to do. When I left school I actually started working in a law firm.

What were you doing at the law firm?

I was a legal secretary, I used to ride my push bike to work from Boondall to Sandgate. I was sailboarding over this time and Dad would ring me at work in the afternoon to let me know whether it was windy enough for us to go sailboarding. I would ride my bike from Sandgate to Shorncliffe and meet him there. Some days we would not be home until 8 o'clock at night. What a wonderful lifestyle that was—no stress. Certainly not the lifestyle of a small business owner, and it was good at the time.

Where did you go after the law firm?

I then moved to Perth and I worked in law there for about a year, got itchy feet and saw an advert in a newspaper for a travel consultant/secretary, and figured I can do that. So I went for the interview. There were probably about 70 or 80 applicants, and they interviewed 20, and I was lucky enough to get the position. I had no passport and had never travelled outside Australia, I had no travel experience or done any courses, yet I got this position; must have been fate. I was the secretary to the manager and they trained me in domestic travel consulting as well, but within a few months, the consulting outweighed the secretarial work and my boss had to get another secretary and I moved into the consulting side.

Do you have a partner in life?

No, I'm single at present, but would love one.

I believe you have a daughter?

Yes, she has just turned two.

How do you balance work and home life? For example, do you have domestic help?

I have a nanny who works from Monday to Friday from 9 till 5, and to be honest if I didn't have her, it would be impossible. I'm very lucky. I have also got a cleaner whom comes once a week for a few hours.

So what led you into your own business?

It was the change of owners where I was previously working, and having a supportive husband at the time. Even now we are where apart, he still says I'm one of the best travel consultants in Australia which is nice (and he is probably one of the most demanding corporate clients we would have, so that's a compliment), so I think it was having that support of someone telling you that you can do it, and knowing that you could do it better than most.

Did you have a business plan when you started out?

I never really had a business plan, because I suppose I knew I could do it, I was confident that once I had the clients' business, they wouldn't go anywhere else. I think it was because I had been doing it for so many years and doing it exceptionally well that I didn't even think that I would fail. Then once the business was off the ground, I had to make sure I employed the right staff, because in my business it's such a service-orientated field.

What was your target market initially?

The corporate business market, no special travel type just basically everything. But that has definitely changed now, especially over the last few years.

How did you get your name out into the marketplace in the early days?

I think it was more the referrals than anything no real advertising as such in the first few years.

Did you network through anybody in the early stages, with other travel firms or airlines for example?

No, I hardly ever go to travel functions. If anything, I get more business by going. For example, down to Melbourne for the BRW's Fast 100 Awards and mixing with other companies and other business people. That's where the business comes from more than mixing with airlines and the industry. But then, I do have fabulous relationships with the airlines and the industry in general, and that's mainly because we are reputable and ethical, and they know we're not one of the standard agencies out there.

What would you say were the most challenging stages in the early days of starting the business?

Probably thinking that I was going to make a lot of money within the first year, and in reality it's a lot harder than you think. I found that a bit of a challenge.

Staff was a huge challenge and if you didn't have the right people, the business would go nowhere, even though you might be great at what you do, if you don't have the right people behind you, then you're in trouble. All the staff, no matter what experience they have had, I have found I still need to train to get to the standard I require.

Is it best getting people who are experienced or getting somebody who's green and train them to your way of thinking?

I've done both. If you'd asked me that last year I would probably have said to get them greener to train, but this year I'm thinking no, get them experienced and mould them. Get them with enough experience to do the base work but then mould them into the core values of what we want and what we need. Because I worked in law for so many years, my expectations are extremely high, presentation is the utmost, whether that be with emails, phone manner, documentation or dealing with customers. I think one of my advantages is that I've actually bought that over to the travel field where I feel professionalism is generally lacking.

Were there any personal sacrifices that you made?

Not really; I'm not married anymore, but I wouldn't say that broke down because of having the business. I would have to say that time was the biggest sacrifice. When you don't have a child, then that doesn't matter—you could be there till 11 o'clock at night. But the hardest thing I find now is feeling guilty that you're not at home with your child and then when you are feeling guilty that you are not at work. I believe that if I did not have a child my total focus would be on my business and I would be so much more successful than I am now. Though in saying that I would not change a thing; Jemima is the best thing that has ever happened to me.

In the early days, what sort of hours did you put into the business?

It would have been something like 7 am to10 pm easy, Monday to Friday. I did also have the afterhours service at that time but as there were fewer clients this was not used as much.

And now, what sort of hours do you do?

Now it's slightly different. I've just put on a general manager. My nanny works from 9 am to 5 pm Monday to Friday so I am in at work by 10 am and then try to leave by 4 pm in order to get home by 5 pm. That is not always the case, and at busy times I have my mum either doing an early or a late shift for me. I wanted to be able to spend that time with Jemima in the mornings and afternoons. I still do a lot of work outside the office as I'm totally set up with wireless laptop, Blackberry, etc, you name it I love technology. Even if I'm away in Melbourne I work in between meetings and I'm hooked into the office. So in a sense, the time in the office is less but I am still working before and after.

What was the annual turnover from last year?

It was $4.42 million.

What percentage of your own money did you initially invest into the business?

I would say it was about $7000.

Have you ever had to obtain external funding?

No, I keep re-investing back into the business. I've just leased another 86 square metres of space to expand our offices.

What year did the business first start making a profit?

First year, that was 1999.

Do you deal with debts and creditors yourself or do you have an external company that handles that?

Initially I was doing it all, but now I have an in-house accounts manager.

Do you currently have a partner in the business?

Brad, my ex-husband, is still a 20 per cent shareholder.

What percentage of the market would you say is corporate travel as opposed to leisure?

Our corporate market is around 90 per cent of our business.

Does the business call for you to travel a lot yourself?

No, not really.

How many employees do you currently have?

Four at the moment.

Do you currently network with any other businesses?

I am a part of a group called YEO which is Young Entrepreneurs Organisation, that hold regular forums for business people to network.

What do you think have been the highlights so far—in owning your own business?

My highlight would have to be the growth of the company, in respect to the last three years and being recognised by *BRW* as one of the Fast 100 Australian Companies three years running, that's certainly a highlight. Considering world events we have had to deal with over this time such as SARS, September 11, the Ansett collapse yet we still managed excellent growth, well enough to be placed on Australia's top 100 fastest growing companies—that's pretty cool. Another highlight would be referrals—I love the thought that we are doing something right that people want to talk about.

What's your main role in the business now?

Director, but my role is focusing on sales, marketing and also still assisting some of my VIP clients and mobile consulting.

Tell me about the VIP and mobile consulting?.

Say you were a first-class client, and you and your family wanted to take a big around-the-world trip, whether it was business or leisure, you would contact me to organise a time when I would take my laptop and meet with you, arrange all your travel requirements there and then, booking it no matter where we are. A lot of companies in the past did business through their PA, and half the time the PA would get details wrong or it was just doubling up, so this way they can just ring and say, ;Sandra can you come over?' It's got to be the business/first class market otherwise it would not be feasible. To be able to do this to its best advantage you need to be extremely experienced with fares and destinations.

How would you describe your management style?

I would say easy-going, friendly style, but when I need to be tough on people I can do it but diplomatically. If I have to kick butt, I do, and I think at times you have to be a little bit dominant and forceful in business.

In general, what motivates you, is it money, sense of achievement, growth of business, recognition?

All of those, definitely. I believe you need these in order to be in business otherwise why would you do it. Achievement is a big one, and also recognition of helping others, for example, one of the staff did a booking to Europe for some people, she was chasing them at least three or four times for payment due to the ticketing deadline looming but never heard back. When they finally contacted her, the airline had put the ticket up $300 per person and as far as she was concerned, that was it—she did everything she could. I happened to hear about it and said, 'No, hold on, let's see if we can get the airline to waiver the ticketing deadline and see if they'll ticket it for us,' which they did, and we actually managed to get the old fare, saving them the $300 per person.

And how would you prioritise your time on a daily basis?

With having so much to do, I'm trying very hard to be a list maker. I find if I don't put everything down, I can lose track of what needs to be done. Having the Blackberry helps to keep organised. It's a little organiser and mobile phone in one. It 's like carrying your computer around with you. It synchronises with the office so for instance I could be sitting here and as emails are hitting my office, they are also hitting my Blackberry. It is a calendar, an email system, telephone plus more all in one. When I am out and about I can check my emails and if there is anything urgent I can on-forward to one of the staff to do.

What techniques do you use to achieve your goals?

If I can have my office focused on the company goals then it is a win–win for everybody. Some of the techniques I use to do this is by having the team's input in virtually everything. For example, we have five minute daily meetings with a quick who has what on, who might need help, and review our daily measurements. Then at the weekly meetings (usually 1.5 hours) we talk about good news, the measures, any customer or employee data, our quarterly targets and if anyone needs help with achieving them. We also have a quarterly meeting where the staff set the targets for the next quarter, come up with ideas to improve the company, and if all are achieved they then get to choose what their reward for that quarter would be. Examples are weekends at Versace with Day Spa treatments, or a helicopter trip to Byron Bay with lunch at Rae's.

Do you think the business puts a lot of pressure on your relationship with your daughter?

I don't think it puts pressure on the relationship, but as she is so young I am sure time will tell. I know that I certainly work extra hard on it. At the moment, if anything it puts pressure on me—feeling guilty for not being there all the time. I think that having a nanny assists in giving her some stability, and at the moment she seems very well balanced, very happy and very smart (obviously takes after her mum).

To relax and unwind what do you like to do?

I spend most of my spare time with my daughter—going for walks, pushbike rides and picnics as well, that would be the most relaxing thing that we do. She also loves to go shopping, whether for groceries or clothes, must be that quest for learning. I also make an effort to go away on the occasional weekend.

Have you had any mentors along the way?

Probably the biggest mentor that I've had has been Brad, my ex-husband. From a business sense, he is very driven and a true entrepreneur, so I suppose I've always looked at him as a bit of a mentor. We have a good relationship for the sake of our daughter, but we also still communicate very well when it comes to business.

Are there any motivational books that you would recommend?

I do not have a lot of time to read, but with respect to growing business, Verne Harnish's *Mastering the Rockefeller Habit* is one that I have read and implemented with in my company. It gives you strategies and basis fundamentals to take your business forward. I know that whether I have 4 or 50 staff the strategies and systems I now have within the company could handle that growth very easily.

Do you go to motivational or management seminars?

Yes I do—YEO have fabulous local or international events with world class speakers that I have the opportunity to attend. I also do check for local events that I may benefit from, though finding the time with home and business is usually the problem.

What was the best advice that you've been given?

I would say take time to employ the right people would have been the most valuable.

Where do you go from here? What's your plan for Skelton Travel for the next five years?

Obviously grow and expand the business. I believe the next five years are going to be a challenge with airlines and wholesalers reducing commissions, but we need to just refocus and put new strategies in place. And still focus on my BHAG (Big Hairy Audacious Goal) to have 100 per cent business and first class travel. If we can achieve that we will certainly be around for the next 10 to 20 years.

What's your annual forecast for next year?

We did $4.42 million this year and with the growth planned for 2005 we're working towards $5.68 million.

THREE KEY STRATEGIES FOR SKELTON TRAVEL'S SUCCESS

1. Offering an exceptional service. We have this little saying on our planning pyramid: 'To provide a service that exceeds expectations of the elite traveller', I think it's one of our points of difference. People say they do it, but I believe we really do.

2. Get the right staff and look after them.

3. Have planning strategies in place—weekly and daily meetings to give it the structure that it needs. And giving the staff the big picture so they can see where the company is heading.

SANDRA'S WORDS OF ADVICE

1. Employ the right people and talk more within the company, verbalise what you are thinking.

2. Be aware of and know your business, know your product and know the clients and the type of people you're dealing with. Have a plan or a strategy of where you want to be in 12 months, 2 years, 5 years and plan on how you're going to get there. I think by having those strategies of your daily, weekly, quarterly meetings, it makes you accountable; it makes the staff accountable; you can see how the company's growing.

4. Location, that really depends on the business too. To be honest, in my business I don't need to have a street front, I could be based anywhere with travel. But, some businesses you may need to look at locations, especially if it's a retail type of business.

5. Specialise in what you are exceptionally good at and that's what you need to build on.

6. Don't expect it to be easy. I know a lot of people who've gone into business and probably like me, thought that they'd be driving fabulous cars. Thought this is going to be easy, I can do this, but it's not, it's hard work. You need time, a clear focus and dedication. If you lose some of your focus, you can bet that the whole company will lose the focus as well.

CHRISTINE TAYLOR
AUSSIE POOCH MOBILE

It was Christine's love for animals that lead her into the pet grooming business in 1985.

At 16 years of age she left school and began her childhood dream of working with animals. Starting a part-time grooming and dog clipping business, using an old bathtub in the family garage, she'd pick up people's pets and take them home to groom.

Christine learnt the secrets of customer service and business from working in her parents business, and quickly realised that she needed to create a service based that was unique, bearing in mind she wanted to make life easier, and more convenient and affordable for her customers. After a lot of thought and research, she expanded her business in1991 to include Mobile Hydrobathing Trailers, travelling direct to the customers homes, this proved to be a success.

With Christine's tenacity, passion and determination she pushed the business to higher levels. Franchising and expanding the business to more than 154 mobile units in Australia and throughout the world. Today Aussie Pooch Mobile has units in New Zealand, United Kingdom, New Caledonia and Malaysia, caring for more than 25,000 dogs per month.

Christine's attributes much of her success to her supportive husband, family and team of dedicated staff and franchisees.

Christine was recently awarded the Franchise Woman of the Year for Qld in August 2005.

Aussie Pooch Mobile will continue to expand, including into the US market in 2006.

Can you tell me about Aussie Pooch and what services you offer?

Basically Aussie Pooch is a franchise with an all mobile hydrobath service, so the franchisees go out to the people's homes and wash and care for the people's dogs.

They are also offered pet care advice and support. The actual animal service we provide entails washing the dog, cutting its nails, cleaning its ears, brushing it, deodorising, and then we give the dog a free treat as well. We also have pet products on board, so it's an added service to your door. The actual franchise administration side of the business is where we support the people that are actually out on the road, we offer them support in the way of on-going development and research, supplying them with the products and everything that they need in order to provide the A1 excellent customer service to their actual dog owner.

Do you do general advertising on behalf of all the franchisees?

Yes. How the franchise system works is that the franchisee pays a royalty and an advertising levy back to the franchise, and for that we develop our customer newsletter and franchisee operator newsletter as well, the advertising covers that plus obviously we look after their corporate advertising, the Yellow Pages, local papers, the pet expos, the trade expos and things like that, which we attend to and organise for them.

Do you manufacture your own products?

We don't manufacture them ourselves but we do have our own labelled products. By doing this it helps build the brand. And with the amount of dogs we bathe every month it's proven to be a good thing to have the best products out there.

Can we go back to your grass roots, where did you grow up?

I grew up on the north side of Brisbane. I have one older brother. My parents had a bait and tackle shop and I grew up in a self- employed background, helping them do all the wonderful things that come with bait and tackle. I always had a love of animals, horses and dogs, anything I could bring home.

And you did your schooling locally in Brisbane?

Yes, at Sandgate State High. I dropped out about three months into Year 11.

Did you do go TAFE or do any additional studies?

I learnt basically everything I needed to know on the job back then. These days I attend many industry related training seminars and I've undertaken some marketing courses and things like that, but I haven't been to uni or that sort of thing.

Do you believe your parents influenced your decision to go into business, through their business with the bait and tackle shop?

Yes, when they sold the shop, they supported me in starting the dog grooming and clipping parlour. Mum used to come around and pick up dogs with me because I didn't have a licence and I was offering a pick-up and delivery service.

Did you always want to work with animals?

Yes. I did my work experience at school when I was 16 and wanted to be a vet nurse.

When I left school I was working with my parents, and one day a week I started going to work for free at the dog grooming and clipping parlour and learnt some basic skills.

And then where did you go from there?

I started the dog grooming and clipping parlour, and I had set up some other businesses on the side as well, I had a telephone answering service, and I also played around with a pet shop for a short while, then some kennels came up for sale so we bought kennels, it was amazing we had all these different businesses. I basically learnt as much as I could about business in general.

And then I went away on a holiday for a belated honeymoon and came up with this idea of having these little blue trailers trailing around town, going to people's homes washing their dogs. I've always been a bit of an ideas person, and because we were on holidays at Cape York Peninsula, I had time on my hands to actually think about different things and that's where I came up with the idea for Aussie Pooch.

Basically on our return from our month-long holiday, I set about getting Dad to put the trailer together for me. I then put procedures and systems in place to start our first Aussie Pooch trailer. And then it just grew from there. Basically there was one trailer and then we added another one and another one and another one and I then fell pregnant, I could see that I personally couldn't do everything that needed to be done, so I proceeded to look at ways to expand the business to reach more people and that's when franchising came up and that's how I began franchising. While I was pregnant I put together all the manuals and systems and everything that we had, I think we had six units on the road and then the seventh was franchised.

It certainly sounds like you were always going to go into business for yourself?

Yes. I've always been a bit of a ideas person, I wasn't afraid to get out and give something a go and get my hands dirty, I think people not believing in me has been a secret to my success, because who would ever have thought that you could make a success of washing dogs. It's been a good ride.

When did it actually become Aussie Pooch?

It became Aussie Pooch about five or six years later.

And you were 16 when you started?

Yes, it was 1990. The first couple of mobile units on the road were actually called 'The Great Aussie Pooch Mobile' and then we had a meeting with a few support people and decided to drop 'great' and my mum's idea was to add the corks to the dog's hat in our logo.

What specific steps did you take when you started the franchise side of the business?

Well, we learnt as we went along. I'd learned a lot of things from previous businesses and put those things that were successful into the dog grooming and clipping parlour. The process we took when we started franchising was simply that we had a manual from the Franchising Council and we basically went along the lines of following the procedures and developed a detailed Operations Manual, which is like the bible on how to be an Aussie Pooch operator. As the business has grown the systems have changed and the manual increased has from 40 pages to 150 pages.

What was your target market in the early days?

We tried to identify what our target market would be, and it just came back to anyone who was passionate about dogs, anyone who is a dog owner, could use our service. So it didn't matter whether you were a qualified solicitor or a shop owner or a shop keeper or someone that was on unemployment benefits, it truly didn't matter what walk of life you'd come from, provided that you had that relationship with your dog. Because obviously if you care about the dog, then you're going to want to do the best by it, so we had to set about educating people on what was best for their dogs. And that's the same process we've taken when expanding into overseas markets. Also, nobody knew what a hydrobath was, and it was just on the forefront when it started in like a bit of a recession, people were like, 'Oh this will never work.' I thought if it works now it'll work anytime.

How did you get your name out into the marketplace in the earliest stages?

I was very fortunate that I'd won a Young Achiever of the Year Award. Here I was a woman in franchising at 21 years of age, in a business that nobody had every heard of; it was like the Beatles coming to Australia. It was awesome and really good fun.

Did winning that award result in any extra exposure?

Oh absolutely, there were TV programs such as *Brisbane Extra*, *Today Tonight* and *Harry's Practice*, also there were newspaper editorials. I soon learnt that if you wanted to get your name out there you had to tell people about it.

Has television been the best form of advertising for you?
Initially TV was a great medium, but these days we don't televise to promote the business.

What do you use these days?

When a new franchisee is launching the business in their area, we advertise in local papers, we go to local pet shows, dropping pamphlets also works, and we attend vet open days, as well as going to shopping centres to set up displays; anywhere that gets a large amount of people in the smallest amount of time.

I would imagine that you need to network with vets and pet shops?

Absolutely, even dog minding and training services and that sort of thing.

Who else do you network with?

We encourage our franchisees to build relationships with people in their community, not only people in our industry but other businesses as well, so lawn mower and garden services, pool maintenance people, dog food delivery companies, you name it and we try and build a rapport with them to try and 'you scratch my back I'll scratch yours'.

We also network through the franchise community and we tend to give a lot back to the Franchise Council itself.

Did you have a formal business plan when you started out?

My husband and I formulated a basic business plan, and I reached that within the first two years. It was the five-year plan of 20 units, with 10 on the north and 10 on the south side of Brisbane. I think plans are great because you get your ideas down on paper, but at the end of the day, any plan in the world isn't going to work unless what you put there is actioned.

How did you break into the international market?

Our website was a great idea. And our network of people and customer base within Australia helped. People from England and other countries would phone and say they've never seen anything like it, and we'd send them a video about the company. Nowadays, the Internet helps us so much with communication and exposure.

Were there any major obstacles or challenges along the way that you had to overcome?

Not knowing, and having to learn from your mistakes, which really turned out to be a positive thing, because the business has been made stronger as a result of those mistakes.

Can you give me any examples?

Little problems like dealing with water restrictions and having to deal with councils, knowing you need to get a special licence to use water to run the business while there's water restrictions.

Were there any great sacrifices you had to make when starting out?

We were very fortunate that the business paid for itself as we went along, and that we had a very good support team. Having a close network of friends, and family around us certainly helped. As for sacrifices, I suppose time, but with anything you've got to put it in time and energy to get the rewards.

What sort of hours per week did you work?

I would be up at 6 in the morning and I wouldn't finish work until 8.30 at night.

And now do you work just Monday to Fridays?

We normally have weekends off, but occasionally I would do an all–nighter if something needs to be finished.

In the early days how many nights would you work a week?

When we first started franchising with the manuals, it would be nothing for David and me to sit up till midnight, 1 am, 2 am in the morning, at least one night a week. I mean that doesn't happen all the time now, but it certainly did then, especially dealing with the UK, and the different time zones. Now I only work 30 or 40 hours per week.

What percentage of your own money did you invest into the business in the beginning?

We invested 100 per cent of whatever we earned from our other businesses back into it. I think the most we put into it was a car we sold for $10,000.

Have you had to obtain external funding over the years as the business has grown?

We've only used a line of credit as an overdraft.
What year did the business first start making a profit?

It was in 1992

What was your annual turnover for the overall business last year?

It was $4.6 million.

And what is your forecast for 2005?

For 2005 it's $5 million.

Do you deal with debts and creditors internally?

We have an accounts lady a few days a week to deal with that but I oversee it all.

What do you think are the advantages and disadvantages of having a franchise business?

The franchise business is a fantastic business to be in. It gets other people believing in what you're doing and it allows you to get other people involved in the business. The franchisees are dedicated because they've personally invested into the company and they have support when they start out and throughout the whole process of running the franchise. So it's very much a win–win situation. The disadvantages, I don't think that there are any disadvantages. I just think that if you're going to go into franchising you have to be prepared to care and listen to what the franchisees need and what.

What countries do you currently franchise to?

Malaysia, New Caledonia, UK, New Zealand, and Australia of course and in 2005 we're expanding to the USA.

How often would you travel with business?

I spend on average, probably two or three months a year travelling overseas and interstate.

How many employees do you have?

There are five employees.

How many franchisees are there?

There are 134 in Australia and 20 internationally.

What have been some of the highlights so far?

It's a buzz every time we get a new franchisee on deck, someone else who believes in you and the product. I'd have to say it was also a highlight being nominated as a finalist for my first award in the Young Achiever of the Year Awards in 1993 and then winning it in 1994. And then winning the Queensland Telstra Business Woman of the Year Award in 1995 and being a finalist in 1999. There have been numerous personal awards, but what is rewarding is when the franchise system and team have won awards and there have been over 22 various awards won over the years that we've been in operation.

How old are you now?

35 years old.

And do you and David have children?

Two kids, a 7-year-old boy and a 12-year-old girl.

How do you balance domestic arrangements with work and home?

At home we have a housekeeper and I could not do it without the support of both our families. David and I have learnt to be really good with managing our time productively. And the kids are pretty good too, my daughter comes in here a couple of days a week to help out; they're at an age where we try and get them involved.

What's your role within the business on a day to day basis?

These days I basically support the people that support the franchisees. And I deal with the international expansion, yet I'm still involved in the marketing and advertising side of the business.

How would you describe your management style and what culture do you build within the business?

I lead by example and I'm very passionate about what we do. We build a culture that is very caring, and enthusiastic.

What motivates you, money, sense of achievement, growth of business, recognition, helping others?

I would say it would have to be the success of our franchisees.

How do you prioritise your time?

I have a task book and I've trained everybody that's in management to do the same thing. I find you've got to write down everything you need to do to prioritise what needs to be done first. And that comes back to personal things as well.

What techniques do you use to achieve your goals?

Basically I break the goal down in depth and work through it from there. So I set achievable goals and basically think carefully before I set them.

If you had to start over, would you do anything differently?

No. I think you've got to crawl before you can walk.

What do you do to relax and unwind?

We tend to spend a lot of time away as a family camping.

Have you had any mentors along the way?

I don't really have business mentors as such. But how I would live my life to the very end is how my grandfather did. He was happy to have people around him and he lived every day to the fullest until he died. My grandfather was as sick as a dog, and he'd be walking down stairs with emphysema and an oxygen machine attached to him to do gardening.

What was the best advice you were ever given, with regards to your business?

Not to give up on your dreams and to set achievable goals.

Where does the business go from here and where do you see yourself in five years from now?

I can see Aussie Pooch or the Pooch mobile continuing to dominate the Australian marketplace and expand worldwide.

THREE KEY STRATEGIES FOR
AUSSIE POOCH MObile'S SUCCESS

1. Gathering the skills and knowledge that you need before you start the business.

2. Believing in yourself and in what you're doing.

3. Enjoying the process and having fun.

CHRISTINE'S WORDS OF ADVICE

1. Set achievable goals, know where you're going.

2. Believe in your ability to succeed.

3. Have determination and be prepared to work hard.

4. Reward yourself and recognise when you have achieved goals.

5. Create a network of friends and advisors around you, that could help support you.

6. Show empathy when dealing with people, whether it is with staff or franchisees.

Simone Babic and Kristina Noble

Citrus

In 1996 this amazing duo had the foresight to jump on the bandwagon when information technology was just in its embryo stages in the world of e-commerce.

The result was Citrus, an online marketing agency that offers integrated services in Internet communications for over 20 key companies such as STA Travel, VRC (Victoria Racing Club), Drake International and Foster's, just to name a few.

Brought up in an entrepreneurial family, the sisters attribute a lot of their success to the foundations laid by their parents when they were growing up: 'We had always planned to go into business for ourselves and saw that online communication was going to be the way of the future.'

Simone and Kristina rode the wave of the IT boom and crash in 2000 and survived, maintaining continual growth, profits and success, based on their determination, ethical standards and consistent approach to pricing and customer service.

They've built a strong team of people around them, believing their staff play an important role in the success of Citrus. Employing a team of 17 highly skilled professionals who are passionate about the Internet and skilled experts in their fields, makes Citrus a market leader in the fast, ever changing future of technology.

◆

How would you summarise your business?

SIMONE—Citrus is an online marketing agency, in short. We develop strategies for our clients around how they're going to use online and how to best integrate it into their marketing mix. We deliver this through our service offering encompassing web development including e-commerce, email marketing, online advertising, online branding and search engine optimisation.

It all depends on what clients want to do online and how they want to use the Internet for their business, we advise them on the best way based on our extensive experience. They might already have an existing website and then engage us to develop an email marketing strategy for them to drive people to the website. It can be a whole range of things, it just depends on where their business is heading and what their objectives are. We have acquired a lot of experience with different types of clients and different sectors, so we have knowledge that we can draw on when we're looking at clients and advising them on where they should go with their online strategy.

Can we go back in time to your childhood, where did you grow up?

SIMONE—Kristina and I (we're sisters) both grew up in Glen Waverley in the outer suburbs of Melbourne.

Do you come from a large family?

SIMONE—Four girls in the family—16 years difference between the eldest and the youngest. Kristina is the second and I'm the third.

Do you believe your childhood influenced your decision to go into business for yourselves?

SIMONE—Yes, we had a very strong entrepreneurial father and mother who came to Australia from Croatia when they were 20. It was tough for them—coming to a new country, they were young, they had a one-year-old child, they didn't speak the language, they didn't know anyone here, and they created businesses that they still own today. Dad now oversees the running of several companies. He was always encouraging us to go into our own business and to take the same paths they did. I remember even when I was young, it didn't occur to me that I would have to go and find a job, I always had the mentality that I would go into my own business, because it's just something our parents instilled in us from such a young age.

We all used to work in Mum and Dad's business on holidays. Every spare moment was at the business, it was a very strong family and business culture. We grew up with the mentality that if you work hard and put a lot into something that you love doing, then you'll be able to live the sort of lifestyle that you want.

Did you complete your schooling in Melbourne?

SIMONE—Yes we did—to Year 12. I did the VCE and then went on to Melbourne University to do information management, which was focused on the Internet—a Bachelor of Information Technology

Kristina, did you do any studies when you finished school?

KRISTINA—Yes, I did a Bachelor of Economics, a Graduate Diploma in Accounting and some short computing courses. That was all at Monash University.

Did either of you have any great schooling achievements?

SIMONE—I suppose it depends on your view of education, doing a degree for me was literally just for getting the piece of paper. When I look at where I've come to and my journey over the past 30 years, I believe I really started to flourish, learn and get the most out of life and how to do business when I was in business.

Simone, what was your first job?

SIMONE—My first job was Citrus. In fact I think I was still at university when we started Citrus—I was doing my final year. I didn't have a lot of experience when it came to anything in business because I had never really worked anywhere else. I'd worked for my father and mother, but that was just as growing up—school holidays, not like going out and getting a job on my own accord, and having my own experience in that respect.

How old are you both?

SIMONE—I'm 30 now, and Kristina's 33.

Are either of you married?

SIMONE—Yes, we're both married. Neither of us has children as yet.

Are your husbands involved in the business?

SIMONE—Kristina's partner, Peter is. He's the CEO and has been with Citrus for almost five years now. When Kristina and I restructured the business Peter became CEO.

We get involved at a strategic board level and are no longer day-to-day dealing with clients and staff.

What led you to start Citrus?

SIMONE—We identified the opportunity back then, and thought e-commerce was going to be the new medium for technology and communication globally and it had to have a massive impact on where the world's going. That was so exciting in itself—being in an industry that was redefining the way the world was communicating, and being part of something that was so dynamic and moving so quickly.

What were your first steps in starting Citrus?

SIMONE—Our first step was to buy a computer. Kristina worked at Grant Thornton (a chartered accounting firm) in the IT department. When we started the business, she had a client base from that job, and she was able to win a few clients from the contacts and networks she had made, while I was learning about the Internet, doing the design and programming, and I would also take care of the clients doing account managing as well.

So she was salesperson and I was the designer, programmer and client service. A lot of it was self taught. You tend to find that the best people out there in the industry are mostly self taught because the universities and courses just didn't cover enough. They probably do these days, but they didn't back then.

What year did you establish Citrus?

It was 1996.

Did you do any market research?

KRISTINA—No, we didn't.
SIMONE—We were both very young and very keen, eager and motivated, but probably a bit naive as well.

What was your target market originally?

KRISTINA—We were basically targeting small to medium-sized enterprises, and getting a feel for what was happening in the industry, and then we started to look at larger companies after that. One thing that was maintained since the beginning was that we always look at how being online can help someone else's business. So that pretty much was the culture we built from the start, and we still maintain that today.

How did you get your name out into the marketplace?

KRISTINA—Word of mouth was a huge factor for us in growing our business. Right at the beginning we did the usual things like putting an ad in the Yellow Pages. Our real focus was on networking, having face to face meetings, cold calling, attending many industry functions and speaking engagements, things like that to get known in the industry.

Did you network with general business organisations or mostly companies associated with the IT industry?

KRISTINA—Both—we networked with everyone. From Microsoft to organisations within our industry, suppliers, potential customers, advertising and women's networks as well.

Did you have a business plan in place when you started?

SIMONE—We decided to test the market before we did a business plan, it was very difficult to make realistic sales projections when it came to the Internet. After we had a few runs on the board and saw that the venture was viable we put together a business plan.

KRISTINA—We do a lot of planning right across the business now, from sales, marketing, recruitment and finance. We focus on researching the market and, our competitors. Fortunately we were that way oriented because we were brought up in a business environment and my background in accounting helped, we saw the value in planning and so we did.

Did you get an outside firm to help you with that or did you both work together on it?

SIMONE—At the start we did all planning, but probably two years into the business, we conducted a couple of business plans with an external organisation. That was good because it gave us a little bit of focus and redefined some strategies, which way we were going to move forward and so on. We got value out of that—it was definitely worthwhile.

What would you say were the major obstacles and challenges you had to overcome in your first year of operating the business?

KRISTINA—That was so long ago. The main challenge was that people didn't really know what the Internet was, so it was a conceptual sell the whole time. You'd go into a meeting with someone, and you'd need to be in there for a long time explaining the actual Internet and what the medium was about. We found we were talking to a lot of organisations that weren't necessarily going to do anything.

Also being so young and being female was another issue. It was difficult to actually get credibility in quite a male-dominated industry. We were learning on the way and there were a lot of skills that we needed to bring into the organisation that we didn't have ourselves and didn't necessarily understand. for example, neither of us really understood the really hard-core technical programming that went on so we had to bring those skills into the organisation fairly quickly. That was an issue in terms of recruitment—making sure we got the right people on board, building teams was very important.

There weren't a lot of people out in the marketplace when it came to building the team. There were a lot of firms starting up and there was a shortage of good employees who were skilled, and the ones that were, were demanding quite high wages through the dotcom boom period. We had people who were in their early 20's demanding $90,000 for a salary.

Were you affected in the dotcom crash?

SIMONE—We've always run a very ethical business, built great customer relationships and charged fair prices. We didn't capitalise on the boom like a lot of organisations did, and that's what saw us through the crash. We had built good relationships with our clients and they saw us through hard times as well.

What would you say has been the biggest sacrifice that you've made in starting the business?

SIMONE—There were a lot of personal sacrifices—like when our friends were travelling and enjoying themselves at that young age—doing trips around the world for a year, backpacking—we were working—and working long, long hours.

What sort of hours would you have done back then?

SIMONE—We were getting in easily by 7.30 in the morning and working till 10 at night, sometimes we'd work till 4 o'clock in the morning or we'd stay the night at the office—we just did what we had to do to get the work done and push to the next level. I made a decision probably two years ago, not to work Saturdays and that's been good. You really can get swept up in it all and I think that's one thing we've learned over time—you really don't have to—if you set things up properly and work smarter, you don't need to work the long hours and every weekend. However, it does take time to set things up properly, especially early on in a business, so it's realistic to expect longer hours at that stage.

Did you ever have difficulty dealing with men in business?

SIMONE—It is much better these days; however, there is still a long way to go. With sales we had difficulty—it wasn't just a matter of us being young. Being a female in business you can't let that stop you, in fact you can use it to motivate you further.

Do you think it's because of the industry you're in?

KRISTINA—I think it could be to a degree. If we were in another industry like fashion, it might be different.

What percentage of your own money did you put in to get your business off the ground?

SIMONE—Being a service business, we didn't really need to worry about that too much because we've grown organically. It was basically just being able to live, and all you need is a couple of computers.

Did you start making a profit from the start?

We started making a profit in year two.

As far as dealing with debts and creditors, do you do that internally?

KRISTINA—Internally. I've always managed that side of the business. We've got skills to be able to manage all the budgeting and cash flow. That's never been a problem.

Is Peter the only other partner within the business besides the two of you?

SIMONE—He is a partner and there are no other partners—just the three of us.

What do you think are some the advantages of having a partner?

SIMONE—I think there are great advantages—you can bring lots of skills together and create something quite formidable. I definitely wouldn't shy away from partnership, but it needs to be the right sort of partnership. I think that critically, there needs to be an exit strategy set up for the partners and terms of working together need to be clearly defined at every level in the partnership.

KRISTINA—How do you and Peter balance business and home—working together and being partners?

KRISTINA—You need to set some boundaries about when you talk about work. We always really enjoy talking about work, but it's not sustainable to do it all the time, so we try to set some boundaries and days off when we're not talking about work. On Sundays we avoid work, but apart from that, we haven't had any issues about managing that—it's all been fine.

Do you do business outside of Australia?

KRISTINA—We do have some outside of Australia—Singapore, New Zealand, and the US.

Does the business call for you to travel regularly when dealing with your clients outside Australia?

KRISTINA—We've done a bit of travel, just on the suppliers side of thing—looking at different technology that's available around the world, but not on the client side. We can pretty much handle all of that remotely.

How often would you travel with the business?

KRISTINA—Recently we've been investigating some different technologies, so we've travelled probably twice in the last year for business. Prior to that, not a great deal.

How many employees do you currently have?

SIMONE—Seventeen and they're all in house.

You mentioned earlier that you do a lot of networking, is there any networking organisation you could recommend to someone new to businesses who wants to network?

KRISTINA—I would attend all networking functions like the Australian Institute of Management, Australian Businesswomen's Network. There are a few out there—most are worthwhile looking into.

What would you say have been some of the highlights so far in running your own business?

SIMONE—I think that there's definitely a lot of personal satisfaction that you get from seeing something grow—really seeing your vision come to fruition. That's definitely an ongoing highlight. And the other highlight for me is the freedom of being in your own business. That would definitely have to be at the top. With the freedom also comes—the choice to do what you want to do, when you want to do it, but at the same time, there's a lot of responsibility that comes with that.

What awards and recognition have you received for the business?

KRISTINA—Various industry recognitions, a recent award was from the Australian Direct Marketing Association—for the viral email and marketing work we had done on Sofitel Melbourne.

How would you describe your management style and staff culture?

SIMONE—I think you can tell that the company was founded and developed by two women—it's a very open culture. We know what's going on with everyone—it's not just a place where you come to work. We know what's happening with our staff in their personal lives as well, because there is such a crossover between personal life and work. As far as our style of reviews—we're very big on reviewing our staff regularly in a formal way. We conduct a lot of personal development for our staff—really just helping them to be the best they can be which I think is a very female way of working. It's not just coming to do your work and going home—it's more of a collaborative approach and culture.

We have high standards, and because we've worked in the business we know the business inside out, back to front. We've set very high standards from the start and our staff are aware of that. I'd describe our management-style as 'tough but fair'. We want everyone to come into Citrus and undergo great self-development, contribute a lot of good to the company and leave saying that was fantastic, it had a great impact on my life, I learned a lot; I contributed a lot and it's time to move on—to whatever they choose to do next.

How do you two motivate yourselves on a daily basis?

KRISTINA—We support each other and talk a lot.

In general, what motivates you both—money, success, recognition, helping people?

SIMONE—All of that really. Dealing with people, financial targets, growing the business, seeing people achieve—that's all part of it—you get a buzz from all of that. Really, I suppose it becomes a natural extension of yourself—of what you do. It doesn't really cross my mind to not be in business. I've always thought I'd be in business.

How do you prioritise your time?

SIMONE—We do a lot of planning—strategic plans. We set goals and then we review those plans. There's no point doing a plan if you don't actually execute it.

How often would you set goals?

SIMONE—We have a couple of planning sessions a year and we set our financial goals annually and review them monthly. We're on top of it the whole time at a strategic level and seeing that everything is moving forward as we had planned. Obviously, plans don't always go as planned. The plan gives us a good record of how we're tracking according to what we projected. This sets the foundation for the following year and basically we keep pushing forward.

When do you think you felt most vulnerable in business?

SIMONE—Probably during the dotcom crash in 2000. There was a lot of instability in the industry. We'd pick up the paper and read about our competitors who were going down, but I think we conducted smart business through the dotcom crash and the boom, and that saw us through. We found when we were picking up the paper every day and seeing everyone going down, our staff were asking questions, so there was a bit of instability on all levels. You need to consolidate and pull everyone together and say we're not in that same boat because of x, y, z. But it was tough doing business during that period because everyone pulled back their spending budgets. It did have an impact but we got through it, which is the main thing.

If you ever had to start over, would you do anything differently?

SIMONE—Hindsight is always interesting and I think the experience was brilliant exactly the way it happened. As always you just need to throw yourself in and go 100 per cent because that's how you learn. The fundamental difference for future businesses is that we would do things smarter and that's due to the knowledge we have built up. For instance we would look at using our networks better, more emphasis on work-life balance, different funding options and expansion strategies.

As far as mentors, who have you had along the way?

SIMONE—Our father and mother are long-standing mentors for us. Even to this day when we take on things we ask their advice. They have accumulated a lot of business experience between the two of them. It's always effective going to a place where you're able to discuss business issues openly and freely.

Do both of you read motivational books?

SIMONE—Yes we do—all sorts of personal development books. I think they're a great resource for people.

Do you do regular training yourself to update your skills?

SIMONE—We're always undertaking different courses. I don't think there's a silver bullet for this sort of thing. There are life coaches out there, there are books, different levels of reading that you can do, there are different people you can talk to, talk to people who are running businesses as well—there are a whole host of things that when you're in a business, you want to tap into.

What's the best advice you were given as regards to your business?

KRISTINA—I think some of the best advice is to always operate with a very clear financial plan. And to work hard—it's going to take a lot of hard work. You need to get your head around that because if you're not prepared to do lots of hard work, then you're not really going to get anywhere. If you don't have the energy for it, don't do it because it takes a lot of energy. It actually becomes a huge part of your life.

Where does the business go from here—in the next five years?

KRISTINA—We're constantly taking the business in new directions because that's the nature of our industry, so we're looking at pushing it forward with a strong online marketing focus—that's been a huge growth area of the business and is continuing to happen.

We're potentially looking at the Sydney market, but before that we need to focus on the business internally to prepare it for the next growth stage, and that's where we're at. Just making sure that the staff, the infrastructure, the systems and processes and everything are in good shape and can sustain a growth spurt.

Three key strategies for Citrus' success

1. Good communication skills—that's not necessarily a strategy on its own, but it's something that underpins everything. Taking care of your staff is a huge thing that we earmarked right from the start—developing relationships with them, being able to discuss things in and out of work with them. We wanted to understand our staff, understand their motivators, so that both parties are able to get the most out of the relationship.

2. Always take care of our clients. In any dealings with people—whether it's suppliers, clients or staff—ensure it's mutually beneficial—it needs to work on all levels. Operating with integrity too.

3. Financial and strategic planning. We don't really operate with a 'we did better than last year so that's great' mentality—we like to know where we're going. You just can't underestimate how important planning really is.

Simone and Kristina's words of advice

1. Make sure your financial planning, that is, cash flow, sales budgets and targets, expenses—are all in place—that's really your plumbing.

2. Surround yourself with other business people, do networking and have mentors. Sometimes it's easy to get stuck in your business and not be able to see outside, so talking to other people gives you great ideas and strategies, and helps you look at things with a new perspective.

3. Take care of your clients and your staff and any interaction you have with others, and operate with integrity.

4. Make sure you have work/life balance—time for yourself. That's really important because again having time off allows you to get perspective. Think about why you're doing it and make sure you're clear on what your motivators are.

5. Take care of yourself. Sometimes you can put yourself at the bottom of the priority list. It's important not to do that—you're far more effective if you're looking after yourself.

6. Strategic planning—make sure you develop a strategic plan that you're working towards, don't just put it in the bottom of your drawer. It really should be reviewed monthly. Have someone external sit on your Board to provide you with accountability and guidance.

KRIS FREEMAN
FREEMAN PRODUCTIONS (AUSTRALIA) PTY LTD

Kris launched Freeman Productions in 1998 when she was eight months pregnant, after securing a large pharmaceutical account distributing over 385,000 calendars Australia wide.

In eight years she has worked from the ground up, building a highly successful calendar production company achieving great success with sales of more than $1.5 million dollars.

Freeman describes her business as a project management company that specialises in the production of customised calendars for large corporations as well as small businesses.

She believes her success has been fundamentally based on the win–win principle she has created, which means that everyone involved in her business must win. This together with the systems she has in place has secured her success and enables her to offer incredible guarantees to her customers.

Kris' proven ability to listen and interpret her client's needs and requirements has been a major factor to her success.

In 2003 she won the Best Manufacturing Category and Queensland's Best Home Based Business Award in the 2003 Australian Micro Business Awards. In 2005 she won the Australian Government Micro-Business Award in the Telstra Queensland Small Business Award and is a finalist for the national title.

How would you summarise your business?

We specialise in creating and producing calendars that uniquely represent a company, so they can give them away to their customers as a thank you gift. But we don't just sell calendars. We're actually selling a service. We say we're money generators for our clients.

To set ourselves apart from the other calendar companies in the marketplace, we tender to organisations not just to print their calendars for them, but to do everything—come up with ideas, suggest themes, image selection, research dates, design, typesetting, proofing and printing, we create a selling brochure, and distribute the calendars Australia wide, we report monthly on sales, and handle all enquiries—so that our clients can concentrate on their core business, and after we've done all of the work for them, we'll thank them by paying them a commission on sales for the privilege. So it's money for nothing for them.

In 2004, Australian industry peak bodies earned over $300,000 through the use and sale of our calendars. We also sell all of our calendars (including our standard range) by brochure, which is something unique to us.

How many clients do you currently have?

We have 1631. Our goal is to have 10,000 or more.

Do you supply calendars to companies outside of Australia?

Not at this point in time because there is still so much work to be done here in Australia. But we get most of our hits from the US on our website.

How old were you when Freeman Productions started operation?

I'm 36 now, and started the business when I was 29.

I believe you are married with two children; is your husband involved within the business?

No, he is an Inspector for State Crime Scene within the Queensland Police

Service. He has a very limited role within the business. I do use him like a business adviser when I have a particularly challenging problem. But that's about it for him.

Do you mind giving me some background on yourself; where did you grow up?

I grew up in Manly West in Queensland with my family, until I married at 20.

Do you come from a large family?

I am one of five children and I am the second youngest.

Did you go on to university, TAFE or college?

I graduated from school in Year 12 from Wynnum State High. I went onto TAFE college and studied subjects that were of interest to me and that I felt would benefit me in achieving my goals. First I did stenographic studies. Then I studied psychology, police administration, law and marketing. All subjects from particular diplomas that I was interested in.

Were their any great schooling achievements?

Art was my best subject, which is where I get my creative side from. Prior to starting this company, I was the Vice President of the Queensland Wildlife Artists Association Inc. At school, I received certificates of merit in at least one subject every year but there was really nothing outstanding—I was your average student.

Do you believe your childhood, or parents influenced your decision to start your business?

Yes. I believe my mother influenced me. I can recall one time, when my older sister and I were having one of our daily arguments, and I went to my mother and asked why won't you help me? She said to me, 'Kristine, this is your life and I'm not going to interfere with it. You can either let your sister upset you or you can choose not to. So what are you going to do? Make a choice.' And with that, I stormed off and cried some more.

But that statement had a profound effect on me. Because, it's like anything in life, it's all about choices. You can either choose to be successful or you can choose to fail. You can either choose to see failure as a negative and give up or you can choose to see it as a positive guiding force to learn from. I was raised in a very strict environment and I consider myself fortunate to have been raised that way. It gave me strength with a 'never give up' attitude. My mother passed away in 2004, and right till the end she showed how incredibly strong she was. She passed on that strength of character to me and it has helped me succeed in business. So yes, I believe my childhood and my mother had a great impact on my decision to start a business.

What was your ambition when you left school?

I always wanted to be in business for myself but I just didn't know how I was going to achieve it. I did, however, change my mind a couple of times along the way. When I met my husband I thought I wanted to be a police officer and then thought I'd be a wildlife artist. But, at the same time I was always searching for ideas to start my own business.

What was your first job?

My first job was as a stenographer in the Office of the Commissioner of Police, and then as an administrative assistant in the Scientific Section, which is where I met my husband who was a police officer in the photographic section of the Queensland Police Service.

Why did you leave?

I wanted to be in business for myself and so I set a goal to become a personal assistant to general managers and managing directors of large companies, so that I could learn as much as I could from them about business.

Where did you go from there?

After leaving the Queensland Police Service I worked within Treasury and Loans at Suncorp Building Society for two years. I then worked for Lloyds Ships who made multi-million dollar luxury yachts for another two years. After that I spent a 3 month period with the Vox Group which was Chandlers and Errol Stewarts. I spent the next 4 years at John Sands Printing which included John Sands Greeting Cards and John Sands Calendars.

I learnt valuable information from each company that would eventually hold me in good stead for the success of my own company. I learnt all about money and investing, how to budget and not overspend, how to treat people kindly and with respect, to encourage them to do their best, how to stay ahead of the times and spend your money to use the best technology available to you, and of course, all about calendars and the printing industry.

After being promoted to the position of Customer Service Manager for Norcross Calendars (formerly John Sands), the company was bought out by Allen Calendars who made everyone in Brisbane redundant. They decided not to produce customised calendars any more. That was when the door of opportunity was opened for me.

What happened then?

The redundancy was obviously the perfect opportunity to go out on my own.

I wanted to start my own company because I had a vision for how business should be done.

The longer I worked for other companies the stronger my desire was to start my own business. I was so disappointed in the treatment of staff and customers in general and felt that far too much weight was placed on profits rather than people.

Did you create a business plan?

Yes. There is a great site called www.planware.org where I created both my business and strategic plans. It gives you the basic framework and examples. It's very simple and easy to use.

What year did you establish Freeman Productions?

February 1998. One month before I gave birth to my first daughter, Eliza.

What market research did you do before you commenced the business?

Having spent the previous four years in the calendar industry, I felt I had enough information on my competitors to be able to succeed. I knew their SWOTs and what I needed to do to improve on the service that was currently being offered in the marketplace.

What was your target market initially and has this changed over the years?

My initial target market was the pharmaceutical industry, which we continue to work heavily in. We have now also created a small business range to sell our calendars via brochure to the business community as well. Now that our systems are running well, we are also ready to duplicate our business into other industries.

How did you get your name out into the marketplace in the early days?

We created a website straight away in 1998. Our competitors have only just last year created their first websites. We also placed a small block ad in the yellow pages, only to realise that it brought far too many of the wrong customers to us. We removed that ad to have just a line ad in following years. We did no other advertising. It was all direct target marketing—tendering to our preferred customers.

Did you have many contacts that you networked with in the early days to help you get started?

I joined the Women's Network Australia straight away and did mentor sessions to give me confidence and assurance that I was headed in the right direction. It was not until recently that I even found the time to actually attend many networking events.

Were there any major obstacles or challenges that you had to overcome in your first year operating the business?

I started my business 1 month before giving birth to my first daughter, Eliza. When I was eight months pregnant I won the tender for the Pharmacy Guild account, which instantly brought me an account with over 385,000 calendars and 914 customers. Six weeks after giving birth, my husband won the Michael Duffy Fellowship, which sent him overseas for five weeks. While he was overseas his fifteen-year-old son was forced to come and live with us because he had personal problems. Needless to say, with a newborn baby and all of this going on while managing an account of this size, it was quite a challenge to co-ordinate and ensure customer satisfaction and delivery success and at the same time keep my family together. I employed my mother to work with me and I worked around the clock between my responsibilities as a mother and wife. Very quickly, I had to learn how to manage my family and business in a unified, balanced and organised way.

Were there any sacrifices or compromises you had to make in the early days to get the business off the ground?

When you are balancing family and a business at the same time, time is of the essence. Every minute of time is valuable. My husband and I sacrificed our social life, which was the hardest thing to do, and we went without luxuries while the business was developing.

How many hours per week did you put into the business in the first year?

I worked in small allotments around the clock. I guess it was probably ten or eleven hours a day, mainly done through the evening when everyone else was sleeping. Since the beginning of 2004, I've worked school hours 9 am to 2.30 pm with only occasional night work.

In the early days did you find it difficult dealing with men in business?

No. In fact, apart from being a woman I had the extra challenge of either being pregnant or having newborns when tendering for business or services and that was often to men. To give you an example, when I tendered for the Pharmacy Guild of Australia account, I was a young, pregnant woman who had never had a baby before, and no real experience at running a business. Yet they believed in me and gave me the account. Of course, it was the best thing they could have done. In eight years I have grown their account by over 61 per cent and they've had no late deliveries. But they could have discriminated against me and they didn't.

If you had to start over, would you do anything differently?

I wouldn't give up my social life and my friends. Alan Jones says, 'No success, ambition or goal is worth sacrificing friendship,' and I think he's right. I should have strove harder to ensure that I was more social. Had I got home help sooner, it probably would have relieved some of the pressure on my family life and business.

What was the annual turnover of your business last year?

In 2003/04—a little over $1.5 million.

What percentage of your own money did you initially invest into the business?

A $20,000 overdraft that I paid off in one week.

When did the business first start making a profit and what year was it?

The first four years of my business I ran at a loss. In 2001/2002, the same year I gave birth to my second daughter, Tanisha, we had a 44.5 per cent sales growth. That was the same fiscal year that I turned my business around by growing my profit margin significantly.

Do you currently have a partner within the business?

No. I had a partner when I first started the business and our ideas were conflicting and it simply did not work for me.

What do you think are the advantages and disadvantages of having a partner?

The advantage may be greater capital and someone to liaise and make decisions with.

The disadvantage is that there is a divided authority, possible friction between partners, and less flexibility. If you don't both have the same vision, then it can appear like a tug of war and eventually too much tension will cause a break. I recommend that a contract be written to safeguard both partners.

I have a contract with all of my clients and my suppliers. It provides the basis for a good working relationship because there is a very clear understanding of everybody's expectations.

Where is your printing operation done?

We subcontract our printing locally to Harding Colour in Tingalpa, Brisbane.

How do you manage distribution, interstate and internationally?

Distribution is a fundamental part of the business, and making sure the calendars reach customers on time is our priority. We use Australia Post's eParcel. Each Post eParcel consignment carries a barcoded address label which is scanned during the dispatch process enabling the delivery status to be viewed on-line. It also enables us to get a signature on delivery.

What process do you go through to come up with new calendar concepts?

Most of what we do comes about through keeping in close contact with our customers. Speaking with them, finding out their desires, and combining that with our knowledge of the marketplace, we come up with the ideas and concepts.

When we are selecting images for our single image range, we actually create a survey showing 18 images and send them out to 5000 customers and ask them to rate the images. We then collate the data and pick the top six images. As an incentive to complete the survey, all completed forms go into a draw to win a $100 gift certificate at their local liquor store.

When we create a new product like The U-CAN-C Calendar, we printed 700 samples and sent them out to our prospective customer list and asked them for their feedback. We then made changes to the design based on what they had to say. We like to involve our customers as often as we can. This way, they take ownership of the products and are more inclined to buy them because they had input. We create new calendars every year, two years in advance.

How many calendar concepts/styles do you have?

Currently we have single image calendars, 12-page calendars and computer calendars within our standard business community range. However, the majority of our calendars are customised for specific client groups.

Which are the most popular selling calendars?

The majority of our business is within the pharmaceutical industry—90 per cent. In terms of actual calendars, our Motivated Animals 12-page calendar tripled in sales in 2004 and we sold out and had to reprint twice.

Does the business call for you to travel? If so how often?

To tender to new clients I will travel only once or twice a year if necessary.

Do you currently network with other businesses?

Not really, other than attending some luncheons through The Women's Network Australia and Bayside Women in Business. I do, however, see the benefit and hopefully this year I will be able to make more time to network.

What have been some of the highlights so far for you in running your own business?

There have been lots of highlights, but the most significant ones are:

Being able to grow my business successfully from home while raising my two beautiful daughters and keeping my marriage of 16 years together has to be the thing I am most proud of.

I created Freeman Productions in February 1998 and our sales grew from nothing to well over seven digits within five years.

I flew to Canberra and won my first large pharmaceutical account when I was eight months pregnant with my first daughter, Eliza.

In one year (the same year I gave birth to my second daughter, Tanisha) we grew our sales by over 44.5 per cent and turned our business around to grow our profit margin significantly without increasing our prices across the board.

In 2003 we won the Best Manufacturing Category and Queensland's Best Home Based Business Award in the 2003 Australian Micro Business Award. And in 2005 we won the Australian Government Micro-Business Award in the Telstra Queensland Small Business Awards.

Being able to give employment to an incredible team of people (Sarah, Sam, Roby and Kylee) who are self-motivated, positive, dedicated and committed to achieving our vision.

What is your main role now within the business?

I manage the day to day operations of the business. I ensure that we are on target to achieving our strategic plans. I set the plans in motion for our company growth. And I make sure that the few million details that it takes to run any business are kept in check.

Describe your management style and culture.

I have a very open and honest management style and I encourage my staff to feel as though they have ownership in the company. Our employees get involved with strategic planning and have a crucial role in shaping and maintaining our culture and direction. Our culture is reflected by the people we have now employed. A favourite saying we have posted on our noticeboard is:

'We choose to have fun.
Fun creates enjoyment.
Enjoyment invites participation.
Participation focuses attention.
Attention expands awareness.
Awareness promotes insight.
Insight generates knowledge.

Knowledge facilitates action.
Action yields results.'

How do you motivate yourself on a daily basis?

For me, it's all about attitude. I really don't have a problem motivating myself to achieve.

I visualise a lot and often I've completed a day in my head before it's started and I know what I'm to accomplish in that next 24-hour period. It's very easy when you love what it is that you do. Also the books I read help motivate me and a great site that I recommend is www.asamanthinketh.net.

In general, what motivates you most—money, sense of achievement, growth of the business, recognition, helping others?

I'm motived by the opportunity this business gives me to become the kind of person I want to be, to help people and to be able to give back.

I'm also motivated by my desire to provide my family with a good life. To have lots of time to raise my children, have money to donate to charities and other projects I'm interested in, have time and money to take care of my health, and to be able to travel the world with my family (yet to be achieved, but one day soon).

How do you prioritise your time?

I live by to-do lists. I write a to-do list every day for business and my personal life. I certainly don't get through everything. But without it I wouldn't be able to accomplish as much or stay on top of my life. I haven't yet found the perfect balance for my life, but I am certainly closer to it than ever before.

What techniques do you use to achieve your goals?

I write all of my goals down and I review them regularly. They have to be SMART goals—specific, measurable, attainable, realistic and have a time line.
I believe setting goals has been absolutely instrumental in terms of achieving my successes. I have very defined goals, and have a very clear vision as to how to achieve them. But even if something gets in the way, I simply set a new course on how to get there. Once a week my staff meet to plan the week ahead to ensure we are on target for achieving the timely production of our products. This is an open forum and an opportunity to talk about our future direction.

As a female, have you ever felt vulnerable in business?

I think the only reason I've felt vulnerable is because of the pressure I've placed on myself. And I would suspect a lot of women in business probably place the same sorts of pressure on themselves. The superwoman dogma does take affect without you even realising that it's occurring. We want to be the perfect wife, the perfect mother, the perfect business woman, the perfect boss, the perfect friend and so on. This superwoman effect is what exposes our vulnerability. There have been times when I've felt alone and unable to cope. But it doesn't last long. I pick myself up, dust myself off and work out a way to solve whatever problem is in front of me.

Has the business put pressure on your relationship with your husband or kids?

When it comes to my children, I have tried to place them first, and so I have worked around them. I've tried to give them as normal a routine as possible. But I wouldn't be honest if I didn't say they haven't experienced any pressure from the business.

There has definitely been pressure placed on my relationship with my husband. And it has taken a great deal of understanding, patience and hard work from both of us to keep things together. But we both understand that we are making a short term sacrifice in our time together for a long term gain. The lack of time we have together is not a forever thing.

How do you both balance domestic arrangements with home and work? Do you have external help?

I get my house cleaned three times a week and my cleaners are brilliant. I know with absolute certainty that both Annette and Brenda add incredible value to the quality of my life.

Have you had many mentors or role models in business?

I've always tried to find someone throughout all areas of my life that inspires me or who can offer me guidance or assistance to improve myself. Lynette Palmen from the Women's Network Australia has been an excellent mentor particularly for her community work.

Trevor Clarkin, General Manager of Gold Cross Products and Services for his great support and belief in me. He constantly uplifts me and gives me such great hope for the future.

Doug Booth the founder of my printing company was another mentor. Unfortunately he passed away in August 2004 from cancer.

But most of my role models are motivational speakers and the authors of the books I read.

What motivational books would you recommend?

If I had to recommend four, they would be *Awaken the Giant Within* by Anthony Robbins for goal-oriented people and those starting out in business. *The Cashflow Quadrant* by Robert Kiyosaki for people who want to move from job security into financial freedom. *The E-Myth Revisited* by Michael Gerber to learn how to create the system that will set you free. And *Good to Great* by Jim Collins for businesses who want to be the best in the world at what they do.

What is the best advice you were ever given, with regards to your business?

Set up the system and get the right people working with you so that you can work on the business rather than in it.

Three key strategies for Freeman Productions' success

1. I have a unique business idea.

2. I have a very clear vision.

3. I care a great deal about my staff and my customers.

These three factors have been paramount to my success.

Kris's words of advice

1. The choices you make affect everything. Make sure they are positive ones that guide you towards your vision. If you made a wrong one, as I often have, simply learn from that, don't spend hours looking backwards, go forward and get back on track as quickly as possible.

2. Your vision of your future must be bold, daring and imaginative, if you want it to come true. You need a compelling one that will give you the strength to never give up.

3. Be value based. Know what your values are, and in everything that you, make sure your behaviour is in line with these values. Don't allow the opinions of others to sway you. Create a win-win principle for your business.

4. Identify your strengths and those responsibilities you enjoy. Build your business utilising those strengths. And then hire someone to do what you don't do well. But when in doubt, don't hire, keep looking.

5. Define success in your own terms. It is so easy to let others, usually very well intentioned friends, and family, define your goals. Take control of your destiny by deciding how you define success. And then write your goals down. It's the only way to make your dream come true.

6. Trust your instincts and believe in yourself. Always be true to yourself. I love this quote: 'The size of your success is determined by the size of your belief'. If you believe you can you, you will.

LINDA LOWNDES
MICROSKIN INTERNATIONAL PTY LTD

After leaving school at the age of sixteen, Linda Lowndes entered the hairdressing industry. After extensive training Linda became one of Australia's award-winning hairstylists. From there Linda decided to travel the world working with some of the most famous people in the hairdressing industry. Linda's work led her to experience platform work for the world congress of hair in Paris. Linda decided to extend her career by completing a film and television make-up course in London. By combining the two trades, Linda spent eight years working in the film and television industry in London. During this time Linda worked with some of the most famous celebrities and travelled the world time and time again.

Upon returning home to Australia to start a family, Linda had to rebuild her career and a new business from the ground up. This was the successful beginning of her first business, Latona's Make-Up Suppliers. Linda established her own professional cosmetic range called 'Latona's'.

Latona's Make-Up Suppliers is one of the leading suppliers to the film and television industry. Latona's imports and exports worldwide. The Latona's range can be found in make-up artists' kits and shops all over the world. With Linda's expertise and reputation, she was asked by Weta Workshop to be the colour design specialist for some of the character make-up for the epic production of *The Lord of the Rings*, Latona's supplied the Weta Team over the entire four-year period of film and production of the movie. Latona's has also worked and supplied products to the Weta Team on some of the world's most famous motion pictures ever made, such as *The Matrix*, *Star Wars*, *Moulin Rouge*, *The Thin Red Line*, *Peter Pan* and many other quality films and television productions filmed in Australia and internationally. Linda's has created a reputation that is recognised worldwide.

It was during this time when Linda's first business was thriving, that she was approached by a young girl who wanted to camouflage her skin condition for her school formal. Linda knew that there were no products on the market that would correct her skin condition successfully and feeling sympathy for the beautiful young girl, Linda had an ingenious idea. Not realising the extent and challenges that lay ahead for her, she embarked upon her sevenyear journey of research and development to finally create the Microskin product.

Linda used her skill, techniques and knowledge from being a professional make-up artist, as well as her passion, willingness and stubbiness not to be defeated attitude, to work towards finding the ultimate, unique solution for skin conditions. From Linda's success in her first business, this has given her the opportunity to fund her vision and take Microskin to market.

Microskin is a liquidised, simulated second skin that aids people suffering from skin conditions such as birthmarks, burns, vitiligo, sun sensitive skin conditions, surgical and skin graft scarring, tattoos, acne damage, broken veins and capillaries and many other skin-related conditions. Microskin breathes and does not have a thick make-up appearance. It is waterproof and flexible and will not rub off onto your clothes and furnishings. Microskin can be used by men, women and children.

Linda's innovative product speaks for itself with her patients being her biggest advocates. Linda says that her greatest reward is to witness the incredible shift in her clients and how they perceive themselves.

Linda's plan is to take her product world wide, giving people the chance to have a life changing experience. Microskin is already a diamond sponsor for the website www.birthmarks.com as a new innovative product.

Could you tell me about a bit about yourself and where you grew up?

I'm 38 years young, I was born in Sydney and moved to Queensland at the age of 8 and lived on Bribie Island till the age of 17. Then I moved to Brisbane to pursue my career.

Do you come from a large family?

No, I have one sister, Vanessa, who is three years older then me.

Where did you complete your schooling?

Caboolture State High. Keith Urban, the singer, was one of the good things that came out of Caboolture High! I finished school in Year 10. All I can say is they weren't my best years; I struggled to keep up with the system.

But you know that old saying when the teacher says to the student 'you will never amount to anything'? I guess those words have haunted a lot of people.

Did you go onto university, TAFE or college?

After I left school I went to TAFE in Brisbane and completed a hairdressing apprenticeship under Benny Togninis from Tognins Hair workshop.

Do you believe your childhood or parents influenced your decision to start your business?

After the death of my father at the age of five my mother, sister and I had to support each other. My sister Vanessa was my protector and guarded me with her life, she felt responsible for me as my mum had to work to support us.

My mother taught both of us that it was important to stand on our own two feet and be independent, work hard and respect others. I believe she gave me the strength to believe in myself.

I decided to start my own business so I could share my knowledge and expertise with others.

What was your ambition when you left school?

I wanted to become a hairdresser and travel the world. Which I did.

What was your first job?

My very first job was at the age of 12. I worked at the local corner beach shop, making hamburgers, packing lollies (and eating them at the same time 'two for the mouth, one for the bag') while watching the kids play on the beach.

I guess at an early age I started saving my money because I didn't have to buy any lollies. The lady who owned the shop was like my second mother, she gave me some words of advice. Every week instead of getting paid, she would put my money into a bank account. As my money started to grow on the odd occasion I would ask her if I could I buy a bike or other things like that. She would say think about it, and if you really want it come back to me. Time went on and by the age of 18, I asked her, 'Vivian, can I buy a block of land?' She handed over the bank book to me and I was overwhelmed to see the total amount.

What an amazing lady. So where did you go from there?

I began my hairdressing career with Benni. This man was one of the hardest trainers there was in Brisbane. He would push his staff to breaking point to be the best; I was one of them. I won countless hairdressing awards and recognition throughout Australia and the industry. I believe that it was Benni who instilled this 'perfectionist attitude' that is still inside me today. I can't accept second best or failure and sometimes this is not the best trait to have.

I believe you're married; is your husband involved in the business?

Yes, I've been married to Barry for 10 years. He has been very supportive over the years and recently he joined the Microskin team.

Barry also has a successful business, Retail Investigation Services. Over the years Barry has shared some very useful strategies for reading people and not laying all your cards on the table. I have also learnt how to read body language. These are very useful tactics to have when people try to bluff you or intimidate. I should get Barry to write a book, as it has worked for me. I used to be a push over ... not any more!

Do you have any children?

We have two boys. Joshua aged 10 and Pierce aged 5. They are good natured and help me in my business.

How do you balance domestic arrangements with home and work?

Balancing work, home and the children can be very trying at times. Between both Barry and I we share everything: schooling, parties, soccer trips and shopping, also the 'friends thing' we missed out on due to our work commitments. We work so hard and any time left over time is given to the children.

Do you have any assistance like a nanny or housekeeper?

I wish. The only nanny I have is the real thing ... my mum and my stepfather. I have never seen a man with such patience as my stepfather, he is our lifesaver. He takes the boys out and they'll go hunting for tadpoles in a creek for up to five hours!! That deserves a medal. My patience is half an hour! It's always, 'Hurry up, Mummy has work to do.'

Lets talk about Microskin, what led you to start the business and why?

I read an article about a little boy who was condemned to a life of confinement due to an abnormal skin condition which affected the skin's pigment. I cut out the article and stuck it on my wall as inspiration and a goal to work towards.

I then met a young girl who was 16 years of age who came to see me at my other business (Latona's Make-Up Supplies) and her one wish was to look like the other girls at her school formal. This young lady had a heart condition and the medication that she was on produced further complications and turned her face blue.

I guess this young girl is the reason why my career path changed so dramatically. I knew I had a challenge ahead of me but when I saw this young girl smile I knew I was heading in the right direction.

What year did you start working on the Microskin idea?

I started working on Microskin in 1997 when I was 31 years old.

What were the first steps you took in starting the business?

My first steps were to find patients that had birthmarks and were willing to become trail patients over a period of time. I choose birthmarks because they are one of the most challenging conditions to visually correct. I researched night and day to have an understanding about different skin conditions. I then began a seven year uphill battle to develop a formula that was compatible with the human skin and to also create a software program that would visually correct an affected area of the skin. This was one of the hardest things imaginable, at one stage I thought I was going mad. There was no peace of mind, I couldn't even sleep without doing mathematical sums in my head and each time I got it wrong it was a disaster. My trial patients would cry and cry. The whole process was very stressful and mentally tiring to everyone involved. If there was one thing out of place the Microskin system would have a domino effect and fall over. Step by step I would have to pick up the pieces and find the problem. Thank goodness that task has been completed and all trial patients are now smiling.

What market research did you do before you commenced the business?

Once I established that the market had very little to offer—other products were gender biased, they didn't have lasting power on the skin and were matched only by naked eye from a choice of maybe 15 colours. It was then that I knew Microskin would outlast, outperform—it could be used by any gender without appearing like make-up.

During the research stage, I became a member of a birthmark association and society for cosmetic chemists.

What was your target market initially and has this changed over the years?

Initially my target was helping people with birthmarks, but I have come to realise that Microskin can assist many people suffering from a wide range of skin conditions. Microskin will be releasing two new products in the New Year, that will be sold in retail outlets around Australia.

Did you have a business plan?

Yes, we had a business plan drawn up outlining the direction of where we saw our business. Detailing trials of the product, testing, manufacturing, labelling, advertising and launching Microskin into the market, we also set time lines, and budgets within the business plan.

As far as getting your name into the marketplace, what been your plan?

In our business plan we decided to target the medical profession, support groups and the general public.

The plan is to get as much exposure as we can through media, such as newspapers and television, such as *A Current Affair*.

Because I've previously worked in the film and television industry, I have established a great reputation in my field and I believe this would also be a great avenue to tap into and pursue.

Did you have any industry contacts that you've networked with?

The only networking is once again through the film and television industry as for other networking I've had to stumbled the whole way through the process, sometimes falling from great heights.

What makes your products so unique?

Microskin is unique because it is not just a product; it's a system that can provide a solution and an answer to people that suffer from skin related conditions. Microskin also has the ability to aid in protecting sun and other light sensitive skin conditions.

The Microskin Colour Enhancing System has taken three years for me to write; it's an additional software program to coincide with a generic software program. My additional software allows me to reproduce a correction formula for each individual patient using advanced technology that can read the human skin and then the Microskin formula can be mixed immediately on the premises. Microskin is waterproof, flexible and will not rub off onto clothing or furnishings. Microskin acts and looks like the human skin.

How many product lines do currently produce in Microskin range?

At the moment there is Microskin and Microskin Removing Serum, Activating Serum, Microseal Powder, Microskin Skin Care Range and The Application Kit and the two new products that are due for release in the New Year.

Do you have plans to export to the international market?

Yes. Currently we are based in Brisbane with plans to open other clinics in Australia, the UK and America.

Until that time some of our international patients are travelling to us for their initial consultation, fortunately for them, they will not have to return to visit us again as their personalised Microskin formula is stored on our private and confidential database. We can then ship their Microskin products anywhere in world. Also we will be exporting the two new products and their range world wide.

Are your products made in Australia?

Yes. All Microskin products are made in Sydney by our own formulator.

Does the business call for you to travel?

Microskin needs to attend international conferences relating to the medical fraternity and related support groups. In the near future we will be travelling overseas to scout for new premises for our expanding clinics.

Do you currently network with other businesses?

Not often. I joined a women's networking group, which I haven't had time to attend yet but will in the near future, hopefully to lift my networking skills.

What have been some of the highlights so far for you in running your own business?

I guess you could say the highlights would be watching the people who are on my product trial blossom and turn into individuals with more confidence than they could ever have imagined. Another highlight was being nominated a finalist in the Business Ideas Grants in 2004.

Have you received any other recognition or awards for the business?

Yes. I was awarded as a national finalist for the Yellow Pages Business Ideas Grants in 2004 and Microskin was recognised as one of the most innovated products developed in 2004. Microskin has also received funding from the QLD government Comet Grant.

What has been your biggest sacrifice?

I haven't taken a wage for seven years! I had to work three jobs to finance my venture. Travelling away a lot and working on feature films, I have worked ungodly hours and lost time away from my family, sacrificed my health and well being, my relationships with friends and family, loss of identity and worst of all I forgot what it was like to buy a new dress!

My mum and dad gave me their retirement fund and my husband and I put the money from our house on the line. If that is not scary I don't know what is! At the end of the day all the sacrifices that have been made will be rewarded.

How many hours per week did you put into the business in the first year?

As for hours per week, one week rolled into the next month, rolled into the next year … Seven years later, I have lived, breathed and slept for the people and the Microskin product, obsessive I know.

Have you found it difficult dealing with men in business? For example in manufacturing, finance institutions and banks?

Firstly, it doesn't pay to be blonde because I've found that some people don't take you seriously. Secondly, no-one would believe what Microskin had to offer. They would insult me, degrade me and humiliate me. I have so many stories that would shock you. All I can say is don't despair, stay strong and focused.

Have you ever felt vulnerable in business?

Yes. I believe all women feel vulnerable and doubt themselves in business at one point or another. Women have more than just themselves to deal with, for example, family, husband and children. Sometimes it can catch up with you.

What is your turnover forecast for 2005/06?

Mid 2005 to 2006 is $2.7 million for our one clinic in Queensland.

Has Microskin been solely funded by yourself or have you had external funding?

Microskin was solely funded by my family and I. Recently we have received funding from the Queensland Comet Grant.

Does the business deal with debts and creditors itself or do you use an external company to assist you in this area?

We handle all our own creditors regarding stock control and ordering. Regarding our debts, our patients pay on a consultation fee basis.

Do you currently have any partners within the business?

Microskin is a family owned business.

What do you think are the advantages and disadvantages of having a partner?

I find one of the disadvantages of having partners in business is that usually there is only one person that puts in the hard yards. In the beginning I had investors/partners but I found over a period of time Microskin was not moving forward, and was in danger of collapsing. I believe unless it's their idea or invention to start with they do not have the same motivation that is required. If you decide to take a partner choose very carefully and don't take just anyone on board.

What's your main role within the business?

My role in the business is the whole box and dice. When your finances are limited you use every resource you can possibly find. I have one very dedicated staff member who has been with me from the beginning, Eloise Thorpe. Eloise and I can pull rabbits from hats. We have gone from writers to interior designers and the rest. It's amazing how fast you can learn how to achieve things on a budget. One great tip is to speak to family and friends. Someone who knows someone, who knows someone, might consider doing contra deals if you both have something to offer each other. This is a great money saver. Always use your resources.

What is your management style and culture?

My management style is to respect each and every employee or patient that walks through my doors.

With my staff, I listen to their opinions and what they have to offer and I treat them equally. We have so much fun together.

How do you motivate yourself on a daily basis?

I think after seven years of bringing Microskin to the market, I have stayed focussed. I believe I am happy and motivated most of the time.

In general, what motivates you most—money, sense of achievement, growth of the business, recognition, helping others?

Helping others would have to motivate me the most. To see the change in the people, that provides me with great satisfaction that money cannot buy. It is a personal sense of achievement that motivates me to continue and grow with the business. Good fortunes will come from my hard work and dedication.

How do you prioritise your time?

I focus on what is important to my business, family and friends.

What techniques do you use to achieve your goals?

I try to remain focused through the good and bad times. Stay true to myself and respect others.

Have you had many mentors or role models along the way?

Richard Branson is my most favourite role model. He sets his goals and achieves them. His book would inspire anyone.

What other books would you recommend?

For those non-readers I can highly recommend a short but sweet book called *Who Moved My Cheese?*, also *The Present* and *The Magic of Thinking Big*.

I also highly recommend that you go and buy a pack of angel cards, I swear by them. When you need someone's opinion, go to the cards, ask the question, and listen very carefully to your inner self and the answer will be there inside you. Remember other people's opinions are not always right for you and your business.

Do you personally undertake management training to update your skills?

No. There has been no training to date, only life skills.

What is the best advice you were ever given, with regards to your business?

This one is regarding legal things. If things are going wrong with your partner, formulator or investor, you could find yourself in a legal battle. You should not have to fight for what is yours. Once you have entered into legal litigation, the only winners are the lawyers.

A wise man said to me, 'When you receive legal documents, screw them up and file them in the round bin.' I followed his advice and it's worked. If you wish to do business with someone and you can't afford a legal contract to be drawn up, write down your requests in great detail and ask them to sign on the dotted line before proceeding. You will find that this will protect you just as good as a legal document. File it in a safe place, provide each member with a copy and take a deep breath because this could be your life saver in the future. It was for me.

Where does the business go from here, what's the plan for the future over the next five years?

We will expand Microskin and open new clinics around Australia then go global. Our goal will be to continue to cater for the people in need of a solution to aid them with their skin conditions.

Three key strategies for Microskin's success

1. Dedication and commitment.

2. Good business ethics.

3. Staying true to yourself.

Linda's words of advice

1. Always follow your instincts.

2. Take your time.

3. Stay focused on the main goal.

4. Don't be swayed by other people's opinions. They don't always know best.

5. When you have been knocked down get up again, and again, and again.

6. Keep your invention or ideas to yourself. Sign people involved to a confidentiality agreement. People will take things from underneath your nose. It's amazing what you miss that goes on behind closed doors.

IVANKA BELIC
LITTLE WORKERS

At the age of 17 Ivanka immigrated from her homeland Croatia, to live in Australia, where she spent the next 15 years working for Ansett Airlines.

Having always had an interest in fashion and design, she trained in interior decorating at the Melbourne TAFE, it was her passion and enthusiasm for fashion that led her into her own business. In 1995, Ivanka started to design and make children's clothing from home and within a short time she began selling them at the Brisbane's Riverside and SouthBank markets.

Her customer base grew to such a point that she could no longer operate from home and this motivated her to look for an alternative location where she could continue to expand the business.

In 1998 Ivanka bought a high set Queenslander in Paddington, Brisbane that she and her partner renovated, and attached a connecting retail outlet and a warehouse. This became her head office where she now sells and designs her clothing ranges. Since establishing Little Workers the business has taken off, achieving over 150 per cent increase in revenue over the past 5 years. Ivanka employs 20 people with specialised skills that help her design, manufacture and distribute over 100 designs in 13 different sizes.

These days Little Workers distributes to selected boutiques throughout Australia and exports to the USA, Japan, NZ, UK, Singapore, New Caledonia and Saudi

Arabia. Ivanka has found the international interest and demand for her designs overwhelming, increasing her export business by 250 per cent in 2004.

Her designs have been applauded by the Australian fashion industry, resulting in numerous awards such as; the 2004 and 2003 Australian Fashion Awards, in 2002 they won the Gold Coast Fashion Awards and the RAQ Viewers Choice Awards. They've been a finalist two years running in the RAQ Fashion Design Awards and between 2000-2004 they consecutively won the Quest for Small Business Award and were inducted in to the hall of fame.

How would you summarise your business?

Little Workers is an Australian fashion house for children. Little Workers garments and accessories are distinctive and exclusive, offering designs with a point of difference while being 100 per cent Australian.

Tell me about your background. For example, where did you grow up?

I emigrated to Australia from former Yugoslavia in 1978 when I was 17 years of age.

Do you come from a large family?

No, I grew up as an only child with my godparents.

Where did you complete your schooling?

In Melbourne.

Did you go on to University, TAFE or College?

Melbourne TAFE, I didn't attend university.

Do you believe your childhood and godparents influenced your decision to start your business?

My godparents ran a successful publishing house in Zagreb. They had old-fashioned views, high values and impeccable taste. By the age of ten, I answered the business phone, took orders, wrote up invoices and helped pack the orders.

My godparents have been the biggest inspiration in my life and carved the path that I later followed which led me to start my own business.

You mentioned that you immigrated in 1978, did you settle in Brisbane initially?

I joined my mother's family in Melbourne; I originally came to Australia with the intention of learning to speak English and returning to Zagreb. I met my partner and moved to Brisbane in 1992.

What was your ambition when you left school?

I planned to go to university in Zagreb in Yugoslavia to study veterinary science after mastering English in Australia.

What was your first job?

My first paid job was at the age of 16 with the local TV station, organising extras before and during filming. I worked on two films, both historical and associated with World War II and Tito.

Where did you go from there?

I worked for the TV station while awaiting the approval for my visa to Australia. Once in Australia my first job was waitressing at the Top Air Restaurant at Tullamarine airport, and the beginning of a long term association with the airlines and airports.

Could you tell me a little about yourself? Do you have a partner in life, are you married?

I am 44 years and have been with my partner, Greg Dixon, for twenty years. Greg runs a building business of his own and helps on the home front with our daughter. In the earlier years Greg would set up the fixtures at the markets before the sun had risen; these days he is only associated with the business on an advisory level and helps with maintenance and carpentry.

Do you have only the one child?

Yes, I was 33 years and employed as an Ansett Flight attendant when our daughter was born. Soon after Yazzy (now 11 years of age) was born I remember thinking that our lives were just beginning and that we had not truly lived until we had a child. Our priorities shifted and our lifestyles and commitments changed.

How have you balanced domestic arrangements with home and work?

Balancing domestics and business life requires careful planning and balancing with the help of my partner Greg. When problems arise I am fortunate to be surrounded with dedicated staff that step in and lend a hand to help sort the relevant obstacles.

What led you into designing children's clothing?

I made clothes for my daughter, and from the beginning I had friends who admired them and we even had strangers in the street stop us and ask where my daughter's clothes came from. I started pondering what life would be like after Ansett. I wanted to find a way of making some pocket money, doing something that I would enjoy and that would work in with raising my daughter.

How did you get the range out into the marketplace in the beginning?

A friend suggested I hold a party for a group of her friends, with babies of similar ages who were struggling to find suitable baby clothes. Little Workers was born that day at the first party, lots more partys followed over the following four years. My hobby soon grew and I found that with the demand I had to source fabric suppliers, professional sewers, cutters and pattern makers to complete the orders.

What year did you establish the label as a business?

A year or so later a friend offered to sell the Little Workers range of clothes at the Brisbane Riverside Markets. That was such a success we're still there every Sunday. My partner Greg came up with the name. In November 1999 we opened our own Little Workers concept store in Paddington, Brisbane.

What were the first steps you took in starting the business?

While I was trading at the Riverside markets I found that my hobby was evolving into a business and I recognised the potential it offered if I chose to carry on with the label. My vision of expansion was limitless providing I invested the necessary resources, but I didn't want the business to get out of hand by growing too big and too fast. I've taken it steadily as I wasn't prepared to invest the time or attention required; I still wanted to balance the business with my home life so I could be available for my daughter's upbringing.

Where did you initially start designing and manufacturing the outfits?

The business was based at home in the early days and I would work hours around my daughter's schedule.

What market research did you do before you commenced the business?

The Brisbane Riverside Markets, we found, was the best place for us to test our clothes in the marketplace. The feedback was great and in the early days the demand was there and the business grew very quickly.

How did you get your name out into the marketplace? For example, did you advertise in the early days?

The markets and basically word of mouth was our only form of advertising in the beginning and still going strong to this day, referrals and repeat business are widespread and that's my most valued compliment. Whatever it was about the label people loved it, it was different and we attracted clients who came from Tasmania, Northern Territory, New Zealand, everywhere.

Today our designs are showcased in seasonal ranges and promoted digitally on an active website with ordering and payment facilities. New buyers can explore our Little Workers extensive range of children's wear and accessories (current and previous season), and enquire about other products and purchases online.

The business has also grown due to the use of the Internet; it has enabled us to provide new customers with descriptive information quickly and accurately. The web is also used for market and product research.

In addition to the website we also distribute seasonal catalogues featuring the ranges to 15,000 clients.

Did you have many contacts that you networked with in the early days to help you get started?

Besides the girls that started me on the party plan, no, I didn't. I concentrated on providing customers with what they needed and asked for, and as our range was reasonably small the turn around time was a week or two so we could respond quickly to the demand.

Did you have a business plan? If so could you explain the process you when through to create one?

Yes, initially we followed guidelines set out in the government publications for new business. One was called Easy Plan—an introduction to business planning and the other was a small retail business self-assessment kit. Both publications are easy to follow and well worth obtaining by anyone who is looking at starting a new business and are appropriate for a variety of businesses. Later I involved my accountant as well as a variety of experts to guide us along. In order to achieve long term strategies a business plan is essential. It also needed to be measured and reviewed on regular bases.

What makes your designs so unique?

The range of designs and sizes progressively grew over the years and Little Workers has become known for its unusual designs, and competitive prices, originality and quality, while still remaining 100 per cent Australian made. Little Workers' design process starts with selection of fabrics and trims available to us in Australia, we use extensive flowers (silk and cotton) that complement our ranges of clothing and accessories. Unusual trims such as vinyl, diamantes, Swarowski crystal, and faux fur and vinyl have become part of our signature mark and have helped with our branding.

We don't compare ourselves with what is available in the marketplace but rather process existing clients' demands and requests. The fashion industry is fickle and changes all the time and we aim to express current moods and trends, adapting them to suit active children and the Australian climate. According to our clientele Little Workers designs clothing that is interesting and show stopping, and that children love to wear and make a point of asking for.

How many outlets or distributors do you supply to in Australia?

In November 1999 we opened our own Little Workers concept store in Paddington, Brisbane. Besides that we supply 40 stores nationally.

Where do you export to the internationally?

We export around the globe with Saudi Arabia being our largest wholesale export market. Last year export accounted for 20 per cent of our overall sales. Next season we plan to advertise in the oversees publication of the *Bambini* children's fashion magazine, which is distributed worldwide.

How did you break into the international market?

Little Workers' first few export orders originated from the Riverside Market. Store owners on holidays found us there by chance, liked our designs and placed orders. Others came to us by recommendation of existing customers and the later ones were either introduced to Little Workers by Austrade connections or our website.

Are your clothes/ranges made in Australia?

Yes, all our garments and accessories are 100 per cent made in Australia; to be specific all our makers are from Queensland spanning from Bribie Island to Beenleigh. I am passionate about Australian made products and the importance of retaining industries and future jobs in the country and would never take our operation off shore.

How many employees do you have?

In-house we have six staff and we outsource work to twenty people.

Does the business call for you to travel and if so how often?

Yes, it does but I prefer to conduct as much business over the Internet or phone, and with modern technology today it seems an acceptable way.

My last trip overseas was six months ago to Korea and Hong Kong to source new fabrics and trims. Domestic trips are mainly to trade or fashion shows with no more than six trips a year.

What have been some of the highlights so far for you in running your own business?

I consider myself fortunate that I enjoy the best of both worlds in a business where I can express my creativity while being able to enjoy normal family life.

Winning the awards has been one of the highlights of running my own business. On a day-to-day basis, hearing and seeing children express love and admiration for our designs is an ongoing one. Knowing that their happiness will last way after they leave the store, in fact every time they wear our garments, is a great achievement for me.

What awards of recognition have you received for the business?

We've received numerous accolades from our peers such as: Australian Fashion Awards in 2003 and 2004, RAQ Fashion Design Awards in 2002, the Gold Coast Fashion Awards in 2002 and the Business Achievers Awards in 2000, 2001, 2002, 2003.

Were there any major obstacles or challenges that you had to overcome in your first year operating the business?

Little Workers did not have major obstacles as we grew slowly and on a demand basis. We measured and tested our product regularly and adapted accordingly. At times staffing caused short-lived problems, but those were soon overcome.

Did you sacrifice anything to get the business off the ground?

Sacrifice is a strong word. I have invested finances, imagination and my time but I don't see that as a sacrifice, only an investment.

How many hours per week did you put into the business in the first year?

Initially my working hours were suited around my daughter's schedule and would have amounted to an average of six hours a day, which is what I still do now, limiting the working hours to suit my daughter's school hours. In order to achieve this I have established a strong team of staff and I am a great believer in that the staff I employ have to be the best available in their required fields.

What has been your average percentage increase each year?

Little Workers' turnover has grown steadily over the years and is currently sitting at an increase of 10 per cent per annum. We currently manufacture in excess of 30,000 garments a year.

What percentage of your own money did you initially invest into the business?

My initial investment was the superannuation payout from Ansett and I have continued to re-invest profits made back into the business, to assist in expansion. We pride Little Workers on being self-funded and proudly independent.

Did you obtain external funding? How did you go about sourcing it?

Financial backup has been established with a commercial arm of the business's financial institution and is awaiting expansion implementation to be drawn upon.

When did the business first start making a profit?

Little Workers has always made a profit accept for the year of introduction of GST, when customers' spending slowed right down. As well as the introduction of GST, people were dealing with the effects from September 11 and the collapse of Ansett.

What's your main role within the business?

My role in the day-to-day business is to lead and create opportunities. Over the years I have learned to delegate and trust the team that I've appointed to handle the tasks set.

I liaise daily with clients, agents and suppliers and oversee the shipments ensuring they're meeting deadlines. I also like to spend sometime on the shop floor and keep in contact with our consumers.

What is your management style and culture?

I cultivate a team culture at work and aim to employ the best people. I appreciate that staff are my most valuable asset. When new employees join us they are trained and given authority and responsibilities, they feel part of the team and become self-motivated.

How do you motivate yourself on a daily basis?

As for my motivation it is something that comes from within and is inspired by various factors.

Mixing with high energy, successful and positive people and not allowing negative self talk helps me stay motivated. I consider myself fortunate for having the opportunity to enjoy the best of both worlds by developing a business where I can express my creativity while being able to prioritise time with my family and work.

In general, what motivates you most—money, being creative, sense of achievement, growth of the business, recognition, helping others?

As I said my driving force is multifaceted and all the factors stated come into it.

I must say that some give me more pleasure than others, but I would not be able to single one motivator above others. They are all as equally important.

How do you priorities your time?

Family matters come first and the rest of my time is scheduled around it. As for the business priorities, if I am not available my staff are trained to deal with priorities during my absence.

What techniques do you use to achieve your goals?

Diligence and determination. Persistence when it comes to solving problems.
 I don't give up, if obstacles come my way. My persistence is well known and admired among my friends and family.

As a female, have you ever felt vulnerable in business?

I can happily say that I have never felt vulnerable in business, certainly not for being a female.

Have you had many mentors or role models along the way?

I have had mentors and role models all my life, and expect I always will. Of late Allan McGirvan, a motivator and Trevor Jorgensen, an export advisor, have both been invaluable. Also Peter Hackworth and my wonderful accountant Kay Lawrence; Paula Bebee, insurance broker, as well as my solicitor, bank manager, logistics manager. All have plenty of expertise and lots of knowledge to share. To be philosophical, I believe that the teacher will appear when the student is ready.

Do you read motivational books, and if so what do you recommend?

I do read motivational literature regularly and draw upon it: Gerber, Kiyosaki, Robins and Abraham spring to mind and are great reading. For anyone starting a new business now I highly recommend *The Next Economy* by Elliot Ettenberg; it is a must read. Another great book is by Wendy Evans—*New Business in 90 Days*. One needs to search to attain new knowledge and broaden their perspective on existing practices. All motivational books will either reinforce or inspire you to adapt to a new way but inspiration alone is not enough until you take action.

Do you personally undertake regular management training to update your skills?

As an organisation, the team (including me) at Little Workers regularly attends seminars and workshops relevant to our industry provided by the Chamber of Commerce, NRA, Institute of Export and the Government.

I believe you are a great supporter of children's charities. Could you tell me a little about this?

We have been supporting a variety of Australian and international charity organisations associated with children. I will tell you about the current one for the 'Door of Hope': a group of orphanages in Johannesburg in South Africa and Uganda. The saddest bit about them is that they have installed a hole in the wall in order to encourage unwanted babies to be dropped off to the orphanages rather than have them left in the parks and on the street. Orphanages there need everything and experience shortage of basic items we take for granted.

After we got approached for a donation of clothing we decided to clear a few lines and have ended up with 500 garments in sizes relevant to children currently in custody.

I obtained a list of NGOs from the government seeking a willing party to assist in shipping the parcel to Africa and found the whole exercise very disappointing. Some of the comments from the people were equally as appalling and after four days on the phone I was no closer to having the clothes shipped thaan the day I started out. We are still seeking the support from the airlines and logistic companies and hope that soon we may have a positive outcome.

What is the best advice you were ever given, with regards to your business?

The best advice I was ever given was to never stop believing in myself.

Where does the business go from here, what are the plans for the future over the next five years?

My aim is for Little Workers to be recognised as a leading Australian children's label, designing and manufacturing in Australia. To have several representatives in each state and to increase our export portfolio in Japan and the USA.

What would you say is your personal future goal?

I am passionate about improving the quality of life for our children's generation and without businesses being based in Australia the opposite will occur.

My aim is also to educate Australian people that only with their support will Australian companies survive and flourish and where possible we should make a choice to buy Australian made products, to ensure a better future for our country and our children.

Three key strategies for Little Workers' success

1. Originality.

2. Quality.

3. Best customer service.

Ivanka's words of advice

1. Start with a dream, have a vision—a clear vision—and see yourself reaching your goal.

2. Do your homework, research the market, test and measure.

3. Get the best staff and advisors that you can afford, good people are found not changed.

4. Know the budget intimately and do not stretch the friendship often.

5. Add value to every relationship with clients and staff.

6. Be determined and persistent and learn how to communicate well.

Business Contacts

Associations for Women-Owned Business
Industry groups, councils, associations and organisations
www.business.com/directory/small_business/women-owned_businesses/associations/

AusIndustry
Ph: 132846
An Australian Government unit within the Department of Industry, Tourism and Resources. They can assist with grants, tax concessions, duty concessions and access to venture capital.
www.ausindustry.gov.au

Austrade
Ph: 132878
www.austrade.gov.au
Provides export and investment services to Australian companies and international investors.

Australian Businesswomen's Network
Ph: 1300 720120
www.inspiringwomen.com.au

Australian Federation of Business and Professional Women
Ph: 02 62572775
www.bpw.com.au

Australian Financial Review Boss Club
Ph: 02 92822298
Network functions with guest speakers.
www.afrboss.com.au

Australian Institute of Company Directors (AICD)
NSW: 02 82486600 VIC: 03 92119255
ACT: 02 62485954 QLD: 07 32214325
WA: 08 93227400 TAS: 03 62242559
www.companydirectors.com.au

Human Rights & Equal Opportunity Commission
Ph: 1300 656 419
www.hreoc.gov.au

National Occupational Health and Safety Commission
Ph: 02 62791000
State laws, links to other states on website.
www.nohsc.gov.au

Nescafe Big Break
Ph: 1800 630630
Business competition that gives away over $100,000 each year for business ideas.
www.nescafe.com.au

Operation Livewire
Ph: 1800 241041
A business planning competition. Personal mentors, work books, weekly seminars to assist in preparing business plans. At the end of the program there is an opportunity to win cash prizes.
www.shell.com.au/livewire

Telstra Business Women's Awards and Alumni Group
Ph: 1800 817536
www.telstra.com.au/tbwa

The Employment Advocate
Legislative rights and regulations.
Ph: 1300 366632 Ph: 02 92460400

The Women's Business Centre Australia
Ph: 1300 660367
www.wbca.com.au

Wageline
NSW/ACT/NT: 1300 363264
Federal Awards and Workplace Relations Act
QLD:1300 369 945 VIC: 1300 363 264
SA: 1300 365 255 WA:1300 655 266
www.wagenet.gov.au

Westpac Women in Business Program
Ph: 02 92606419
Ph: 07 32271437
www.westpac.com.au/womenbusiness

WorkCover
NSW: 1300 1050 Qld: 1300 326128
VIC: 1800 136155 SA: 13 1855
ACT: 02 62050200 WA: 1800 670055
State Government agency that supports workplace safety and workers
compensation injury claims.
www.workcover.nsw.gov.au

Business Organisations
New South Wales
Australian Businesswomen's Network
Ph: 1300 720120
www.inspiringwomen.com.au

Centrum Events
Ph: 02 99839406
Businesswomen's network.
www.centrumevents.com.au

Eastern Suburbs Businesswomen's Network
Ph: 02 93659750
www.swissgrand.com.au

Small Business Development Devision
Ph: 131145
Victoria

Victoria Women's Trust
Ph: 03 96420422
www.vwt.org.au

Businesswomen's Breakfast series
—Melbourne
Ph: 02 99839406
www.centrumevents.com.au

Small Business Victoria
Ph: 132215
www.sbv.vic.gov.au
www.businessaccess.vic.gov.au

The Australian Institute of Management
Ph: 03 95348181
Outstanding Women's Breakfast Series
www.aimvic.com.au/apps/events/

South Australia
The Business Centre
Ph: 08 84633800
www.tbc.sa.gov.au

ACT
Women with Ambition
Ph: 02 62673888
Ernst & Young women's networking functions
Email: karing.howman@ernstyoung.com.au

Chamber of Women in Business
Ph: 02 62950896
www.cwb.org.au

Canberra Business Advisory Service
Ph: 02 62605000
www.canbas.com.au

Queensland
Women's Network Australia
Ph: 07 32728222
www.womensnetwork.com.au

Department for State Development QLD
Ph: 07 32248568
www.sd.qld.gov.au

Cairns Businesswomen's Network
Ph: 07 40523888
www.cbwc.org.au

Townsville Businesswomen's Network
Ph: 07 47783488
www.businesswomen.com.au

The Sunshine Coast Businesswomen's Network
Ph: 07 54458454
www.scbwn.org.au

Western Australia
Women in Business Western Australia
Ph: 0417 909679
www.womeninbusiness-wa.com

Small Business Development Corporation
Ph: 08 92200222
Ph: 1800 199125
www.sbdc.com.au

Momentum Women's Forum—For Women Networking
Ph: 0417824619
www.momentumwf.siss21.com.au

Tasmania
Business Tasmania
Ph: 03 62335712
www.tdr.tas.gov.au